The Best Ladled Pans of Rice and Penne

T0347056

BY THE SAME AUTHOR

Oxford Student Pranks: A History of Mischief & Mayhem
Britain's Most Eccentric Sports
As Thick As Thieves - Foolish Felons & Loopy Laws
The Man with His Head in the Clouds
The Unbeatables
Oxford Examined: Town & Clown
Norse & Nordic Oxford
Oxford Z-A: 1000 Years of History in 26 Letters (*illustrated by Korky Paul*)

The Best Ladled Pans of Rice and Penne

62 Snapshots of Oxford Life

Richard O. Smith

Signal

Signal Books
Oxford

First published in 2020 by
Signal Books Limited
36 Minster Road
Oxford OX4 1LY
www.signalbooks.co.uk

A catalogue record for this book is available from the British Library

ISBN 978-1-909930-84-1 Paper

Cover Design: Tora Kelly
Typesetting: Tora Kelly
Cover Image: © Andrew Manson
Printed in India by Imprint Digital

CONTENTS

ATTA GIRL

In front of me a tourist is taking a photo of a gargoyle sitting astride a drainpipe. Just to clarify, the gargoyle's the one straddling the drainpipe. The photographer is using a lens the size of an anti-aircraft gun.

It's the sort of reason for pavement obstruction that occurs in Oxford. Then a woman elegantly dressed and mannered, perhaps in her mid-60s, stops next to me - ensuring the pavement is now completely blocked.

"I like you," she says to me mischievously. My brain attempts to process this information and quickly concludes that no-one has ever expressed this sentiment out loud to me before. My face is puckered in confusion.

"I was in the audience when you spoke to us recently," she clarifies, "and I love your columns." "Thank you," I say, genuinely grateful, if a little flummoxed.

Sensing the pavement is being blocked, Great Taste Lady moves on after chatting briefly, leaving me preoccupied with the thought that my wife won't believe me when I recount this pleasant incident later.

"I don't believe you," says my wife, dutifully, five hours later. I protest with the tiresome indignation of a truth-teller. Although public recognitions from strangers, and their resultant outpourings of praise for my work, happens to me all the time - at least every four or five years.

Great Taste Lady kindly namechecked two columns I'd written as her favourites. One, she informs me, is titled *Atta Girl*.

After relaying this lovely encounter to my wife, she adds a reasonable detail: I never wrote a column called *Atta Girl*. "Isn't that a famous short story by the multi-million selling American humourist David Sedaris?" I mulishly insist Great Taste Lady must have meant one of my columns instead.

"Ah, here we are," says my wife, determined to claim the last of my good mood, "it's not by you - it's Sedaris." A quick google search on my wife's phone confirms *Atta Girl*, or even more accurately, *Atta Boy*, is a column written by him not me. I hate the Internet.

A book reviewer did once kindly brand me "the English David Sedaris" in a broadsheet newspaper. "I'm flattered to be given the moniker," I informed my wife at the time, "but it's not a comparison based on sales or commercial impact." "Or talent," my wife points out, mutinously. Admittedly it's fairly unlikely Sedaris is known as "the American Richard O. Smith."

"I'm not anything like David Sedaris," I plead. "What are you doing on Saturday?" asks my wife. This is a trap. "Okay, I'm doing litter picking around my neighbourhood."

One thing most people know about Sedaris is that he's a compulsive self-appointed litter picker. Sussex County Council has even honoured his litter vigilantism by naming a dustcart after him.

"Look, that's a one off. I'm just joining the Clean-up Rose Hill litter pick day." "Why don't you email Oxford Council and ask how much litter you have to spike to get your name on a dust truck?" says my wife. I choose to ignore this. Although I immediately start to compose an email to the Council in my head.

The next day I spend three hours picking up litter. Four youths departing the plush Rose Hill Community Centre ask me what I'm up to. I tell them I'm doing community service. They accept this explanation unhesitatingly; had I said I was engaged in voluntary communal litter picking, they'd have likely floundered in failed comprehension.

My wife makes a suggestion. "Why don't you write a new column called *Atta Girl*? Then you can legitimately say a nice lady in the street outside Magdalen once said it's the greatest thing you've written."

"I can't just write a story randomly called *Atta Girl*," I contest. "Besides, it's self-evidently an American expression. I'd be more likely to catch myself saying 'Ye-haw'."

Instead all I can think about during the long hours of harpooning cigarette packets and thoughtlessly discarded KFC wrappers is how I'd like to spear the litterbugs responsible and toss their lifeless corpses into an unmarked black sack too.

"Have you thought of a column yet you can title *Atta Girl*?" asks my wife while I'm washing my hands for the fifth consecutive time after the litter pick. "No," I reply honestly.

From the Community Centre - where we gather for post pick photos for the local newsletter - I cross the footbridge to Sainsbury's in search of snacks. As I leave the supermarket, two girls in their mid-20s pass me walking in. They are wearing expressions that signal they've endured a difficult day.

"I don't know about you," remarks one to the other, "but I intend to fill up my trolley with nothing but chocolate." "Atta girl!" I exclaim to myself.

BACKTRACKING TRAIL

I'm recruiting a crack team. If we're successful a big prize awaits. And since the odds are raised, so, accordingly, must we do the same to our game.

So far I've enlisted a ten-year-old child who's the daughter of my friend Matt who'll "definitely come along to help but I may be quite late." My wife has also been reluctantly signed up. Basically we're replicating the *Ocean's Eleven* movie, assembling a dream team to deliver a sparkling jackpot - had *Ocean's Eleven* planned to grab a cuddly toy retailing at £3.99 from an underfunded library rather than the weekend takings of a glittering Las Vegas casino.

Not for the first time in my history of humiliations documented via this column, the situation is my wife's fault. During a recent library visit she discovered that a cuddly Paddington Bear toy is on offer to anyone who can solve something billed as 'The Library Trail'.

Moreover we only have two hours to solve it. "Let's synchronise watches," I say, determined to impose a military-esque discipline and vocabulary upon proceedings. Everybody ignores me and gives their attention to the clue sheet. "What time shall we meet after the trail?" asks the ten-year-old. Preferring us to 'rendezvous' rather than 'meet', I say, "We'll rendezvous here at precisely fifteen hundred hours." "What?" Bridles my wife. "About three," I confirm, while my wife's eyes look skywards in search of absolution.

"I've conducted reconnaissance of the library, and anticipate mobilising our column…" I say, before stopping on account of the fact nobody is paying attention. Before I can commence a prepared *Henry V*-like pep talk to my team ahead of their quest - containing several phrases that I'm sure will be a shoe-in for the next edition of *The Oxford Dictionary of Quotations* - everyone sallies forth, eager to start the trail "and avoiding you" as quickly as possible.

The Library Trail comes in the form of a worksheet containing studiously difficult questions about books aimed at both child and adult readership. Hence knowledge is required of which murder weapon was used in a particular Agatha Christie scene, whereas another question relates to Katherine Rundell's Costa-winning novel *Rooftoppers*.

Having once done a double act performance with the latter at Blackwell's bookshop, I have the celebrity author's number in my phone. "Er, why don't I just text her and ask which character in her bestseller played the cello?" I suggest. "Because that's lazy. We should look it up in the books. They have them all in the library, that's why it's called the 'Library Trail'. Otherwise you're cheating by contacting the author." This is unimpeachably correct. Thank goodness one of us retains sufficient integrity - and fibrous morality - to be adult about proceedings. Yes, it was the ten-year-old who spoke that sentence.

We dash around the library speedily flicking through books as diverse as Michael Bond's *A Bear Called Paddington* and Graham Greene's *Brighton Rock*. This could easily have led to mix-ups: "Paddington knew, before he had been in Brighton three hours, that they meant to murder him."

There are questions on adult thrillers and the fairy-tale *Snow White*. Following recent revelations in the age of #MeToo, the Seven Dwarves should probably be renamed Gropey, Handsy, Touchy, Feely, Rapey, Grabby and Squeezy - to more accurately reflect male showbiz-industry personnel.

My friend Matt, like a pub quiz cheat, uses Wikipedia. But at least he's consulting it with library resources. The ten-year-old - her moral fibre evidently not quite as fibrous as earlier - confirms this is definitely allowed.

But there's a concern that sloshes around our collective stomachs making us feel uneasy. Admittedly it doesn't say the Library Trail is for children. There's no specific age limit on the form. But the prize is surely indicative that it may be a competition exclusively for children: a Paddington Bear toy. To circumnavigate this concern we put our ten-year-old companion's name on the entry form. But include my wife's mobile phone number. Between us we solve all the questions and hand in our answer sheet to a librarian.

Paddington, his destructive relationship with marmalade unchallenged throughout all 34 books, was the most famous creation of the late Michael Bond. Paddington is at least unfailingly polite, although responsible for inevitable destruction. Such unswerving politeness was modelled on the author's father who reportedly wore his hat (similar to Paddington's) even when paddling in the sea on holiday. His justification for such eccentricity? In case any ladies would pass while paddling, thereby enabling him to raise his headwear in greeting them.

Fully a week after we'd forgotten all about participating in the Library Trail, my wife's mobile rings. "Yes!?" she answers impatiently. There is no requirement for her to add, "This really, really isn't a good time," given that sentiment has already been tonally implied.

"Hello, I'm calling from the library," says the voice on the other end, unflustered by my wife's impassive phone manner. On realising the caller is from the library, her mood suddenly changes - as does her voice. And name. "Oh, thanks so much for ringing me," her voice suspiciously raised at least an octave to impersonate a ten-year-old.

The next day I'm dispatched to collect the prize. My resolve is unanchored by the requirement to impersonate a child. The only cover story I can think of to explain the discrepancy between my middle-aged appearance and the age declared on the entry form is one involving abnormal growth hormones. Then there's the gender dichotomy to address too. Approaching the librarian's desk I feel a pinch of anxiety. I decide to tell them the truth. My friend's ten-year-old daughter did it, but with help from me and, er, two Oxbridge postgrads.

"That's alright, dear," she says, unlocking a cupboard and picking out one of what must be about sixty identical small Paddington bears. "Anyone who entered receives one," she says unassumingly.

This was not how *Ocean's Eleven* ended.

"I know personally one of the authors featured in the Library Trail," I say boastfully in an ill-conceived attempt to claim back some lost status.

"That was useful for the quiz then," she says, without allowing me to impress her with the celebrity author's name. Instead she has her own boast: "We had a lady here this morning who knew Agatha Christie." Aware that I've just been crushed in a game of Celebrity Author Namedrop - a game that I'd instigated - I proceed to stress test the unlikeliness of this brag. "Wow. How old was she?" I ask. "Not old," confirms the librarian. "She lived in Cholsey when she was little and got to know Agatha Christie who lived in the same village."

Yet again I'm a victim of my own rodomontade posturing. Thanking the librarian, I grab my Paddington bear and harrumph down the library steps. At least, I console myself, our effort will be worth it when I see the ten-year-old's face glow with delight upon presenting her with the hard-won Paddington prize.

"It's nothing like as big as I was expecting," she announces later when I hand her the prize. "You or the library could have removed the £3.99 sticker," adds my wife.

"Please look after this bear," I say, giving them a hard stare.

THE ASSIGNATION

My quiet corner of a supermarket café is exploded by the loud arrival of a suited man. He ignores several empty tables before deciding to select one next to me while shouting into his mobile.

I quickly conclude that he must be entering a radio phone-in competition to list the maximum number of business clichés possible in sixty seconds. "This requires out-of-the-box thinking. Pushing the envelope. Ensuring we're singing from the same hymn sheet." Then he adds one I haven't heard before, that may risk him being disqualified from the competition: "We need to fork through the compost one more time on this one." Unless he's discussing "the way forward" with his gardener, this is a decidedly odd linguistic addition to business-speak patois.

Never once does he leave a speaking gap for whoever is on the other end of the line - assuming there is some unfortunate having to listen to this. Other than me. And anyone else within a 90-metre radius.

Then a woman in her late-40s, expertly dressed in a woollen purple and black outfit with complementing accessories, strolls towards us and sits alongside me on an elongated sofa facing the businessman. She has exceptionally fair hair - just on the blonde side of silver - and suspiciously white teeth. She flashes a bright, dazzling smile that suddenly lights up the room - as if a man had just said "try it now" after changing the bulb in a lighthouse.

"Oh, hi there," says the businessman with an unconvincing casualness, banging his knees on the table as he jumps up almost involuntarily to greet her.

"What's good here?" she asks him, as if contemplating whether to plump for the braised pheasant with porcini before remembering it's a supermarket café on Botley Road. "Er… they do a good sausage roll," he says, presumably regretting his words even as they are forming in his throat. "Perhaps a sandwich then?" she quickly concludes. "We have to order at the counter." "Oh, of course," she concedes - signalling that she's not used to frequenting establishments so squalid that you have to actually go and fetch the food yourself. Whatever next?

Her vocabulary, referring to 'chaps', 'scrummy' and 'being blotto' reveals an unashamed poshness. "Did I mention that I've bought a boat?" asks the businessman. "No," she replies. Unwisely. Her conversational naivety allows him to raise anchor on an uninterruptable voyage of vanity. "I was warned that boats are the quickest way to lose £50,000 - even ahead of an ex-wife… ha ha… but…" To her credit Bleached Teeth Woman gets up and walks away mid-anecdote. "Just going to order," she says. "Oh, okay. Me too."

"Oh, thank you. Perhaps you can get me a sandwich then?" Clever. "Something vegetarian." She smiles again, forcing me to shield my eyes with a newspaper from the equivalent phosphorescent luminosity of a supernova.

She sits alone at the table, but only a few inches from me on the shared long red sofa. I steal a 1/10th of a second micro glance at her - a risky procedure in case she smiles again and temporarily blinds me like looking directly at the sun. She then rushes to join the businessman briefly in the queue - presumably to amend her order - and trustingly leaves her cash-stuffed open purse on the seat next to me. They return with three pre-packed sandwiches and a sausage roll. Then something bizarre happens.

He kisses her. Properly kisses her. "Not here," she chastises him. Ignoring her own advice, she lunges at him, and they kiss holding their breath like pearl divers.

Classily dressed and in their late 40s, both instantly regress to acting like teenagers at a bus stop. My free Waitrose coffee and newspaper are an inadequate distraction from the breathless *in flagrante delicto* that's happening exactly 1.5 metres to my left.

Eventually resurfacing for air, Posh Lady announces: "I must be going." She furiously brushes her expensive dress as if she has just undergone physical entanglement with a moulting dog rather than a suited middle-aged businessman, before announcing: "I'll take my sandwich to go. See you there." "See you there," he repeats. I forget and am a nanosecond late shutting my eyes when she smiles again - like someone flicking on stadium floodlights.

Suddenly she's gone, leaving only a perfume trace behind her like an airplane's lingering vapour trail. No doubt on her way to somewhere unimaginably exotic. "See you in Didcot," he calls after her. When my vision returns the businessman has gone too, their assignation over.

He's taken a bite out of one of his two sandwich halves. I temporarily consider claiming this abandoned lunch, but realise that even impoverished freelance writers like me have their standards and dignity.

So I only take the sandwich that hasn't been bitten.

STATE OF THE HEART TECHNOLOGY

Sun's out. Temperature's perfect. And I've got a rare day off work.

Although all three occurrences are rare, the latter is undisputedly the rarest. Being a freelance writer is a lot like being a panda. Kindly allow me a chance to explain that analogy. You see pandas have chosen to eat one undeviating food source that is very low in nutritional value. Thereby consigning themselves to investing virtually every waking minute munching bamboo to obtain sufficient nutrients for survival. And given how little freelance writing pays as a profession, that's pretty much the same life for me. Rendering me indistinguishable from a panda. Apart from the two black eyes. And a refusal to mate in captivity.

Strolling towards the shops by myself on a sunny Monday morning, I feel relaxed and content. Invigorated with life, I experience a surge of optimism.

Five minutes later I'm dead.

Well… very, very nearly dead. Suddenly I begin to feel profoundly unwell. So unwell I genuinely believe I'm dying. The fat lady's about to hit her final note. The curtain operator's reaching for the cord. The Grim Reaper is sharpening his blade.

Moments earlier I had cycled calmly into the town centre and parked my bike. Unaware at the time, my last decisive action on this planet was to press the button at a pelican crossing.

The little man turns green. I turn greener. Instantly I feel acutely unwell. Believe me, no previous experiences of illness can aid me as a reference point for just how chronically ill I suddenly feel. Plus I'm vibrating with terror. That's the last thing I can remember.

An unknown number of minutes later I am unaccountably lying down in the middle of the road. A dual carriageway no less. I have no idea why. My brain scans the situation and responds with: "Why does the floor go upwards?" Followed quickly by: "Get up off the friggin' road! There's probably a lorry coming!"

Picking myself up, I attempt to struggle to safety. Somehow I make it to the side of the road. Thank goodness this hectic highway is implausibly traffic free. Yet my feet seem to be rebelling against a lifetime's control by my brain. I'm wobbling. Lucidity returns intermittently allowing me to process that I'm still in immense danger.

There's an unhelpful metal fence stopping me from escaping the dual carriageway and reaching the sanctuary of the pavement. I feel like someone lost at sea unable to battle any longer, about to cease struggling and relent to the inevitable waters closing above them.

I experience no heart palpitations. Instead I host an overriding feeling of dizziness and disorientation. I feel like a phone battery displaying '0%'. Feel so, so ill. This. Is. It. Of all the places to die, at least there's a lamppost nearby - handy for any roadside shrines.

Desperately I need to sit down. Only there are no public benches. Thanks austerity. Instead I cling onto a nearby wall like ivy. The seconds combine into minutes. Soon I realise something alarming: I no longer know who or where I am. Then I sink into bottomless nothingness. There's no bright guiding light. No choir of angels. No tutting St Peter to greet me at the Pearly Gates with the words: "Hmm…I'm going to need a couple of helpers to wheel out your sin file."

There's a loud bang. The cause turns out to be my right knee collapsing and hitting the pavement. Mighty hard. Then no recollection whatsoever. Later I awake on my back - on a decidedly uncomfy pavement. I'd been out cold for an incalculable amount of time. Blood is seeping through my clothes from cuts I don't recall getting. My right knee, leg, arm and chest hurt - but thankfully not my head. I think.

I crawl onwards and find a bench. I sit on it for nearly an hour. After five minutes I remember my name. Followed by where and who I am. It's a literal lifesaver that bench.

At least my timing's good for having a suspected cardiac arrest. If you must die of a heart attack, terribly inconvenient as I'm sure that's always guaranteed to be, then at least dying at 9am on a Monday is preferable to experiencing a fatal episode at 5pm on a Friday!

People load final acts and words with undeserved significance. The most appropriate final words anyone should say is: "Dial 999 now!" When asked to renounce the devil on his deathbed, Voltaire replied: "This is no time to be making new enemies." Undeniably witty, but had Voltaire later requested a glass of water his final words would have been less memorable, but on the plus side he might not have died of dehydration soon afterwards!

Thankfully I make it home, where my wife bullies me into visiting either my GP or A&E. But I'm a guy. And evidently would rather die than risk causing a mild fuss. I never visit my GP. But I dial the surgery and expect to be told the next available appointment will be in late spring next year. "I collapsed in the street this week and lost consciousness …" "Can you get here within an hour?" "Yes, but I have to work today as I'm on deadline to file…" "If you can't get here within an hour then you'll need to go to the hospital." Crikey, this *is* serious.

An hour later I'm in a doctor's consulting room. He cannot conceal his delight at being presented with an interesting case, rather than the usual stream of patients with an achy digit from excessive texting who've just googled "finger cancer".

Thank goodness for the wonderfully dedicated doctors, nurses and support staff of the NHS. There's a good reason why Britain's real state religion is the NHS. "It's a choice between a seizure, stroke, epileptic fit or a heart problem," announces the doctor. Ominously. None of these selections appeal to me. It's like a Tory Party leadership choice. He asks if anyone came to my aid. "No, but it's quite an unpopulated street given its proximity to a nasty dual carriageway."

"Did you wet yourself?" asks the doc. "Er… not since Timothy Spence's birthday party." (I don't tell him it was Timothy's 30th.) "Did you bite your tongue?" "No." "Did you experience any feelings of being very unwell before losing consciousness?" "Yes." After a few more evaluating questions he's eliminated three of the four probable candidates. "It's likely not a seizure but a cardiovascular cause." I look at him on the cusp of really wanting to say something, yet somehow holding back - wearing an expression akin to Lee Mack allowing a spotted *double entendre* to pass unacknowledged. "A heart problem," he confirms. "Oh," I nod.

He interrogates me further. I sense early on this is not a time to attempt humour. "Did you bite your lip?" "Only when my wife said she she'd lost weight recently." Told you.

Then he measures my heartbeat. Instantly I detect from his body language it's not good news. He actually recoils. Unplugging his stethoscope from each ear, the doctor exhales a displeased sigh. It's not the sort of noise you'd reserve for coming home and discovering a missed parcel delivery ten minutes ago. Instead it's more the sound emitted after returning home and discovering the house you'd diligently locked up that morning has been replaced with a smoking crater.

"You'll need to cancel any plans you may have for the rest of the day," he says portentously in full missive-issuing-tone. "Brilliant," I think, "are we going on a surprise outing?" Once I was walking through Soho to meet the comedian Holly Walsh in the bar of the Soho Theatre. I had been in Soho for barely two minutes when an inadequately dressed woman approached me and enquired: "Would you like a nice time?" "Fantastic," I thought, "can we go to Alton Towers?"

"I mean you'll need an urgent ECG - either here or at the hospital. It can't wait until tomorrow," says the doctor solemnly. My heart, with scrumptious irony, is now working particularly hard. An image puffs into my mind: Eric Morecambe shouting behind his jacket lapel at his heart: "Keep going, you fool!"

"The heartbeat is slow, there almost a missed beat, and kind of secondary echo beat." He can tell by my open mouthed terror that he needs to say something reassuring next. "It can very likely be treated with a pacemaker."

The news arrives like a clap of thunder on a bright summer's day.

He consults with another doctor while I wait outside. Later I'm ushered into a different room at the surgery where a support worker offers me a drink. Surely no one gets offered a drink by the busy staff unless you're not expected to make it past mid-afternoon? "What would you like to drink?" asks a kindly tall lady with a face that's evidently been exposed to more than her fair share of stress in life. "A quadruple vodka please," I say, "with a shot of cranberry juice as I'd better be on a health kick now." She laughs sympathetically. "Tea, then?" I nod. Even though I don't drink tea, I recall reading somewhere that coffee may be bad for the heart. Or is it good? I don't know. But I'll need to find out. Soon.

Within three hours I'm at the hospital. A nurse is unpeeling and placing adhesive strips all over my body, like someone completing their Panini sticker album against a very tight deadline. Another nurse in a blue uniform wheels in a cart containing impressive-looking state-of-the-art cardiological monitoring equipment and starts clipping wires to my stickered torso. Everyone is friendly and professional. No-one attempts any light innuendo or bawdy banter - both staples of British hospital-based comedies. I begin to feel misled over the depicted reality of hospitals by Barbara Windsor, Kenneth Williams and the rest of the *Carry On* team.

When I visited my psychologist friend Helen in a maternity ward recently, a nurse prefixed administering an injection by saying: "You'll just experience a small prick." "That's what got Helen here in the first place," I replied - almost involuntarily as a comedic reflex. (Come on - if you don't convert those when the opportunity arises, they'll confiscate your comedy licence.) Instead of a Sid James cackle or an "Oh matron!" I received a tumbleweed silence. And feared having my own #MeToo posting.

I receive an urgent ECG. Consequently I'm fast-tracked a cardiologist instead of a more traditional seven months spent on the waiting list. Diagnosed with an irregular heartbeat, I am banned from driving for six months. Also I'm not allowed to have baths on my own. And no, this does not allow me to ask a female friend to join me. Clarifies one of the nurses. Needlessly. But at least it's lascivious hospital badinage consistent with *Carry On Nurse*.

In addition, I'm told to avoid heights and depths. The latter is bad news for anyone who's just splashed out on their own personal submarine. Oddly the doctors and nurses seem to be more apologetic about relating news of my driving ban than my potentially fatal heart defect. Another doctor reiterates the possibility I might need a pacemaker. "Why, am I going to attempt to break a middle-distance world record?" I say with a flash of mischievousness in my eyes. He liked that.

I receive notification that in order to plan their strategy of countering my irregular heartbeat, I must undergo a 24-hour hospital stay for more heart monitoring. Meanwhile my returned blood tests confirm I have high cholesterol - which is annoying if it means breakfasts will no longer involve fry-ups but nibbling demurely on a blueberry.

Hearing that I've been unwell, my youngest niece comes to visit. "I've made you a present," she announces, handing me a homemade card. Underneath the words "Get well soon" she's drawn a large recuperating animal with a bandaged head. "That's you," she says. It's a panda.

A COMPLETE LACK OF NATIONAL TRUST

I have committed a crime. Criminals report that after your first crime, it steadily gets easier. But I disagree. Here's how I tripped and fell off the straight and narrow, badly straining my morality in the process.

My friend once purchased lifetime membership to an organisation that preserves historical buildings. Since there are at least two well-known institutions fitting that description, I'll leave it there to preserve deliberate ambiguity. Here are the details of the case, m'lord.

Four of us are paying a hefty admission fee to visit a historic Oxfordshire building. However, I can show my friend's life membership card - even though he's not in our party. To be fair, it did cost him an enormous sum several years ago, even though he's hardly used it since getting a job that required him to move instantly to New Zealand. And there aren't that many English stately homes to visit in New Zealand.

All I have to do is pass myself off as my friend at the entrance gate. But my wife isn't helping with the stress levels.

For this deceptive mission I have learned my friend's date of birth and postcode in case I am interrogated and required to recite them to disprove any discovered discrepancy between cardholder and card bearer. There were people parachuted into occupied France behind enemy lines who'd undergone less preparation for their false persona than me. I commit my friend's autobiographical facts to memory. "In order to pull off this subterfuge," I inform my wife, "I have to be someone else." "Yeah," agrees my wife, "an honest person."

Two days later on an unpleasantly cold morning I approach the historic building's entry gate just as the sun disappears behind menacing clouds, silhouetting the black guard hut. Staff click to attention and march out of their sentry post. In my imagination they had torches, jackboots and snarling dogs on chains - but I doubt that was the reality. Nobody asks my date of birth or postcode. Euphoria at slipping past the control point is short-lived, when I realise this is only the hut where they try and get you to take out membership. My friend had been snared here ten years ago.

We approach the main checkpoint for interrogation. "Three full-price adults, plus one free with life membership, please," I announce in a voice oscillating with tension to the border guard, er, I mean helpful volunteer.

"This card allows two adults in your party free admission," says one of the kind volunteers. "No," insists my wife suspiciously, with the 'I' pronoun heavily stressed, "I wish to pay full price." "Are you sure?" asks a volunteer. My wife is very sure. Hence I pay for three adults. Plus I pay the extra for Gift Aid too. Why is avoiding tax more expensive than not paying it?

Sensing an easy add-on sale is available, the volunteer annoyingly informs us: "Guide booklets are £5 each." I buy one - mainly out of transparent guilt. In Gift Aid contributions, guide books and unnecessary extra adult tickets, I've already spent more than I've saved, and haven't got past the gate yet.

We're told to wait a few minutes before a guided tour starts. It transpires we are the only four people on it. "Don't call him Richard," my wife whispers to our friends Graham and Margaret. "Why?" asks Margaret, reasonably, her face creased with concern. "So they don't suspect he's not the name on the membership card."

"I don't think they're concerned about that," says Graham calmly.

"Besides," reasons Margaret, "Richard says that card cost hundreds of pounds and has hardly been used - so they've already got their entrance fee paid." Such an irremovable rock of logic is trivially pushed aside by my wife.

"Maybe," I dare to suggest to my wife, "on this occasion you're wrong?" Distinctly unopen to the possibility that there's a first time for everything, my wife emits a noise indicating this suggestion belongs on the inconceivable side of totally impossible.

Sitting in the café after the tour a worrying thought suddenly enters our otherwise now relatively relaxed mood - like a wasp of anxiety flying into my pub garden of serenity.

"Don't pay by card," announces my wife, in the same tone deployed at the culmination of an episode of *Columbo*. "That will give away your name," she reasons.

"Richard…" says Graham in an attempt to begin a sentence. "Don't call him Richard!" cautions my wife dramatically. She gestures by throwing a hand over her shoulder that café staff may be eavesdropping. A waitress, fully twenty metres away, is obliviously chalking specials on a board.

"I'm not entirely sure you can go to prison for this," I inform my wife as I force the cashier to dig for change while the lights on the contactless payment machine wink their convenience at us.

This is surely the most middle-class crime it's possible to commit, short of shoplifting a polo pony from Waitrose.

Just over a week later we receive a speculative brochure in the post suggesting we join "that organisation we recently visited," I say. "You say 'visited'," clarifies my wife, "I say 'defrauded'."

She picks up the brochure, delighting in it being addressed to me personally and concludes: "They're onto you." We fill out the form for annual membership. According to my wife it's either that or go on the run. I'm now nearly £70 down after my "deception".

My life of crime is over.

THE BEST LADLED PANS OF RICE AND PENNE

A cheerful Oxford café is running a charitable promotion for Shrove Tuesday. Eat a stack of twenty small(ish) pancakes within twenty minutes and you get to consume the whole hefty calorific count for free.

That's right - it's only free if you succeed in achieving the eating challenge. Fail to gorge your way through a pancake pile the size of the Matterhorn and then you have to pay full price. An equally hefty twenty quid. But…given it all goes to charity - specifically Mencap - what's not to like? Apart from indigestion.

My wife enthusiastically relays information about the challenge after discovering it in a shopping centre leaflet. "And it'll mean you'll likely die earlier too," she says, her tone betraying a voltage surge in her enthusiasm for my participation.

We bus into town and indicate to the eatery our willing participation in the challenge. This leads to a choreographed staff ceremony. Two restaurant employees stand either side of me. One asks me if I'm going to win the challenge. "Yes!" I reply with unconquerable optimism. The other addresses the restaurant like a Town Crier, rapturously announcing: "The charity challenge has hereby been accepted." Hearing millennials deploying words like 'hereby' is unavoidably funny, and I allow an unguarded snigger to escape. Don't worry - the millennials will be taking their revenge on me very soon indeed.

No-one else in the busy eatery seems to stop their conversations or even notice the proclamation. Until a waitress arrives, fumbles inside her top in an unsettling act of self-groping, before producing a whistle attached to a fuchsia ribbon. She blows it with the intensity of someone trying to replicate the saxophone solo in *Baker Street*.

Everyone suddenly drops their burgers, pancakes and forks of pasta mid-bite to free their hands for panicked earplugging.

Attention now duly sought and delivered, everybody turns to look at my wife and me. This is most definitely not what I wanted. The restaurant is packed; it's fuller than a centipede's sock drawer. Blushing uncomfortably in the unwanted recognition, I take a timid bite out of pancake number one. And chew. It is quite sweet. In fact it's so sweet I'd doubt whether a bag of sugar would contain a higher sugar content than these pancakes.

Only one minute has elapsed and already I'm nibbling the frosting off pancake number two. Keep this up and dinner is on them. Mercifully by now the attention of other diners has returned to their own meals and murmuring conversations. Busy waitresses revert to their usual job of ferrying plates of pasta, burgers and rice to hungry carbohydrate seekers.

According to my time-keeping wife, as I consume my fourth and fifth pancakes I'm still on schedule to succeed in my sugary quest. Tension is rising like a pie crust at Gas Mark 8. Gorging my sixth, seventh and eighth within eight minutes means I'm maintaining par to reach pancake glory. Lifting up the ninth I'm suddenly aware that it feels somehow heavier. Plus sweat is starting to trickle down my forehead.

I nibble a blueberry. My wife makes a face to communicate: "Don't eat the garnish - classic rookies' mistake." By the time I finish pancake number twelve there are only six minutes left on the clock. The situation is quickly becoming unpropitious. It's not looking good for my attempt to join the world elite of competitive pancake eating at this level.

Polishing off number thirteen takes four whole minutes. I don't so much wolf it down as peck at it like a timid wren. My stab at pancake scoffing immortality is looking decided unlikely - ironically just as my pancake eating mortality looks increasing likely. Hence I concede defeat and bow my head in dejection. I have managed fourteen pancakes and currently have no plans to munch a fifteenth until sometime around the year 2039.

Shortly afterwards two café staff stand behind me and blow their whistles - the high pitch shrill of failure. One holds up a pre-printed sign declaring: "Pancake loser". A tad insensitively in my opinion. Her colleague proclaims aloft another placard, handwritten with: "My buttered mate." Which is a bit odd, frankly. Then, without warning, the situation suddenly becomes even weirder.

Two staff members are augmented by another female millennial wearing an extra small baseball cap struggling to contain her huge hair. All curtail their waitressing work instantly - to the visual chagrin of customers waiting for their orders - and instead stand right behind me. Instinctively I flinch. Then it starts.

They all begin to sing acapella; though not, it transpires, the same words or tune. Halfway through their rendition, another waitresses-cum-chanteuse rushes out from behind the grill to join them with a ladle still in hand. At first she's neither in the right room nor key.

Their "song" is howlingly awful. It's a four-line ditty about an abnormal love of pancakes which is presumably the subject of an attempted banning order by the Diabetes Awareness Association. Sadness leaks out of one of the "singer's" painted-on smiles. The girl with the tiny hat and giant hair has a legible thought bubble escaping above her baseball cap: "I've got a GCSE. I don't have to do this. I could be a successful stripper - if I just had a bit more self-esteem. Help me!" I consider returning to the restaurant later tonight in a brazen attempt to free the staff.

Then the tuneless trio (latterly quartet) ask the rest of the diners to applaud me for raising £20 for charity. I take an actorly public bow, radiating in my public-spiritedness. And try desperately to pull off the convincing look of someone not in any way whatsoever thwarted in their selfish ambition to blag a free pancake dinner. Oh no. It's all about the donating to charity - that's why I'm here. Yeah. It is. (Awkward cough.) Definitely. Well, possibly.

Besides, I could easily have cheated had I venally possessed the immoral gumption. Slipping pancakes under the table would have been easy. In the world of competitive eating contests there's likely more cheating than in international cycling. And on that note: surely the moment defining when the game was finally up for international cycling not being infested by drugs cheats was the year that Amy Winehouse was the surprise winner of the Tour de France?

Cheating is not uncommon in eating competitions. As a journalist I once covered the World Pie Eating Championships in Wigan for my resultant book *Britain's Most Eccentric Sports*. Disqualification awaited a previous podium finisher when it was discovered his pies had been laced with cough medicine to ensure they slipped down. Boo.

In later years the competition rules were altered to determine the winner by the speed of consuming one pie rather than by aggregate number. This concession to the healthy eating lobby was too much for some: presumably those who replied to their doctors' express concerns of "have you considered taking up a sport to benefit your health and fitness?" by replying: "Yes, elite pie eating."

One year the annual pie eating contest was deferred as an organiser's dog had broken into the store room where stock was being amassed for the next day's World Championship and proceeded to gorge the lot. At least the occurrence provided a definitive answer to the longstanding question: Who ate all the pies?

I donate my £20 to charity and ensure I also leave a decent tip for the waiting staff - in case the waitress blows her whistle again and holds up a sign daubed: "Loser AND lousy tipper." Or even worse: they threaten to sing again.

THE UNDERAGE DRINKERS

My agitation reaches what I incorrectly assume to be its highpoint for the day when someone squeezes in front of me to get served first.

However, it's definitely not going well. "Three pints of cider," says the pusher-in-er. This, to her visible frustration, does not result in three glasses being placed under the draught tap. Instead of cider, the barman dispenses a polite but unwavering directive. "I'll need to see some ID." The fact the girl couldn't look any more underage if she was wearing Peppa Pig branded pyjamas, doesn't bode well for this encounter.

Realising she has no vested interest in reacting to the barman's demand, she decides to ignore it. "Three pints of cider," she repeats. At this point the barman launches a phenomenally effective weapon from an exclusive arsenal belonging to bar staff and bus drivers. "What year were you born?" The size of the pause between her words decaying, and the girl's answer, suggests her 16-year-old - 17 at most - brain is whirling into action. And stuck buffering for a considerable amount of time.

Normally being asked questions appertaining to a level of difficulty covered by "when's your birthday?" are deemed as easy as a question can be. If she's failing at this level, wait until the barman starts asking her about Central American capital cities.

Her thoughts are easy to read: "Er… 20… no, hang on, 19…" It's quite understandable to forget someone else's birthday, but rarely your own. And rarer still to be out by an entire century.

Reacting like she's just solved a maths problem harder than Fermat's Last Theorem, she eventually stammers: "1997?" "You're 22, then?" says the barman instantly, flashing me a look like a prosecution lawyer communicating to the jury, "Well, that's this case resolved. I can catch an earlier train." The girl does the most unconvincing acting since *Crossroads* was taken off air by offering an insouciant, "Yeah, 22." Shirley Temple looked older in her audition tape.

Given the panicked randomness of her answer, 22 turned out to be relatively credible. Had she been served three preposterously expensive ciders, she'd probably have checked her eligibility for a child's discount.

"So I'll need to see ID confirming you're 22, please." "I haven't got any!" she snaps back, with the accompanying mannerisms of a surly teenager mid hissy-fit stomping towards her room.

"I'm sorry madam, but I cannot serve you without ID." This is almost certainly the first time in her short life she's been called 'madam' - at least without the prefix 'a proper little'.

Emitting a truculent snarl, she swivels to depart the bar space and finally allows me to get served. A cloud of humiliation rains on her, causing her to shiver with unrighteous anger. She returns ciderless to two friends who had optimistically seated themselves in the pub.

Finally the assistant editor I'm here to meet arrives. He offers me an occasional column for a trade magazine, adding, "I like the way your columns end with a big laugh." It turns out that he ends proceedings with a big laugh too, when offering a shockingly paltry fee that even Underage Drinker Girl would be able to calculate (eventually) constituted a fraction of the minimum wage. Don't be a freelance writer, kids. I can't remember the last time I bought food in a supermarket before its expiry date. Needless to say I accept the impecunious job offer.

Afterwards I wait at a bus stop outside the Queen's College when a sudden bottleneck in pedestrian traffic causes a pack of undergraduates to stop. They are obviously freshers. The one at the back is projecting his voice to everyone - from Magdalen Bridge to Carfax: "So I'm like, 'I don't like this essay title', and she's like, 'you're at Oxford now and you must expect to be challenged', and I'm like, 'that's not what I mean' so I went for a nap." His sentence is remarkable for a modern teenager in managing to incorporate one correct usage of the word 'like'.

They are presumably en route to another pub or college bar. All are likely 18 and enjoying their recent entrance to both Oxford and adulthood. Such a contrast with the three teenagers I encountered earlier, who although only a couple of years younger, were still ensnared in a pre-adulthood purgatory - disconnected refugees from both childhood and adulthood.

My phone rings. It's my father informing me he has visited my mother and reports she is now incapable of understanding who he is after nearly 60 years of marriage. Alone in a care home room, lacking mobility and comprehension, now almost entirely blind and deaf, I grieve for my mother while she's still alive. Tears rise up with an unstoppable violence. No one notices an adult man crying uncontrollably amongst the crowded bustle of Oxford's High Street in the gathering gloom of a dying winter's afternoon.

So much for always ending with a big laugh.

MALICE THROUGH THE LOOKING GLASS

In an age of digital communication, the really serious stuff is still delivered in paper format: tax demands, jury summons and hospital appointments.

Plopping onto my doormat one morning, and instantly standing out from the accompanying junk mail offering me discount vouchers for pizzas the size of mini-roundabouts, is a letter from the NHS. Somewhat ominously they bugle that I have hit a significant age and therefore *the* time has arrived. Time to be summoned for a particularly invasive hospital procedure.

Of course, the chirpy text points out, it's completely voluntary and you don't have to proceed. And that's perfectly fine. Totally okay. Just as long as you like experiencing avoidable premature death.

My summons is for a bowel cancer check and includes an explanatory booklet titled, from memory, *Twenty creatively convincing euphemisms for explaining we're going to shove something huge a long way up your jacksie.* My favourite euphemism deployed in the leaflet is "flexible sigmoidoscopy". A few hours later my wife is explaining this procedure to our elderly neighbour. "It means they're going to be shoving a camera somewhere where the sun doesn't shine." He looks confused. "No, not Skegness," clarifies my wife.

I consent to attend and notify the NHS. By letter, obviously, given the seriousness of the situation. This only triggers another unwanted visit from the post(wo)man. A few weeks later I hear someone straining and pushing against my front door, like a puma attempting to use a cat flap. On the third attempt the postie succeeds in shoving through a brown box. Wow, a parcel! This mundane morning suddenly got a lot better. Will it be a surprise competition prize? Scrummy chocolates? A cherished book? Should I film an unboxing ceremony to upload onto social media like today's star vloggers? Some hasty ripping quickly reveals it's a DIY enema kit. Oh. It's to guarantee that when the day of the scheduled hospital visit arrives, my bowel hygiene, if not dignity, will be ensured.

An hour later I spot another envelope on my doormat. This one has been hand-delivered. Opening it reveals a handwritten note in scratchy red felt tip. "Hi Richard. Can you help my rabbit?" begins the letter. And there the letter ends. Abruptly.

Things are getting curious and curiouser. But the note's not from Alice regarding a white rabbit. The signature reveals it's from our near neighbour's 17-year old daughter Alison. In a brief postscript she requests my email address and mobile number — as there's evidently only so much handwriting a teenager is prepared to do these days when they could be texting instead.

Agreeing to this course of communicative action, I type an email. With her response the plot unspools before me. For the next fortnight she expects me to feed, medicate and exercise her pesky pet. Alison provides detailed instructions on how to undertake these immensely challenging tasks, while she presumably lies about her age ordering cocktails on some inexpressibly beautiful beach. "Where are you going for your hols?" I ask in one message after I've received another two-page attachment on how to cater for Fussy Flopsy. "Siberia to visit my grandad," she replies. Maybe I was wrong about the pina coladas in Skegness.

I risk RSI scrolling through the extensive briefing documents attached. "He must be fed bell peppers that are either orange or red but

NOT ON ANY ACCOUNT green. Serve shredded lettuce (romaine, UNDER NO CIRCUMSTANCES GIVE HIM ICEBERG)." Talk about a pampered spoilt bunny. Does he insist his salads are undressed but never untossed? Will he send back his carrots if they're diced not batons? Basically I'm looking after the Mariah Carey of rabbits — one demonstrating similarly outrageous backstage rider demands. I'm genuinely expected to pick out the brown circular bits from his special rabbit muesli "as he doesn't like them". "He also needs about 3-4 daily treats and once a week he must be served a raspberry. Make sure IT IS REALLY FRESH."

"Why pick on me to feed Finicky Flopsy?" I ask my wife. Initially she sighs her response, before adding: "Well you used to work in a pet shop." This is true. I was an original pet shop boy — years before Neil Tennant. However, the problem with boasting about my professional pet expertise renders others justifiably expectant that I'm a competent pet wrangler. As I try and pick up the reluctant rabbit for his exercises one evening, it soon transpires my abilities are not so much rusty as corroded to nothingness.

On my second day assuming bunny duties I attempt to pick up the Greens Gobbler. However the Fussy Furball evades me easily — a manoeuvre which ought to be quite difficult in a corner segment of a rabbit hutch.

I can feel the confidence flaking off me. Eventually I catch the Huge-eared Hopper, then wrap him in his favourite blue blanket to create a bunny burrito. At this stage I'm supposed to administer his medicine through a dropper. This, more predictably than Boxing Day following Christmas every year, meets with sturdy resistance. Bunny has two massive front teeth, coupled with a disinclination to allow anyone — especially me — to insert a foul smelling drugs stick down his cabbage shoot.

Outsmarted by Herby the Herbivore, I ruminate over my next move. After all I'm hardly stupid myself; I know rabbits are clever because I've seen *Watership Down*. See. Therefore I revive an old trick from my pet shop days to deceive macaws into swallowing their medication: secrete it in a teaspoon portion of mashed banana.

I place the mushy drug-laced treat into his food dish and observe. Instantly Big Ears hops towards his bowl. After an inspecting sniff, he wolfs — or, rather, rabbits - down the banana first, ahead of chomping his other snacks. I high-five my wife in triumphant exuberance.

Next I walk him around the garden. Not outside on public pavements in case of potential passing dogs and ridicule. The briefing notes explain he MUST be exercised every evening for forty minutes. And that means I have to be exercised for forty minutes each twilight too, even though he's the crepuscular one. Early evenings must be peak time at a rabbit gym.

Afterwards I remove his rabbit reins and place him back in his six -room dual level home. Not so much a hutch as a luxury apartment that I seriously consider renting out on Airbnb while his owners are away. Any posher and he'd have his own hanging baskets and a doorman. Yet my bunny duties are not over. Nor is my terror.

The following day I open His Hareness's hutch and serve dinner. As his personal salad chef, I'm not surprised to see Discerning Bugs twitch with food recognition. He hops towards his freshly prepared bunny banquet. However, I am considerably more surprised by what he does next. Bunny bolts towards me. And bites me. Really, really hard. Blood geysers into the air like a red oil strike.

Clearly the pernickety pet considers his food service to be too slow. And decided to take matters into his own paws by snacking on me. "He. Bit. Me." I say, partly in shock, but mostly in pain. My wife immediately takes the rabbit's side. "Big deal! He's only a cutesy, likkle, bunny wunny wabbit," before her tone quickly alters when I appear bleeding like an expendable character in a zombie movie. She flings open a row of unfamiliar cupboards until locating a first aid kit.

"Can you catch a disease from rabbits?" I ask. "Could I die of myxomatosis?" I ponder aloud, and consider doing the joke about a rabbit that expired after being fed ham toasties instead of specifically requested cheese toasties, complaining, "They mixed me t…" "And don't do your stupid joke about mixing me toasties!" "I wasn't," I lie.

"Don't bleed on their floor!" cautions my wife. Unsympathetically, in my view. "I thought rabbits were supposed to be vegan," I protest ineffectively. [The rabbit can't possibly be a vegan - because if he was he would have told me by now. Probably as soon as he first met me! Sorry, vegans.] This one is evidently a devout carnivore. He'd much prefer a slab of rare red steak to accompany his salad.

Two days later I am shivering with apprehension in a hospital waiting room alongside four strangers. Had we been huddled together in a marooned lifeboat floating aimlessly towards an empty horizon, I doubt if our expressions would be glummer.

I'm not here for bunny induced injuries, but the date has arrived for my colonoscopy. A man of a similar age but dissimilar waistline to mine is called before me. He ambles towards the waiting nurse at a speed akin to a sloth realising he's going to arrive early for an appointment.

Then a nurse booms out a name. Unlike the appointment I once endured to have my ears syringed — yeah, they still call out your name in the waiting room for that too (I know) - I hear her and therefore respond accordingly. "Follow me," she says and walks me along a corridor so long I conclude we can't possibly still be in Oxfordshire when we finally arrive at our destination: a windowless interview room. Patiently she explains the procedure and cleverly calms me down. Right up until the point when she says, "And we have gas and air for the pain." Anything comparable to childbirth, I ponder, is unlikely to be painless.

Once again they check I wish to continue. To galvanise myself into proceeding and not declining cowardly, I imagine my funeral. Graveside, my wife is snivelling uncontrollably into her handkerchief. Then I realise my burial appears to be taking place in summertime and she suffers with bad hay fever. My father is there too, asking the priest if this will take long as he's got a horse running in the 2.50 at Pontefract. My friend Helen heckles the vicar, pointing out religion is a manmade construct to avoid confronting the random futility of existence as we cling to a boulder hurtling pointlessly through space.

Confronted with this vision of my avoidable demise, I decide to live as long as possible. Hence I indicate my willingness to proceed with the cancer scan. Besides, I need a longer rest before tackling the epic walk back to reception. "Does anyone drop out at this stage?" I enquire, motivated by genuine curiosity. "Occasionally," confirms the nurse. Really? After paying for hospital parking?

From here I'm taken to a changing room where I put on a backless hospital gown and a pair of black plastic shorts resembling fetish wear that contain an ominous hole in the back. As a heterosexual male I don't find this at all reassuring.

Making small talk on the way to theatre, the friendly nurse asks me about the plaster on my hand. I explain about my rabbit sitting duties and how the Bitey Burrower had mistaken my fingers for carrots. She explains there are no nerve endings in the colon. Unlike my fingers. However, she warns me, my gut will be expanded with carbon dioxide, enabling the camera tube to navigate through my large bowel, and this will cause some discomfort.

For reasons that are never quite established, a team of three other people are also in the treatment room — perhaps they're live streaming the event on Facebook? After a minimal exchange of awkward social niceties, I'm asked to lie on my side and present my naked bottom to the doctor who's kindly trying to preserve my health. The barefaced cheek of it.

The doctor inserts something resembling a shower chord into my rectum. Surprisingly he seems able to push it in immensely deep without causing too much discomfort. I conclude I must have a massively capacious arsehole. Which surprises me, given I didn't go to public school.

"You can view the procedure on screen," says the nurse with more enthusiasm than the situation warrants. I glance upwards to see a monitor relaying live footage of tunnelling inside my intestines. That's the title sequence of *Dr Who* ruined forever. Watching the screen I half expect to see a flying Tardis. Though thankfully no nasty Ddalek-like polyps (potentially cancerous growths) seem to be appearing. The whole experience looks and feels surreal, like Alice disappearing down a rabbit hole.

Suddenly the lower part of my stomach hurts. Real kicked-in-the-googlies type agony. I start wreathing in pain, flapping and floundering like a haddock on a trawler deck. Instinctively I grab the tube and breathe in the gas. Or is it air? Whichever, it doesn't seem to be nullifying the pain.

"That's not right," says the proctologist, causing my anxiety to spike. It's the last thing you want to hear from a health professional mid-examination; especially one peering into one of my least publicly displayed orifices. Oh well. Goodbye kind world. I'm going to miss you, even if you won't miss me that much.

Perhaps they've now found a field of malicious Cybermen polyps that will require immediate removal. Or a tumour the size of Piers Morgan's head? Or, should they give Donald Trump a colonoscopy, Pier's Morgan's actual head?

"It should be the other end," propounds the nurse. That's a basic error the proctologist has made there, I think, if he's supposed to have gone in orally with his camera. "You're not breathing in from the correct bit," explains the nurse, her patience deflated like my colon when she pauses the carbon dioxide pump. When I identify the right tube the pain quickly recedes, if not my embarrassment. So that was why the proctologist made his remark. Phew.

Later I recount this to my friend Clare who has endured a colonoscopy recently too. Firstly she dismisses it (as "just like period pain") then, secondly, dismisses me as "a wuss" for requiring Entonox (less formally known as 'gas and air'). "I endure worse every month," she points out.

Before departing I use my remaining few seconds with a proctologist wisely and ask what I can do to maintain good bowel health. After all, bowel cancer is the third most common cancer in Britain, with 1 in every 18 UK citizens expected to experience it. "Eat lots of fibre and drink plenty of water," he replies.

"Your initial diagnosis appears good," declares the nurse after I've got dressed. But it's not all good news. Not at all, I'm afraid: they won't let me keep the plastic shorts with a hole in the back.

However I'm not out of the cancer woods yet. Having been told that the initial signs appear positive, they can't be sure on all fronts for a few days. She reminds me they'll send a further communication. By post, of course, given the importance. Just to keep my anxiety stoked for a few more days. It seems coming to terms with my own impermanence isn't quite over yet.

To maximise my fibre intake, I decide to start a new life. Well, a virtually indistinguishable life except one now involving prunes. I begin by googling the harshly yet unfairly maligned fruit. "There's a prune museum," I announce to my wife. This is true — it's in France. "I assume they get regular visitors," I add to a gathering silence. Eventually my wife sighs her displeasure. I also discover that there's no such thing as a prune bush or tree. Prunes are actually plums. Who knew? This is a fact bomb I intend to enjoy detonating in the future. I also pledge to eat more fibrous greens — aware my diet is morphing into the rabbit's, only without the latter's penchant for red meat.

Eventually news arrives. Sure enough, by traditional letter format given the gravitas of the situation. The postie has delivered an official-looking envelope bearing a tell-tale hospital postmark. Keen for the wounds on my right hand to heal as quickly as possible, I open it with my left to avoid using my bunny-savaged fingers. Mainly because I'm now in a position to report that, if ever questioned what animal bit you, replying "a bunny rabbit" elicits zero respect in public no matter how big a plaster you try wearing.

Then I stop mid-tear and decide to forego unsealing the letter. Since they've communicated in traditional paper format, the news is likely momentous; so I opt to wait until my wife is home before discovering its contents. Besides, with twilight drawing closer, it's time to feed the Broccoli Beast next-door.

Drenched in disquietude, I approach his hutch. For feeding duties I've now decided to wear protective oven mitts. Spokes of sunlight illuminate his twin fangs through the approaching cloud. Fastidious Flopsy glares me an "I'm going to masticate your other hand" look, before flinging a piece of rejected celery at me — presumably because I'd bought cheaper non-organic celery from a budget supermarket. Whenever he repeatedly knocks over his muesli bowl or dislodges his water tube, I'm the one who has to reposition it; he's clearly not prepared to lift a paw to help.

I manage to feed him without enduring another mauling. Returning home I'm relieved to see my wife is now back and so I can confront whatever fate the letter awaits to inform me.

"Where's our oven mitt?" asks my wife, running her hand under the cold tap after placing a pizza in a pre-heated oven barehanded. "Hmm… not sure," I poker bluff with a slither of exasperation in my voice. "Did you know a prune is a plum?" I enquire. She hastily looks around the kitchen, possibly for an improvised murder weapon. "Where are the plasters?" she asks. "Here they are," I say, passing her the box and revelling in actually doing something useful for once. "Are you sure you can spare one?" she asks, "remember you've still got to feed that killer rabbit for another week."

Opening an envelope with one hand is a surprisingly slow process and serves to elongate the tension. Eventually I access its contents and the letter reveals good news. The all clear siren sounds. They — the brilliant, brilliant NHS - have discovered neither evidence of colorectal cancer nor pernicious polyps. Relief floods my brain.

Three weeks later my friend Paul is summoned for the same invasive hospital procedure. "Can I ask for a DVD of the procedure to take home?" he suggests. "It could be called *A Journey Up My Arse*." Talk soon turns to favourite movies. "I've recently changed my fave film of all time," I announce. He leans forward with curiosity. "What movie is your new number one?" he asks. "*Fatal Attraction*."

GRIEF ENCOUNTER

My mother died this month.

Within five minutes of receiving the devastating news, I received another unpleasant shock: a brown envelope pushed aggressively through my letterbox.

It contained an unexpected demand from HM Revenue and Customs. This confirms the old adage that there really are only two certainties in life: death and taxes. My mother would have appreciated that - she always had an ability to finesse mollifying humour out of unpleasant situations.

A few hours later I'm travelling on a bus to Oxford Parkway station to begin a long journey to join my crestfallen father. Sheltering in a tiny waiting area I'm joined by a pair of latte-sipping 20-year-olds. Unavoidably hearing their conversation - conducted at comparable volume to a lost wolf calling to the pack - reveals they are brother and sister.

"Mum is on my case ALL THE TIME!" howls the sister. "So I told her, 'Mum, chill out. I'll get a job, like, one day.'"

I want to shake her until her absurdly pointy hat falls off and scream: "Do you know how privileged you are to have a mother? Mine has just died." But I don't. Although I do start crying again so I stand outside on the uncovered platform. There I am splendidly alone. Probably because it's freezing. And now raining.

The sister is wearing trousers that have so many deliberate holes 'designed' into them that they would make an effective fishing net.

A few minutes after departure the siblings invade my carriage. "That's better," announces the brother, "it was freezing back there." Oh joy. I start to sob even harder.

Between Bicester and Marylebone, Stupid Trousers makes a series of phone calls. During one she announces her credit card details complete with security digits to the entire carriage. On another call she quotes her mobile phone number twice. I enter it into my phone.

Suddenly I'm composing a text. "SHUT UP! Stop shouting on your phone. PS Your deliberately ruined trousers look RIDICULOUS."

My finger hovers over 'send'. But I don't do it. As we reach Marylebone I realise this is my last chance to press 'send'. Trust me;

her annoyingness - invulnerable to shame - is sufficient to justify being the message's recipient. Had Gandhi wandered into our carriage he would probably have punched her.

Maybe I'd be doing her a favour. One day she would tell people how her life was turned around when stranger intervention made her see what a narcissistic, whiney, workshy, shouty, stupid-trousers-wearer she was aged 20. A constructive comeuppance. But it's clearly the grief talking … or, rather, the grief texting.

Tubing to Kings Cross I arrive with an hour to fill before my next train. So I walk to the nearby British Library. A security man pushes a wooden stick into my rucksack half-heartedly, like it's a dipstick that has never once registered oil. "You've got a big bag - going anywhere nice?" he says in a friendly manner. I decide against answering, "To arrange my mother's funeral." Capsized by grief, I just about make it into the hushed reading room before I start blubbering again. No one shushes me.

Boarding the train at Kings Cross I locate the Quiet Carriage before sobbing loudly. No other passengers react, although an elderly man rustles his newspaper in presumable protest.

I hear the one o'clock news bulletin on my radio headphones and no one mentions that my mother has died. I've heard how the suddenly bereaved shake an angry fist at the world for possessing the temerity to carry on oblivious to their loss.

Grief is an odd opponent to outfox. Whenever you think it's toppled, the slightest draught of recollection reignites it. Grief is like one of those trick candles you get on birthday cakes that flicker themselves alight long after you've safely blown them out.

When your mother dies you feel less protected - more alone in the world. You've lost your biggest fan. Yet there's admin to do. When someone dies the grief can be overwhelming - but so can the paperwork. Alongside death and taxes there'll always be a third permanence: admin. There is a funeral to arrange, authorities to notify, pensions to stop, registrars to visit, solicitors to be fleeced by. I find these duties simultaneously invasive and a helpful distraction.

Later I discover the unsent text message in my drafts. Briefly my finger hovers over 'send'. Then I imagine my mum calmly telling me to delete the message. I comply. I guess that means she'll always be my mother, regardless of whether she's physically here or not. Which is just as well as I'm clearly not yet ready to make my own way in the world. Though I'm more able than some at buying my own trousers.

As the cold of her absence blows, I miss her. But I must carry on. For starters I really do need to pay that tax demand.

THE LUMP

My father has a large lump just above his neck. My late mother's response to this development would likely have been: "I know. It's called his head." But things are more serious nowadays. Especially as she's no longer around to finesse humour out of situations whose inexorable and unyielding bleakness requires it. She is also unable to fulfil her other expert skill: cajoling.

His lump is growing alarmingly, accelerating through the UK's coinage seemingly used to measure such things. Formerly the size of a 5p piece, it soon requires comparison with a 20p then 50p. It's well on its way to becoming the UK's other units of media measurements: football pitches, Olympic-sized swimming pools and Wales. This potentially cancerous inflation is worrisome to everyone he encounters. From family members to market stall traders, their faces crease in concern

When the growth became the size of a 20p piece my father's friend Linda urged him to seek medical attention. He declined, instead choosing to conform to the stereotypical male attitude that it's just a pimple. Things will get better by themselves. Besides, he'd prefer not to make a fuss. As John Cleese once observed, it's the goal of every Englishman to reach his grave unembarrassed.

Dogmatic wishful thinking will only get you so far, before an inevitable high-impact collision occurs with reality. I ask my father to see a doctor. He declines - citing the reason that, as a retiree, he's too busy. After all, the racing channel isn't going to watch itself, is it?

Although it's essential he sees a GP, he resoundingly refuses. Consequently an asphyxiating sadness risks overwhelming me. Whereas my own cajoling skills are poor, my coaxing arsenal fortunately contains a nuclear option. Hence my wife is duly mobilised to pay my father a visit. She arrives with the sole intention of sheep-dogging him to the doctor.

Given my father is Britain's most stubborn person - and I'm married to Britain's second most stubborn person - this does not bode well. Especially for me. My wife reads out quotes to him from websites detailing how unchecked facial tumours can be fatal. Since he still won't agree to see the doctor, underhand tactics are now decreed necessary.

Ingeniously she inveigles him into the town centre - a trip to the bookies being dangled as a decoy carrot. While "shortcutting" through Boots she brakes hard at the pharmacy counter. "We need to see a pharmacist URGENTLY," she announces as my father recoils in embarrassment. "We're prepared to wait." Her second sentence means my wife is willing to operate a stand-off until closing time, probably beyond - at least until the siege negotiators send in sandwiches.

Ten minutes later a pharmacist appears. He gives my father a concerned glance. Adding to the brewing drama, he pauses for several seconds of wordless contemplation before informing my father with unmissable unambiguity: "You should see a GP immediately." "Well I suppose I could see my doctor," he surmises. Finally.

My wife dials the surgery. Handing her phone to my father she demands he arrange an appointment. The doctor sees him three days later and instigates an urgent hospital referral. "They'll see you within a week," he says, "as this does need looking at sooner rather than later." Unfortunately in a cash-starved NHS buckling under waiting lists and a society that values low taxes over highly funded healthcare, a week becomes considerably longer. As does his facial lump.

"This delay means it won't be cancer," announces my father, still trusting wishful thinking ahead of modern medicine.

When my father's appointment does materialise I accompany him to the hospital where we meet a consultant. She has a soft American accent and a kindly manner. "Normally we'd need a week for tissue tests to come back," she announces, "but my instinct tells me we should fast track this one. I have to inform you that there's a likely possibility it could be cancer." My dad's chosen takeaway message here is: "It's still likely nothing."

Two - rather than the promised one - weeks later the consultant contacts my father. "We need to operate urgently," she says. "Well," concludes my father after receiving an info pack about his impending hospital op to remove the cancer, "it's a good job I decided to get that lump checked out." According to actuarial tables, his predicted cause of death is statistically far more likely to be from strangulation than cancer.

ANOTHER SIDE OF BOB DYLAN

"You know that art gallery opposite the artisan French café close to John Lewis?" says my wife in an outbreak of middleclassness to someone (as yet unidentified by me) on the phone. "Well," she continues breathlessly without pausing to receive an answer, "Bob Dylan's going to be there on Thursday afternoon."

This strikes me as unlikely. Unless there is another less famous Bob Dylan. Perhaps someone christened with that same name just before the other one emerged from the 1960s folk scene as a global household name. After all, I once worked with an actuary called David Bowie (yeah, he knew all the mortality statistics on men who fell to earth, rock' n' roll suicides, etc.)

I hope for his sake that there isn't another Bob Dylan who works in marketing or does something in IT. Consequently he would spend most of his free time posting replies on social media: "I am not *that* Bob Dylan."

So I conclude that another, decidedly less globally iconic, Bob Dylan must be the person appearing at the humble art gallery in our town. Usually the most plausible explanation turns out to be the correct one. Well done me for working it out.

"No, it's the famous singer/songwriter Bob Dylan," confirms my wife to the caller who evidently drew the same conclusion as me. "It's being billed as a world exclusive. His new artwork is being premiered there, before being launched for sale around the world."

Our attention is suddenly taken by a visitor at the door. "Somebody's knock, knock, knocking on heaven's door," I say. This is not a lyrical allusion my wife, who once fell asleep at an intimately sized (by his usual standards) Bob Dylan concert, comprehends. I receive my usual look from her mixing derision with pity.

Peering through the frosted glass I make out the silhouette of my wife's friend Mark. "I'd better tell him about Dylan coming to Oxford," she announces, surging past me to open the door. True to her word, she does. Mark is amazed by the news. Then asks when His Bobness will be gracing our town with his presence. He doesn't much care for the response.

"Thursday? Oh no, not Thursday. It can't be Thursday! I've got to work in Manchester that day. Can't believe I'll miss it!"

He's now wearing the look of an astronomer who just popped out for a fag behind the observatory at the exact moment a spectacular comet whizzed past.

Mark also has difficulty comprehending that Dylan will be visiting a tiny art gallery in our town, but finds it awkward to ask my wife to repeat the news: "Are you, er, hmm… sure… err... umm?" he says, spluttering like a tap with an airlock. "Yes!" confirms my wife unhesitatingly.

Yet Bob Dylan has a history of doing surprising things. He turned up on virtually the last available day to collect his Nobel Prize for Literature and visited National Trust properties incognito by himself while on UK tours. Once he permitted his lyrics to be altered - allowing *Blowin' in the Wind* to be used in an advert for the Co-op supermarket. It's just a shame the lyrics weren't amended to: "How many rows must a man walk down, before he can find the milk?"

The day before the exhibition opening of Dylan's artwork, I check the gallery's website. There's no mention of a personal appearance. "That's to keep the crowds down," my wife suggests. There's also no mention anywhere else online or in the local newspaper.

Quizzed about how she knows that *that* Dylan is definitely attending, my wife offers an unconvincing explanation: "There was a note in the gallery." She shows me it on her phone. It reads: "Bob Dylan - world famous artist - will premier his latest art works here on Thursday, 5-8pm." The statement's ambiguity dawns on her while she reads it aloud.

I check Dylan's itinerary for his so-called Never Ending Tour. He's scheduled to gig in Helsinki, Oslo and Stockholm this month. Not the UK. "Well, he could still come. It's kind of on the way," says my wife, her hands grazed from all that straw clutching.

This setback doesn't stop her continuing to spread the info that Dylan will be there. Imparting such news is met with a remarkably consistent response: "What, *that* Dylan?" As opposed to all the other Dylans who strum a guitar, were big in the 60s and appeared stoned in public. Although fans of children's TV classic *The Magic Roundabout* might have a legitimate reason to seek clarification on exactly which Dylan is expected.

"Well, are you coming?" my wife asks me when Thursday eventually arrives. "Most likely you go your way, and I'll go mine," I reply. My wife is as unimpressed with this reference as if I'd just shown a dog a card trick. Only when I ask if we should take an umbrella on a cloudless day "as a hard rain's gonna fall" does she suspect I'm channelling song titles. "Idiot," she says. "Idiot wind," I correct, for any non-existent Dylan fans listening to our conversation in an otherwise empty house. Her good mood continues to cloud over.

We bus into town and arrive at the gallery. A friendly man who I assume works there, although I never entirely find out, patiently explains Dylan's modus operandi. Apparently the American superstar pencil sketches places of interest prior to crafting them into fully formed Hockney-esque pictures back in the studio. In Britain we remain naturally suspicious of polymaths. It's as if you are only permitted to be talented in one discipline. Though personally I'm always amazed that the two separate skills of songwriter and singer so often arrive simultaneously. And Dylan clearly possesses a third skill as an accomplished painter.

Bold colours are strummed across the canvas like mellifluous harmonies. His capturing of Americana includes paintings depicting urban scenes, the Brooklyn Bridge and the New York diner where Harry met Sally; all littered with the detritus of advertising signs so ubiquitous in the USA.

Professional art critics can be as sniffy as they feel they must be about Dylan's paintings, but the truth is that the pictures are extremely difficult to dislike. The only thing I do dislike about them is the price tag - which means that I still can't take down my 1980s Tennis Girl with scratchy bum poster. £3,500 is a lot for an unframed limited edition print - albeit one signed by a normally reluctant autographer.

A gallery staff member offers us mini pork pies and prosecco. My wife declines for both of us out of politeness and concern for my waistline. "Don't think twice," I say, "it's alright." This garners no response from the curator, while my wife's eye-roll is so intense it's probably audible. When her attention is momentarily diverted by another guest, I exploit the distraction to snaffle a complimentary prosciutto roll. Appropriately the Dylan song *Ballad of a Thin Man* appears over the gallery speakers.

Anyone who has seen Dylan's self-drawn cover art for his appropriately titled 1970 *Self Portrait* album (which could generously be described as containing qualities of childlike exuberance) will be amazed how much he's progressed as a painter over the last five decades. The same is true of the music on that album, a listen considered to be as good as its artwork. Upon release the record received one of the most famous opening lines of a review when *Rolling Stone* magazine declared: "What is this shit?"

We mingle with gallery staff and visitors. Even though I successfully crowbar several more Dylan song titles into the conversations, none receive any response whatsoever.

When the conversation turns to whether there's anyone else around called Bob Dylan, I remark to our conversational huddle: "I used to work with an actuary called David Bowie." "I know," says my wife sighing, "you always tell that story and it never ch… ch… ch… changes."

Dylan, like Albert Einstein, is a testament to what it's possible to achieve in life if you don't waste time brushing your hair. Elsewhere in the gallery we clock a man with similarly dishevelled hair to Dylan. Furthermore he's wearing a brown spotted shirt with white circles. It's a shirt synonymous with Dylan's stage attire.

Fleetingly I feel a frisson of celebrity encounter excitement. My wife's celebrity-spotting antenna has registered his presence too. We shuffle closer towards him to obtain a definitive identification.

Then I realise that this man looks like Dylan did in 1966 - during his classic *Highway 61 Revisited* and *Blonde on Blonde* era. And since it's currently 2019, then it's unlikely to be him - akin to spotting Elvis Presley today adorned in his 1970s rhinestone-studded white jumpsuit pomp. He turns around, confirming he is a fan of, as opposed to, the man himself. My wife finally accepts that the free mini pork pie halves have failed to attract the American cultural figurehead to our local art gallery.

Afterwards on the way to the bus stop the heavens open, prompting us to abandon any remaining dignity and run to the sanctuary of the bus shelter. "This will give us shelter from the storm," says my wife.

My mouth remains wide open and motionless so long that a small bird investigates it as a potential nesting site. "Yeah, I can do them too," she says. Eventually my oral paralysis recedes. "How do you know…?" I ask, amazed. "It was one of his songs in the book."

In the gallery a beautifully bound book of Dylan's handwritten lyrics was on sale. The cost was £1,500, which is a bit steep given it included neither colour nor an index. "Who'd pay that for a book?" asks my wife. "The same people who pay £50,000 for a George Orwell first edition," I say, before adding: "Haven't these people heard of libraries?"

Ascending the bus stairs, my wife's mobile rings. It's her friend Mark calling from Manchester. "Well, did Bob Dylan turn up?" "The answer my friend is blowin' in the wind," I say. "Shut up!" barks my wife, before adopting a more conciliatory tone towards Mark: "Sorry, but my husband keeps speaking in stupid Dylan song titles and it's really, really annoying." "Pah," I say, "Just like a woman."

"Things have changed?" asks Mark. Rather brilliantly in my view. My smirk gives him away. "Oh not you as well!" she says.

OUR FATHER ALMOST IN HEAVEN

I have a customary Sunday phone chat with my father. This tradition is so well established it feels like it originated sometime around the Mesolithic Period, i.e. when Nicholas Parsons was still a teenager. But only really began when I left home in 1984.

One recent Sunday I called Dad and found him disturbingly disorientated. He promised he would see the doctor in the morning. Promised. Just like he had the previous Monday. And the one before that. Going back every Monday until Nicholas Parsons really was a teenager.

The next day I receive a truly unsettling phone call. "Your father's curtains are still drawn," reports a kindly neighbour. "Should I investigate?" Having your curtains drawn at 11.45am is a definable matter for concern - given my father isn't an undergraduate. Besides, there's horse racing form to be studied: my father's daily preoccupation.

"Should I break down the door?" asks the neighbour. I realise this is a time-sensitive situation, so he'll require an answer. And a sledgehammer. And a forwarding address for a repair bill. Luckily a keyholder is located just before the hammerer's backswing is completed. Surprisingly he discovers an empty house.

I phone the local hospital. Yes, they confirm, there has been an emergency admission by ambulance that morning at 4am. Eventually we establish my father had a fall, dialled 999 and was rushed to hospital in a critical condition. Luckily there was no horse racing taking place at 4am, otherwise he'd probably have made the ambulance crew wait until a race had finished before saving his life.

His timing coincided with the worst snow to hit the area in 20 years. Thanks, Dad. Unseasonal snow and ice descended like a potent metaphor, paralysing life. Only time itself marched on unrestrained by the worst the weather could do.

Somehow I travel from Oxford to Lincolnshire (only took nine hours!) to be at his bedside. A journey that necessitates walking the last three miles in a blizzard along a closed road through snow drifts as deep as my concern for my father. Hashtag: Worst birthday ever!

When two solemn-faced doctors greet you at a hospital and ask to speak to you in a private room - having first slid you the tissue box - you have a tiny hunch this might not be good news: "What's this about? Have I won a competition?"

Having been told to stay overnight at the hospital and keep my phone on if going outside (had I ventured outside I'd have died first - of exposure), I begin the grieving process. The doctors have already started the (gorgeously creative euphemism coming up...) "palliative pathway".

My father is diagnosed with advanced sepsis coupled with a declining heart rate and acute renal failure. His temperature is down to 34.1 - this is the sort of temperature you'd normally post after spending the last four hours in a river.

The nurses inform me that his blood pressure is perilously low. I say that's probably because he's stopped reading the *Daily Mail* for six days. Made them laugh.

Yet, after I'd agreed to DNR and been offered a chat with the kindly Hospital Chaplain (apparently you can't ask to see the Hospital Rationalist), a last roll of the drugs dice suddenly improves Senior

Smith's condition. Talk about a comeback. He was 3-nil down with the referee looking at his watch.

Throughout he suffered delirium and vivid hallucinations. Ironically, when his hallucinations began to recede, he told me about a three-foot high black furry animal that had been stalking his hospital bed before I visited. Yeah, I thought - that's actually a new hallucination. Turns out....... the hospital operates a Pets Visit Patients scheme and a few minutes later I find a three-foot high black Newfoundland dog striding the corridor. True. Or maybe I'm now the one having hallucinations?

Further scrumptious irony is to come. My father is a dedicated Brexiteer. Hence I enjoyed informing him that the miracle drug that returned him from the absolute toes-over-the-edge brink was developed through a collaboration with the EU! "At least after we Take Back Control," I told him, "we'll still have leeches."

After fifteen days he's discharged. Outside daffodils daringly poke through the thawing snow. Walking with a frame for the first time, he thanks the wonderful NHS staff for saving his life before approaching me. We stand silently on the edge of hugging, repressing tears. Finally my father speaks: "You don't happen to know who won the 3.10 at Wincanton two weeks ago?"

TOAST IN THE MACHINE

My epiphanic moment arrives too late.

When the darkness softens into dawn's growing light I awake and open an eyelid. Pleasingly it's a Sunday morning and I feel relaxed after a sound, restorative sleep. Buoyed with optimism, at last I feel content with the world. This is going to be a good day.

"I'm not talking to you!" says my wife as I open a second blurry eye, now reluctantly, to greet the morning that's taken a sudden turn for the worse. She then proceeds to explain why she's not talking to me. At uninterruptable length. I can't recall what the offending reason was exactly - though I suspect it was something to do with not listening to her properly. "Why?" I ask. "Why?!" she exclaims mockingly. Swords clank.

Actually it's because I invited my pal Pete to watch the football at ours last night instead of making progress on a necessary household chore we'd allocated to that particular evening. Which - and the prosecution's evidence makes this unprecedentedly clear - I had earlier agreed to do.

"Why don't you go out for your exercise?" she not so much requests as threatens.

Like a politician's parade of promises, I had begun the year by foolhardily listing all the improving things I'll do in the future without believing I'd deliver on such optimistic intentions. One was a commitment to go out regularly for combined bike rides and walks.

Consequently I decide to head into town for a cycle ride then walk - not so much to maintain my fitness levels as to avoid giving up on them completely. This, I calculate, enables me to accomplish a good two-hour shift of exercise - my first dedicated workout for far too long. My time spent avoiding exercise has slowly expanded - matched by my waistline.

Hence my instigated fitness regime. Albeit mainly so I can tell my couch potato friend Pete [name changed for avoidance-of-being-punched reasons] how much fitter I am than him. Even if that way smugness lies.

People often ask me in concerned tones whether I feel vulnerable riding a bike around busy streets surrounded by cars, buses, lorries and vans all dodging for room on the city's predominantly narrow streets. To such a line of questioning I have a stock reply: I prefer to cycle since it always provides me with an opening anecdote whenever I arrive at my destination: "Wow, I just had to pedal furiously into a post box to avoid being killed by a van!"

Most cyclists - and car drivers too, to be fair - are fearful of the reckless deathwishery displayed by some van drivers. Yet in my experience White Van Man is a mythical creature - it's Red Van Man you should really be looking out for. And, upon spotting him/her, immediately cycle headfirst into a hedge to avoid any post office vans.

Some Royal Mail vans appear to misinterpret road signs as not a maximum but a minimum speed, regardless of road conditions. Presumably some of their drivers contemplate: "I know this is a narrow residential street and it's school leaving time, but that road sign clearly says '30' so 30mph at all times I must maintain." Vrr-rooom. Screech. Bang. Ner-ner.

However, early Sunday morning proves to be an ideal time to cycle around Oxford. No commuters, shoppers or school-runners. Offices and schools are closed, the shops are hours away from opening, and college students are never to be seen in the early morning other than those engaged in the well-known Walk Of Shame, tiptoeing back to their college still wearing yesterday's clothes after a night of spontaneous hot monkey loving and anxious to avoid bumping into any friends, tutors or their boyfriend.

I lock up my bike in the city centre and go for a walk, liberated from having an actual destination to speed towards. Instead I have the space and time to stroll past - and crucially notice - details that one isn't normally allowed to observe in the unrelenting furiousness of busy city centres.

Then I spot something genuinely alarming. I'm instantly snapped out of my relaxed Sunday morning mood. My amygdala floods with anxiety.

An aproned woman saunters out of a café holding a tray containing a toaster. Nothing unusual about this scene, you may be thinking, until I add one further detail: it's on fire.

Alarmingly high orangey flames shoot out of the toaster as if a seriously annoyed dragon is trapped inside. Acrid black smoke billows skywards.

Understandably agitated, she drops it onto the pavement. Then pauses while clearly wondering what to do next. I wonder what to do next too. I can feel the courage seeping out of me and pooling around my feet.

Consequently we both do nothing and the flames soon burn themselves out. But the smell is hideous. Plumes of wafting blackness rise constantly like two loquacious Native Americans having an overdue long distance reunion.

Two minutes later after the fire has naturally burnt itself out, a man sprints purposefully out of the café. His gesturing implies: "I'm taking charge here - move back everyone and accede to my authority!" He unleashes the entire contents of a foam extinguisher onto the toaster, thereby creating, where the toaster once stood ten inches high, a snow-capped Alpine peak. This proves that doing nothing in frozen panic is sometimes the correct approach. Now they have to clear up a massive Mount Blanc of foam as well as a carbonised kitchen appliance buried several feet below the summit.

At this time on a Sunday morning there's only a light scattering of people around.

Yet even at this unusual hour a few tourists determined to maximise their time in Oxford with an early start are already about, ticking Oxford's famous buildings off their checklists. Soon a few gather near me, also attracted by the burning spectacle.

An eccentrically dressed girl - who has clearly foregone communicative speech in favour of emojis - stands observing the smoky scene. "OMG," she says, her mouth open so wide that bats may try to roost in it. "OMG," she repeats. "Awesome," says another millennial who may, or may not, be her companion. Then OMG Girl does what young people are trained to do in the event of any emergency. She gets out her phone. Not to dial 999, but to film events.

I recall travelling on a bus through a West London suburb last year when I glanced out of the window to notice a branch of KFC on fire. Thankfully the building appeared to have been safely evacuated, as it was encircled by uniformed staff. All were busily engaged filming the inferno on their phones. I can only hope that one of them had possessed the logicality to actually use their phone to notify the relevant authorities.

But that's today's typical response. OMG Girl will probably be uploading her street toaster fire footage to WhatsApp, MyFace, YouTwit, Instagran, SnappyTwat, HaroldPinterest (users of the latter platform report experiencing frequent frustrating pauses.) (Oh yeah, I'm cool and socially relevant when it comes to being up to date with all the kids' preferred social media platforms - and the topical comedy references they comprehend.)

Again acting more like an emoji than actual person, OMG Girl does a scary face, accompanied by putting her hands in front of her mouth to signify horror like a silent movie actress. Next she reverts to an open mouth pose. Finally she encores with a classic LOL face after the man has deposited most of the UK's foam reserves onto one small (already extinguished) toaster fire. Prior to taking the inevitable smoky selfie.

I return home. "I'm still not talking to you," says my wife. "Oh, by the way," she adds, oblivious to the immediate contradiction, "The toaster needs cleaning out before using it." Examining it reveals a piece of stuck toast now well on its way to becoming charcoal.

"I'm still not talking to you," my wife clarifies before continuing the conversation, "but don't forgot to NOT unplug it first," she jokes. Eventually I remove the carbonised toast. "You have to be careful," I advise, "toasters can easily catch fire. They collect lots of combustible grease at the bottom which ignites when…"

"Oh really?" says my wife, "and how come you're such a self-appointed expert on that subject?" This is a perfect cue. An overpitched full toss instead of the intended attacking yorker that I can merrily whack out of the park of retribution.

I unsheathe my phone. "Well I saw this an hour ago in Bonn Square." Instead of the expected photo there's a video icon. I must have accidentally filmed it instead of taking a photo. "Here's a video I filmed this morning," I say. I press the play icon and a female voice repeatedly shouts "OMG! OMG!" She competes against the sound of the wind blowing. Then, just as I'd expected to see Too Late Foam Guy, OMG Girl walks across my camera, meaning I capture the back of her impressive hairstyle and nothing else. The film ends abruptly after five seconds. No burning toaster or pyramid of foam has been captured for posterity. So I instantly press delete.

"What have you been videoing?" asks my wife. "Have you been filming teenage language students? Are they over 18?" No, I plead, it was a toaster fire I was filming. Or attempting to film. "What toaster fire?" pursues my wife. "That's the reason she's screaming 'OMG!'" Ungenerously my wife checks: "Are you sure she wasn't screaming 'OMG' cos some creepy bloke was attempting to film her?" "No, I…"

The slightest smile escapes onto my wife's face, signalling that she's winding me up. "Anyway, if you could return to not talking to me," I say.

All I have to do now is figure out the best time to inform her I've arranged, before he left last night, for Pete to come around this afternoon to watch the match.

BEAUTY IN THE EYE OF THE COLD SHOULDER

An attractive 20-something brunette deliberately dims the lights and leans forward towards me. She is so close I can feel her soft breath on my face. I can inhale her delightfully floral perfume. I can even see the flaws in her wine-red lipstick application. She repeats the beckoning phrase: "Look into my eyes."

Discovering I possess no capacity to refuse, I willingly comply with her directives. "Keep looking into my eyes," she encourages. She has remarkable eyes. These are the sort of eyes that a poet might compare to something starry or sparkly - like a... er... sparkly star (YEAH, I can so nail poetry).

They are the kind of top drawer eyes that John Lewis would probably sell - if genetic body part farming was something medical science and ethics committees decide to crack in the future.

"Keep looking right into my eyes," she says. No, she's not a hypnotist. But she's certainly mesmerising. "Wow, I've never met an author before," she tells me, gushing admiration.

After the experience I bus home and decide to tell my wife immediately about what has just happened. As a rule, I've long since concluded that whoever coined the expression "honesty is the best policy" most certainly wasn't married. Nonetheless I decide to tell my wife everything about my experience with the attractive brunette.

Arriving home I find my wife scrubbing the kitchen floor. Every micro crumb, minute stain and miniscule mark is scornfully blamed on me.

Opting to change the subject, I make an announcement about my earlier experience with Remarkable Eyes Lady.

"Err...," I say when my wife stops berating me for a nanosecond and I manage to sneak into a conversation crevice, "my visit this morning to the opticians went well. The optometrist was pleased with me."

"The opti what?" says my wife. "Whatever happened to opticians?" She has a point. "Hopefully the optometrist will give you better glasses. Ones that enable you to see all the mess you make." I wonder if the optometrist has a partner. I decide she has, and that her partner, him or her (although I mostly imagine it's a her), must be equally beautiful. Then I imagine them yelling at each other over who was responsible for leaving toaster crumbs.

A week later I collect my new glasses. Just as she - an optimistic optometrist - predicted, they improve my vision. But I don't see her again. Secretly I'm disappointed as with my new glasses she's likely to look even more fabulous. Obviously that's a detail I'm too busy to tell my wife when she catches me surveying the store with the alacrity of a meerkat lookout tipped off to expect an invasion.

However, there is a huge problem ahead. And even though I'm aware that 'problems' have all been rebranded and recalibrated as 'challenges' at some point during the last decade, this one steadfastly remains an old-fashioned 'problem'.

Because both my wife and I know that this visit to the optician - or optometrist - has been preparation for a much bigger challenge ahead. A challenge that makes the collective planning for Brexit a comparative doddle.

"I'd like to book an eye test for my 92-year-old father, please," I inform the receptionist. My father has reluctantly 'agreed' to have an eye test. Never has the adverb 'reluctantly' been more appropriately applied to a situation. "There's nothing wrong with my eyesight," protests my father, narrowly avoiding walking into the reception desk as we enter Specsavers.

After debating whether we require a home visit - turns out they are available - my father decides that we can arrange for a car to drop him sufficiently close to the store's front door. "I don't know why I need an eye test," he reaffirms, "I've never worn glasses in my life."

This is a strange application of logic. A bit like saying: "Well I don't know why I need the fire brigade to attend my burning roof as I've never once required them before."

Waiting outside the consultation rooms, I see the amazing-eyed optometrist who treated me a fortnight earlier. She comes out of her testing room, unhooks a clipboard from the wall and checks her next patient. Then walks obliviously past me. I practise my best smile. There is no recognition whatsoever on her part. Stinging from the rejection, I focus on getting my father safely into the room when his name is called. I'm permitted to stay during his consultation.

The eye test begins. "Okay," says the optometrist primed to expend a week's worth of patience on the next five minutes, "let's try reading the first line." Two letters appear on the screen. Even allowing for the fact I'm sitting several feet nearer, they are huge. Billboard-size huge. They are equivalent size to the 'B' and 'T' that appear on the top of the Post Office Tower.

Nevertheless my father struggles to read them. There are two letters, he calculates. Hence he'll play the odds game. After all, a 26 to 1 x 2 probability of being correct is only 626 to 1. A doddle. "Is it, er, A and K?" It isn't. "I meant G and Q." It isn't that either. "P and Z?" he offers, his bravado now tonally leaking. Before my father is allowed further guesses, such as "is it an ampersand and the Icelandic rune Þ?", the optometrist changes the screen.

The optometrist displays a solitary letter 'H' on the screen. It's so large there's a real danger it will attract a landing helicopter. "H," trumpets my father confidently. "See, my eyesight is fine," he counters with award-winning stubbornness. "When I joined the RAF they said I did the eye test perfectly." I'm desperately willing the optician to ask: "What year was that?" Ask him the year. ASK HIM THE YEAR! He doesn't ask him the year. For the record it was 1944.

Besides, my father has repeated the anecdote continuously throughout the last 75 years that one of the RAF ground staff in 1944 had 'borrowed' the eye chart from the medical bay and hired it out for those having an eye test the next day in order to learn it! An anecdote he's uncharacteristically unforthcoming in telling today.

The optometrist concludes that my father requires much stronger reading glasses. "You should do the car number plate test. Because of your age, you are more likely to be asked to do it by a policeman. Just as I, and your son, are more likely, if stopped, to be breathalysed," he advises with some sagacity. It's literally a sobering thought for us all.

We return a week later and pick up my father's new glasses. Suddenly I spot the entrancing optometrist who treated me. She walks straight past without a murmur of recognition.

Later that same afternoon after we've returned home I hear my father joyously exclaim from the next room: "I can read the numbers in the crossword squares!" before later adding, "Getting new glasses is the best decision I ever made!"

Turns out the bottom line is "T-H-A-N-K-L-E-S-S."

A SHOT IN THE DARK

I am leaning on a lamppost at the corner of the street. No, I'm not a prostitute. Or George Formby. But it is in case a certain little lady goes by.

The little lady in question is my wife and we have agreed to rendezvous at a malfunctioning streetlight. This decision probably requires an explanation.

Following my wife's crusade against pavement fouling by a dog whose deposits suggest must be larger than a morbidly obese bison with a taste for vindaloos, she has now flung herself unrestrainedly into other civic duties. Not only does she have a dream that one day our streets will be pooch poo free, but also that those same streets will be sufficiently lit for pedestrians to appreciate their new excrement-empty status.

Hence she has spotted another civic calling and thrown herself into it with the reckless enthusiasm of a new Coyote plan to catch Roadrunner.

Two lampposts illuminate a vital passageway linking our housing estate with its bus stop. It is occasionally land-mined with dog poo in the dark because one of these essential streetlights is broken. My wife phones the Council to report its malfunction.

Our councillor requires photographic proof of the defective light along with its serial number. Apparently this helps build an evidence file for the outsourced contractors, necessary given that Britain sold off most of its municipal possessions and responsibilities ages ago - probably in a job lot with its soul and grandmother - like someone desperate to raise money for drugs.

Hence we meet next to the dark lamppost. For this purpose we have borrowed a selfie stick - or, as I like to refer to them, "wands of narcissism". In fact I'd rather be mistaken by a passer-by for soliciting under the streetlight than owning a selfie stick. Frankly it would be less embarrassing.

There are numerous daily examples in Oxford of tourists travelling thousands of miles in anticipation of witnessing the Dreaming Spires' undimmable beauty. And then literally turning their backs on it while gurning into their selfie stick. These people are unwilling to have any meaningful interaction with the world unless it has digital validation. Oxford has always suffered a schizophrenia of Town and Gown identities. Yet the city is actually supported by a tripod of Town, Gown and tourism - just please stop it, tourists, with the selfie sticks (the so-called wands of narcissism).

Transcribing the serial number printed on a streetlight requires the medium of light. As already established, our faulty streetlight emits none. Therefore we use a torch to record its darkened details.

Having sought instruction from the Council, we are told to log onto a website called 'Fix My Street'. Here we chart the lamppost's location on a map, diligently entering its postcode. I was unaware lampposts had their own postcodes but we set about calculating it from adjacent properties. Then my wife notifies the individual councillors with a remit for the area on both councils (as no-one knows how the City and County Council partition responsibilities - especially the two councils themselves).

She then attends our local Tenants and Residents meeting to report it, and starts working the room afterwards in an effort to create a grassroots momentum for her campaign. The next day helpful County Councillor Gill Sanders contacts her. She helps to, ahem, illuminate the situation.

A few days later my wife's reporting of malfunctioning streetlight N19A appears in circulated minutes. Then our estate's news-sheet emails to request an interview. My wife's moniker is fast becoming 'Lamppost Woman' - "Well, at least it makes me sound thin," she concludes positively. If this rise in fame continues at a similar trajectory she's only a few weeks away from sitting on Graham Norton's sofa explaining her delight with the choice of Meryl Streep to depict her in the inevitable movie.

However, one week later N19A is still darker than a Norwegian coal house at midnight in December. It looks less likely to emit light than the surface of a black hole.

This situation causes anger to rise spring-like inside my wife, culminating in a gush of emails and campaigning phone calls. Then one evening, her face glowing with sufficient pride to negate the need for N19A, she announces that the streetlight is fixed. This giddy exaltation is unlikely to have been experienced before from political engagement unless you're Obama. Enoch Powell may have pontificated that all political careers end in failure, but clearly my wife and Nelson Mandela are the exceptions.

Two days later I'm strolling down the murky alley. The only other streetlight in the passageway - number DC13 - is shedding about as much light as the police inquiry into Shergar.

I announce the news to my wife as sensitively as possible. Initially her reaction replicates the lamppost: it's like a bulb has been turned off inside her. Then her mood suddenly transfixes. "Right," she declares, galvanised like a superhero looking for a changing room, "Let there be light!" and opens her laptop.

At the time of writing DC13 is still unfixed.

DE BOTTON OF THE CLASS

There can't be many professional philosophers around these days. Surely the heyday for that particular industry would have peaked in Ancient Greece.

There, people probably queued at the job centre only to be told by staff: "Sorry, there's not much call for builders, cooks, soldiers or social media influencers at the moment. Have you considered retraining as a philosopher?"

And yet here I am, in an Oxford bookshop, nervously about to meet one of the UK's (okay, probably the only one who isn't employed in the teaching profession) full-time philosophers.

"I can't believe I'm going to meet Alain de Arse," I say. "Alain de Botton," corrects my wife, "as you well know." Before quickly adding: "Are you going to keep cracking that joke in the misguided belief that it'll eventually become funny?" Zing. Ouch.

Not for the first time in my marriage, I choose to shrug off the put-down. "Also," warns my wife, "if you get too familiar with calling him that, there's a risk you'll probably say it to his face." Yeah, like I'm that big an idiot. I know my elbow from my de Botton," I say. "Still unfunny," she cautions. "Well, Bottom and Botton - you can say either as they sound so ambiguous," I proffer. My wife doesn't consider this observation response-worthy.

Shuffling forward to the author's signing table I have an uncomfortable dilemma to conceal. The front of my book bears a vast circular label in fire-engine-red declaring: 'SALE: ONLY £1.' Yes, admittedly I could have peeled it off. But it's a trophy sticker. It declares my shopping prowess: tangible physical proof that I'm capable of achieving something in life other than dodging the permanent hailstorm of my wife's put-downs, criticisms and verbal disappointment.

As an author responsible for several books that have received good reviews but poor sales (apparently publishers prefer it the other way around), I often visit bookshops. Occasionally for signings, but much more frequently to ensure my titles are - quite literally - customer facing. This is a dirty secret most authors possess. I often pop into WH Smiths to ensure my works are well displayed - though I've never bumped into J K Rowling or Philip Pullman engaged in the same activity. Yet.

Once in WH Smiths I stumbled across a particularly generous January sale table where books had been reduced to £1. Amongst them was Alain de Botton's erudite yet reassuringly readable hardback *The Art of Travel*. Hence I'm here at today's in-store event clutching my bargain purchase.

While queueing I feel a jab of anxiety. I don't want to humiliate the author if he sees I only paid £1 for his hard work. This risks acute embarrassment. As I near the author's signing desk I'm sweating like a POW escapee with forged papers approaching a Swiss border control.

As an author regularly asked in interviews if the Radio 4 sitcom character Ed Reardon - an impoverished and humiliated writer protected by his inability to suffer self-pity - is based on me, I know all about experiencing the burn of literary humiliation.

I was once welcomed back to my hometown in Lincolnshire by Waterstones placing a table OUTSIDE their store. Jutting into the street a huge sign announced: "Giveaway - now only £1". Among strands of tinsel and packs of Christmas cards (in May) were several SIGNED copies of one of my books! Cheers for that, Hometown. I chose to see the funny side, given the alternative is a professional life spent sloshing around in oceanic quantities of bile.

I reach Alain de Botton's signing table. He carefully writes his signature directly underneath the printed version of his name on the book's title page. Like most signatures, it's not immediately legible.

Indeed I'm not entirely sure he hasn't signed it "Alain de Arse" but wisely decide not to check. After I'd carefully handed him my book with the signing page open, Alain then does something I was not expecting.

He closes the book before handing it back to me. At this point he spots the colossal sticker proclaiming "SALE: ONLY £1"

"Oh," is all he says initially. There follows an oppressive pause. Surely he'll be philosophical about it. I ask my brain to come up with a suitable comment to fill the silence. Instead my buffering brain merely shrugs: "I've got nothing. Sorry, you're on your own here." Although it was likely only two seconds in reality, the suffocating silence feels like a geological age.

Finally the celebrity philosopher speaks. "That was a good price, wasn't it?" "Yeah, it was in the sale," I say timidly in an apologetic tone, my need to inform him of its sale status rather negated by the gigantic sticker shouting "SALE". Now my trophy purchase just seems sordid.

I return to my wife who is sitting in seating erected for the author's pre-signing talk. The store's chair-stacking staff eye her keenly, waiting for her to vacate one of the last uncollected seats. They stare at her with unmoving eyes, like a thirsty gazelle waiting for a lion to depart the watering hole. "How did it go?" says my wife. "Fine," I lie. "I didn't call him 'Arse'."

"What did he write in it?" she asks. With all the embarrassment I had forgotten to look. "Er," I stammer. I flick through the book, which turns out to be quite difficult to do one-handed as I'm determined to keep my left hand obscuring the 'SALE £1' sticker for fear of causing further mortification. "I'll hate you 'til the day I die. Love, A de B."

"What?!" bridles my wife.

"Not really!" I say. "Why say that then?" "It's what he allegedly wrote to a *New York Times* literary critic who gave one of his books a bad review." "Oh," says my wife, "he doesn't seem like someone who'd do that. You'd expect him to…"

"…be more philosophical about it?"

"Exactly," she concurs. I decide against saying anything else, content to sun myself for as long as possible in this rare moment of my wife actually agreeing with something I've said. "You'd expect a philosopher to be less querulous in their response," she says. "With his sales you'd expect him to be less aggrieved too," I add. Somewhat philosophically.

As an author who regularly checks Amazon to establish he has written the current 4,768,000th most popular selling book in the UK, I agree wholeheartedly.

Alain de Botton once spent a week as the official Writer In Residence at Heathrow Airport. At the time I recall a fellow columnist of mine setting herself up as Writer In Residence at Slough Bus Station - mainly in an exercise likely codenamed Operation Take The Piss Out of A de B. However, the joke quickly backfired when she discovered early on in her 'residency' that 99% of her public interactions were either timetable related or whether the 5B stopped at the big new Tesco.

"So what was Alain like when you met him?" asks my wife as we depart the store. "He was polite," I confirm. "And I managed not to call him Botton, either."

Picking up on my wife's concerned look, I hastily correct myself: "I mean Arse."

"Arse!" repeats my wife.

"I was going to buy a CD here too," I say.

"What CD?" asks my wife. "One by the band Guy Garvey fronts," I reply, "proving I can tell my Elbow from my…"

"Arse!" confirms my wife.

THE FLOOD

Getting out of bed at 6am I place my right foot into a pool of cold water. I was expecting soft warm carpet instead. My brain whirls into pre-caffeinated early morning action. Hmmm. This has definitely never happened before, concludes my brain. Try your left foot; that might be alright. Then things can be reassuringly back to normal.

I splash my left foot into a similarly squelchy carpet. My brain, still processing the contradictory info of cold water instead of expected dry carpet, recalibrates. And pattern matches for an explanation. Did I spend last night on a houseboat and choose the worst possible time to start sleepwalking?

I wade along the landing. Standing water shimmers in dawn light. The bathroom is submerged. Items are actually floating in it. I allow my wife a few more seconds of blissful oblivion to the crisis before waking her.

Water is trickling down the stairs. Directly beneath the bathroom it is dripping through the ceiling. Huge damp patches encircle the light fittings. There aren't sufficient swear words yet coined for this situation.

Unfortunately my stairwell and hallway resemble the log flume ride at Alton Towers.

My wife and I communicate in a series of shouts, like someone who's mistakenly knocked Caps Lock on their keyboard. WHERE'S THE TORCH? GET SOME SCREWDRIVERS! ARE WE GOING TO DROWN?

I empty the toilet tank and hold the ballcock to stop it refilling. This initially seems to halt the leak, though I realise my plans for the rest of the weekend will have to be modified around staying in my bathroom holding a ballcock. Even so, I allow an exhalation of relief like a cartoon character who's just outfoxed a hairy situation. Solved it. Phew. "It's still leaking," says my wife.

Abandoning the ballcock as an irrelevance, I dash downstairs. Locating the stopcock under the kitchen sink, I turn it as far as I can. Then I drain off the existing water in the system - should there be any water left in Oxfordshire that's not currently on my floor. I have seen this much water before, but only once - from an aeroplane window above the Pacific.

I call my friend Matt. He cycles over and points out that I also need to turn the outdoor stopcock off too. Ah, that would explain...

Helpfully there is a black circular disc in the pavement bearing the solitary word: 'WATER'. This is exactly what is needed in a crisis: unambiguous one-word instructions. In upper case.

This is a job for people with long arms. I plunge my hand fully two feet down and fumble for a tap. With pavement tarmac up to my armpit, I locate it. I turn it. It won't move. My options are now (a) panic or (b) panic. Then I turn it the other way - which I know is counterintuitive and just plain wrong. It moves. My wife shouts from the bathroom that the leak has stopped.

Matt declares the situation to be out of his depth. He leaves, peddling furiously uphill in pursuit of higher ground.

We need to find a plumber. Urgently. Compounding matters, it's a Saturday morning. On a Bank Holiday weekend. This, my instincts tell me, is not going to be easy.

Predictably most don't answer the phone. The first who does realises it's an emergency, but the earliest he can do is Thursday afternoon. Will that be okay? Er, let me check. NO. NO IT WON'T! By then we'd be on the roof, waving our shirts to attract passing helicopters.

A helpful plumber in Abingdon picks-up. He's blocked with appointments, but suggests another. I ring his recommendation. Yes, they can come that afternoon. Five hours later the plumber arrives. He's certainly industrious. Sawing. Hammering. Spannering. Sighing.

Water had been spurting out of a hidden pipe beneath the toilet. The plumber's diagnosis is that the isolation value is broken. So is the filling valve. Together they are creating a perfect storm. Kindly he undercharges me after admitting he could have fixed the problem in less time. "It was my fault for not spotting that other fault earlier," he says.

After the plumber's been on site for one and a half hours the bathroom is drier than a Mormon wedding.

Five days later a surveyor from the insurance company arrives. I've been warned their job may well be to underplay any damage. Send a loss adjuster to Aleppo and their report would probably conclude: "Needs a bit of light re-grouting."

"Wow," he says upon arrival, "This is really bad."

ADVANCING TO THE JAILHOUSE ROCK

"Pucklechurch," repeats the stranger with whom I'm engaged in conversation, "she visited me in Pucklechurch."

Pucklechurch sounds lovely. Let's say it again: Pucklechurch. Pucklechurch! Just like the sort of place Bertie Wooster would visit for a weekend stay in a country house. Where a mix-up would ensue, culminating in his accidental engagement to a darning-needle heiress - much to the chagrin of Bertie's Great Aunt Agnes. Meaning Jeeves would be despatched to Pucklechurch on the next steam train to clear up the mess.

"Pucklechurch is a prison," confirms the stranger. Oh.

My wife and I are attending a charity fundraising event in North Oxford. It had been her decision to mingle.

"Have *you* been to prison?" he asks. I contemplate my answer carefully, in order to avoid saying anything to offend him and therefore possibly returning him to prison. I notice the cheese knife on the buffet table suddenly looks particularly sharp.

"No," I say meekly. "Not yet," I add - just to leave things open and show I have the potential to turn bad. My wife makes a disdainful noise. But I'll have you know I could depart the straight and narrow. Sometimes I eat gateaux with a normal fork - not a patisserie fork. See.

I contemplate whether adding that I once got a detention at school. Moreover I was told by the headmaster Mr Prawnton (and I promise this is true) that I was "probably the only boy in the history of the school's Upper 6th to be given a detention". "Oh, thank you very much, Sir," I gushed with pride. "IT'S NOT A GOOD THING, BOY!" clarified Mr Prawnton. Who must have been under the misapprehension that I suffered from acute hearing difficulties, since he considerately raised his voice like a golfer at the Annual Hard-of-Hearing Golf Tournament screaming 'FORE!'

"Stephen Fry went to Pucklechurch too," the ex-jailbird tells me. I was unaware that prisons boasted posh alumni like Oxbridge colleges. "Can you put your name down for prisons?" I ask. Then instantly regret it. I wish the cheese knife was further away.

Perhaps you can? I can imagine some posh North London parents saying: "Well, Tarquin and I are determined to put little Augusta and Drambuie down for Pucklechurch for when they inevitably get caught with more dope than constitutes a reasonable definition of personal use. We'd hate them to have to go to a state prison like Wormwood Scrubs - you hear of such bad inspection ratings awarded by OFNICK."

"Has he told you what he was inside for?" asks his returning wife. "No," says just about everyone leaning forward with interest to first eavesdrop, then secondly participate, in our expanding conversation. Many new minglers have advanced towards us. Their curiosity couldn't have been more piqued if it was a season finale cliffhanger on Netflix.

"Anyway," says the ex-convict in a much more timid voice, "who wants to try the buffet?" - his confidence suddenly dropped and broken.

"Oh, you'll like this…." says his wife.

Everyone leans forward so far, they risk toppling over.

"He breached his bail conditions after some minor insider trading fraud."

"Misunderstanding, not fraud," the ex-lag hastily corrects; with an effrontery unchecked by humility.

"He got a couple of days inside before they sorted the paperwork out."

"Do you know The Krays?" I ask.

"It was years ago. And it taught me a big lesson," he says, ignoring my witticism. "Was that lesson: You need to be rich?" asks a lady who I now suddenly like a great deal.

Immediately the man's demeanour is decidedly less scary. "It was only for two days, but it was the worst experience of my life. I'm careful now… you know … not to do anything that would risk going back inside." I find my sympathy returning as quickly as it left.

Sensing she has just caused her partner a public humiliation, his wife places a hand on his shoulder and declares supportively, "Ah, he's my rock, aren't you?" "She was my financial rock when I came out," he replies, "as it was hard to get back into the sort of work I was doing before." He then adds: "In those days," to re-emphasise it was all a very long time ago.

"I turned over a lot of Advance To Go cards in my career, culminating in easy money from the bank," he admits, "before I inevitably turned over a Go To Jail card." Proving that sometimes Monopoly can replicate real life; it was certainly prophetic in its realisation that one day all utilities companies would become privatised.

Our collective discussion then turns to: "What was Stephen Fry in Pucklechurch for?" Members of our conversation huddle add guesses, half-remembered facts and the odd theory that proves to be flightless. Some contradict each other. Yet between us we eventually have enough information to come up with the true facts - like emptying our pockets onto the table to pay a restaurant bill.

There is a majority decision for credit card fraud. A quick phone check confirms this. "He used stolen credit cards. Once he used them for luxury hotel accommodation," announces a phonechecker.

Untypically at juvenile court, Fry was represented by a QC: his godfather and eventual High Court judge Oliver Popplewell. Another name that also sounds like it belongs in a PG Wodehouse novel. In fact Popplewell later became the oldest undergraduate student in Oxford University's history when he enrolled at Harris Manchester College to study PPE aged 76. Like a lot of undergraduates, he won't have finished paying off his student loan aged 80.

Visibly anxious to close the subject, the ex-con (albeit for two days) asks again what we think of the buffet food. But the others in our group discussion aren't allowing the topic to be moved on any time soon.

"Do you know anyone else who's been to prison?" someone asks him.

"No. Has anyone tried the potato salad? It's homemade."

Unsympathetic towards the ex-offender's clumsy attempt to alter the subject, the questioner redirects his enquiry at me.

"Yes," I'm surprised to answer. "Yes, I do."

This equally surprises my wife who fails to contain her incredulity. She does a restrained throat clearance, like Jeeves attempting to gain Bertie Wooster's attention, before abandoning all subtlety and broadcasting to the group: "Oh come on, you hardly rub shoulders with underworld figures!" Everyone immediately wants to know: "What did they do?" Murder? Kidnap? Hijack? Run a Zumba class without the appropriate paperwork?

Once I dreamt I was in a prison van being transported to serve a 30-year stretch without parole for murdering Nigel Farage. Imagine my feeling of despair and regret when I woke up to discover it was only a dream.

However, it's completely true that I have a friend who endured several months in clink. "A Norwegian friend of mine refused to do compulsory National Service. He was a conscientious objector," I clarify, "and got sent to prison."

As no one else in our definably middle-class huddle appears to know anyone who has spent time stirring porridge in the slammer, our group disperses. Thereby causing a rush at the buffet table. "I sometimes wonder if I'd be able to endure prison," says a posh-accented lady wearing an outfit that clearly cost what most freelance writers earn in a year, before asking, "is there any vegan almond or soya milk?" and thereby answering her own earlier question about whether she could endure a stay in chokey.

"He's right, you know," says my wife a few minutes later when we discover there are no remaining seats, necessitating us to stand uncomfortably while eating buffet food. "Yeah, I know," I reply, "this potato salad is homemade. It's delicious."

"I mean about it only taking a couple of days to learn you need to be honest." "Er…okay," I say, wondering if this is the prelude to a big confession from my wife.

It isn't. Instead she speaks to the person next to us: a lady in young middle-age with bright post-box red lipstick. She has gorgeous brown hair that tumbles down her back and shoulders. A few lightning strikes of grey appear in her mane as if to add character. I recognise her as an earlier member of our extensive conversation group.

We discover she made the potato salad and compliment her on it. "I might have to steal your recipe," I say. "In that case," ripostes the lady through a smile, "you might end up in Pucklechurch."

RIGHT TO TRIAL BY FURY

Entering the polychromatic splendour of Keble College I am greeted by a smiley woman with big hair and a small skirt. I christen her Schrödinger's Skirt. This is because her skirt is so infinitesimal that it both exists and doesn't exist at the same time.

She is going to be one of my fellow jurors in a criminal trial. Several lawyers are holding a weeklong conference at the Victorian redbrick college. On their last day a mock trial is performed, with members of the public invited to act as the jury. This is done to provide the trainee adversaries with a rare glimpse of a jury's inner thoughts - and to provide me with a rare glimpse of £20.

We are left waiting in the quadrangle where, unwisely for British strangers, we attempt to make conversation. "Why are you doing this?" I ask the girl wearing - and simultaneously not wearing - Schrödinger's skirt. "The money. I'm a student."

After a short briefing we are to be "led by an usher to the courtroom" - or, rather, a bored student takes us to a college classroom. She tells us to follow her, then races off without ever once looking behind her

- clearly she's in a hurry (well, Facebook isn't going to update itself). Luckily twelve of us keep up sufficiently to find the room and are sworn in as the jury - or, more accurately, asked "are you lot the jury?"

She then pops her headphones back in - visibly aggrieved that ferrying us to the courtroom had deprived her of two minutes of bad music.

Here we meet the judge, prosecution and defence counsel. However all the roles are being assumed by real lawyers. Though not, it soon becomes apparent, real actors. A professional defence lawyer stands in the pretend dock and assumes the role of the accused. The dialogue is so bad I begin to feel nostalgic about *Crossroads*. "It wasn't me what didn't do no murder," garbles the accused, offering an inarticulacy of double negatives to untangle.

Luckily the accused reveals in the opening cross examination that he owns a dog called Tyson. Clearly this is all I require to find him guilty. Although I could sit back and relax for the rest of the trial, I continue to concentrate on proceedings. After all, the mock liberty of a mock prisoner in a mock case is at stake.

A loud blast of music suddenly leaks into the room from next door - it's Sting singing 'Roxanne'. "That's appropriate," announces the judge drolly, "as we are also about to hear from The Police. Call police constable World." Oh, they're doing a joke here…geddit? PC World. Just like a proper courtroom, only the judge is allowed to be funny.

After a parched three hours we finally get a coffee break. We trundle to another college building and consume our coffees in a communal refreshment area upstairs. It is easy to spot the students (and freelance writers) present by the amount of biscuit pilfering that is going on. Schrödinger's Skirt shamelessly wraps several hobnobs into a supplied serviette and puts them into her bag. Even I feel a need to be more clandestine in my bickie-pocketing activities.

In the college's refreshment room I spot the accused, witnesses, judge, defence and prosecution. We have been told firmly not to discuss the case. "Nice case," I say to the defence barrister. "Thanks," she replies, wheeling her matching twin-travelling cases out of the cloakroom, clearly planning a quick getaway once the jury verdict is in. Schrödinger's Skirt smiles at my remark before wrapping up some custard creams.

We are sent to the jury room to deliberate and allowed an ungenerous fifteen minutes to reach a decision. One man appears intent on reprising the Henry Fonda role from *Twelve Angry Men* - the title of the film/play rather displaying its ageing sexism. Just like the jury in that movie, we are being filmed too - albeit "for training purposes".

An older man clears his throat to indicate he is about to say something requiring the group's unanimous attention. "This reminds me of a murder I saw out in Kenya in the 80s," he begins. "You saw a murder?!" asks a suddenly startled woman. "Yes... well, I saw it on telly." She looks noticeably less startled. "Shall we give a show of hands?" suggests the same woman.

Eleven of us think he is guilty. Meaning a movie of our jury trial would have to be titled: One Angry Man.

Schrödinger's Skirt and I both agree he's guilty. Collecting our £20 together, we say goodbye in Keble's entrance tunnel. My wife is waiting outside and spots this. "Who's your new friend?" she asks. "And was your case about who stole her skirt?"

WHY I DELIBERATELY CAUGHT TYPHOID

I am mopping a feverish brow as I type. Not for any metaphorical reason, but because I have typhoid. Yes, really.

The reason I have deadly typhoid is entirely the fault of Oxford United FC and our city's mayor. Allow me to elaborate.

After the previous football season had concluded, Oxford United were designated worthy recipients of an open top bus cavalcade culminating in a civic reception in Oxford's town hall. Quite why Oxford is a city but has a town hall is a question for another day. A question for today is why does a bunch of footballers who scraped into a promotion place in English football's fourth tier receive a civic parade for pointlessly kicking an inflated sphere between two sticks arbitrary placed eight yards apart? Especially when several doctors, nurses and vaccine trial volunteers from Oxfordshire recently developed the world's first active Ebola vaccine in our city (or town) - without receiving open top bus recognition. Whose actions are worthier and accomplishments greater?

When an Oxford nurse returning from Liberia informed me of her noble volunteering to tackle the devastating Ebola outbreak in Africa, I decided to volunteer with research undertaken by the Oxford Vaccine Centre for a more effective typhoid vaccine. Last year typhoid reportedly killed 161,000 people (though experts believe the true figure approached 250,000).

Presently the best licenced typhoid vaccines are, according to some studies, only around 61% successful. Oxford is currently trialling a new immunization requiring healthy (for the time being at least) volunteers to, er, be given typhoid. Proper, full on, typhoid - the terrifying real deal. This is my one grand deed for humanity. And humanity had better be suitably grateful and start letting me queue jump in shops. More selfishly it's also a belated opportunity to disprove to myself that I'm a coward.

Surprisingly it turns out that not just anyone can get typhoid. Oh no - it's very exclusive. There's a strenuous audition required first. Who knew fatally infectious diseases were so choosy? To receive typhoid I have to undertake a series of physical and mental tests. Although I initially can't spell typhoid, this apparently doesn't influence my ability to catch it.

After passing my typhoid "exams", a doctor at Oxford's Churchill Hospital, obliged to receive my wife's approval on a form for my participation, reiterates: "Richard's death is very unlikely if we treat the disease in time." My wife reacts to this statement with expressed displeasure. "But there's still a chance, right?" she clings. Already I sense my wife is planning how she'll utilise the extra wardrobe space.

Numerous medical tests later, and I'm sanctioned to receive via (un)lucky dip either an existing licensed vaccine, Oxford University's new unlicensed vaccine, the placebo or a fourth vaccine unrelated to treating typhoid (the latter is like being handed a snooker cue on your way out to open the batting against Australia.)

I commence daily blood tests and return to the hospital a few weeks later to receive a vaccine. "Do you like injections?" I'm asked. This I interpret as a redundant question; they may as well ask someone if they like Piers Morgan.

"Do you still want to go ahead with the trials?" they check before administering the vaccine. "Depends how big the needle is," I think. There's a slight delay before emitting my next word: "Ouch!"

A few days after receiving the vaccine/placebo I return for what is euphemistically termed "the challenge". Rather than being the sort of challenge I prefer (eating two desserts to win a free third one) this "challenge" involves being infected with the potentially fatal live bacterium Salmonella typhi.

On challenge day the drama is ratcheted up by staff wearing protective aprons and what appear to be welder's goggles. "We should invest in some chemicals to make the test tubes bubble and smoke," jokes a nurse empathetically to calm my visible anxiety.

For fifteen consecutive days after being infected I must routinely return to the Churchill Hospital. During daily visits I'm asked to roll up my sleeve. What do they want, blood? It transpires they want a lot of blood, with the justification that it's critical to monitoring my health.

Early one Sunday morning my arrival at the hospital is greeted by a ringing alarm and a security alert. A doctor smuggles me in through the staff entrance to fulfil a necessary appointment at a critical stage in the disease's development. "The hospital's in lockdown as there's been an attempted escape from the ward," they inform me. "Was it a doctor?" I ask.

Temperature is one of the most efficient early-warning methods of spotting typhoid. And with typhoid an early diagnosis is vital if your future plans involve staying alive. Average body temperature usually stabilises between 35.5°-37.5°. Should you be unfortunate enough to contract typhoid it will register around 38 degrees. Though you'll ideally be speeding your way to hospital and adopting an Oxford cyclist's attitude towards red lights as soon as your thermometer hits 37.9. This doesn't sound like much of a margin for error, but like hundredths of a second in 100 metre running, tiny differentials are critical. Life or death critical. Hit 38 degrees and I need to seek medical attention immediately, or my wife gets to claim her coveted closet space.

Throughout the trial I notice a tendency for my wife's sentences to begin with "when you're dead". As in, "when you're dead, is eBay the best way to get rid of your crappy music collection?" Moreover she enthuses, "Balliol's Gerard Manley Hopkins died of typhoid, so Oxford people can die of it," with fingers crossed on both hands.

Returning from another hospital check she casually greets me with a disappointed, "Oh, still alive then?" This attitude is ironic given the precariousness of her own situation living with a likely typhoid carrier. Risks have to be managed. Typhoid is a disease spread by poor hygiene and sanitation. One of the many useful things hospital staff teach me is how to wash my hands. This hand washing tutorial is a necessary life skill and one profoundly undervalued by society. Add it to the national curriculum now.

To become a typhoid vaccine volunteer I must pledge not to prepare cold food for anyone but myself. Guests arriving for tea two weeks into my volunteering are informed of this, yet after initially bridling at the news I have one of the world's most deadly diseases, willingly eat my cake given it's been baked at 190 degrees. Frankly guests would be placed in far greater danger had my wife cooked - typhoid infected or not.

Prep cucumber sandwiches at a church fete with poor hand hygiene and I could wipe 200 pensioners off the electoral role. Handy for this country's political progression; but damaging for my continued plans to stay out of prison. "We will be able to trace an outbreak of any Oxfordshire typhoid epidemic to you," they warn me on the day I receive the infection.

Blood tests are vital to trace the disease. Medical professionals always announce a blood test with the same line: "Just a slight scratch". These "slight" scratches vary from pleasantly painless to "ARRRGH… have you just amputated my arm without anaesthetic??!!" This disproving-I'm-a-coward thing isn't going too well. However the latter response was unquestionably my fault for moving my arm at needle time. Most are done so well that they are impossibly painless. All are vital to ensure my continued well-being.

Eventual relief from the typhoid sweats comes in the form of some powerful antiviral drugs the size of ping pong balls. They are of such a potent dosage that, had Amy Winehouse become a professional cyclist, she'd still be reluctant to swallow them. Quick access to antibiotics provides a typhoid carrier with a 99% chance of survival anywhere in the world. Untreated, approximately 30% of those who contract the disease die every year. Yet general antibiotics' effectiveness risks being undermined by over-prescription, rendering the need for an efficient vaccine even more imperative.

Mercifully typhoid quickly dissipates from my body. Tragically it doesn't for around a quarter of a million people globally each year who die of this pernicious disease. I can't help wonder how differently this horrendous infection might be addressed should it cause 250,000 Europeans to die annually.

I recover almost instantly, though I have to go back to the hospital intermittently for a year to be sure I remain typhoid free. Yet thanks to Oxford, perhaps in a short time the world will have a more effective typhoid vaccine.

An open top bus parade would be nice.

RUDE PEOPLE OF THE WORLD: F**K OFF

Here's a joke. Two men are adrift on a life raft. They've been bobbing on the ocean undetected for weeks, when one of them announces: "I see Oxford United lost again." "How do you know that?" asks his fellow shipwreckee. "Because today's a Saturday."

Leaving a football match prompts me to think of this gag. Oxford has just lost again. Actually it was City not United I had just witnessed succumb, but in Oxford, unlike Manchester, this detail is relatively unimportant. And it is indeed a Saturday.

On my way home I stop off at Sainsbury's in Heyford Hill. Just as I'm chicken-scratching through items unceremoniously flung into the 'Reduced For Quick Sale' section, an agitated stranger suddenly shouts abuse. VERY LOUDLY.

Startled, I involuntarily jump into the air, before returning to earth a second later. The shouter responsible for demonstrating this Newtonian physics is wearing an expensive Nordic-looking grey sweater. He's in his early 60s and, by his dress sense, visibly affluent.

He arrows me and my fellow bargain scrabblers a belittling glance, clearly communicating: "The whole of this store is at my disposal to shop in, not just the tiny bargain trough available for you snivelling guttersnipes." Unfortunately he's also clearly communicating verbally, via actual shouting: "I DON'T CARE!!"

The unfortunate recipient of his hostilities is a diminutive young Asian girl wearing a store worker's uniform. She speaks timidly, yet armoured by a steely determination not to raise her voice in perpendicular contrast to Odious Shouty Man.

"It's not my department," she attempts to explain, "but I'll…"

"I DON'T CARE WHAT YOUR DEPARTMENT IS!!" bellows the bellend. "Find me some saffron!!"

The girl lowers her head and mumbles something incoherent, as if she's been winded by the verbal violence. Eventually raising her head she says softly: "If you could please wait while…"

"No, I'm not going to wait! Don't tell me to wait!!" (I've used two exclamation marks, but nine would have been a more accurate reflection of his chosen volume.)

"I don't have a phone with me," she reasons.

"You've got feet haven't you?! So walk!"

Never has the urge to smash a jumbo-sized jar of reduced price pickled gherkins over a stranger's head been stronger.

Searingly rude, he shouts to her retreating back: "It'll cost you nothing to walk faster!" I'll tell you what else costs nothing: good manners.

"Un-be-li-ev-ab-le!" fulminates Odious Shouty Man, somehow stretching it to six separate shouty syllables. His outrage is ineffable. He wonders along another aisle muttering loudly to himself. "Where's the manager?!" he hollers to what I hope is no one in particular and not me stealthily observing the whole scene unspooling in the Savoury Biscuits/Cereals/Roasted Nuts aisle.

"I don't believe it," he shouts like he's auditioning to be the unfunniest Victor Meldrew impersonator ever. He's an uncorkable Krakatoa of erupting toxic abuse.

Another staff member soon arrives. Similarly uniformed, he attempts to placate the unpalatable and unplacable. "The saffron should be this way, Sir," he says with an ominous calmness unwarranted by the situation, and leads the man on a route past Table Sauces/Coffee/Tea.

"I know where it is!!" fumes Odious Shouty Man with the word 'imbecile' never more tonally implied in the history of human conversation. "There isn't any on the shelf. So I want you to get me some saffron. NOW!" The "Now!" is at least twenty decibels louder than the rest of his sentence.

Logically this is akin to saying: "I know unicorns and permanent world peace don't exist, but bring me both. NOW! Or I'll speak to your manager, imbecile!" Thereby ensuring he'd be unopposable should they ever open up a Nobel Prize for stupidity.

"If there's none on the premises then I'm afraid we cannot fulfil your order today," says the staff member with unchallengeable logic. Only his logic is challenged. "I don't care!" yells the man. "However," begins the store worker at a volume again refusing to match the shouter's, "we can…" Odious Shouty Man is not interested in the worker's "however we can" and curtly curtails it with a "Fetch your manager NOW!!" instruction.

He appears to be dedicating his Saturday afternoon to humiliating people of perceived lower social standing. I know violence is a negative expression that creates rather than solves problems - but I really would be prepared to stare into the eyes of a court room jury and say "I saw nothing" should any of the staff elect to club him to death with a frozen garlic baguette.

Unfathomably rude, he continues his verbal assault on another passing member of staff. "I want some saffron, and I am not prepared to wait any more," he bugles. Like an arse.

The Asian girl and her male colleague walk away together. Once safely out of earshot of the customer's conniptions they chat conspiratorially, probably fermenting revenge.

Meanwhile I take cover in Biscuits/Confectionery/Boxed Chocolates. I want to keep him under surveillance to see how this will end but dare not risk making eye contact with the ogre. I study labels with the intensity of someone about to go on *Mastermind* with ten minutes' notice to answer questions on "Ingredients listed on boxes of Teatime Assortment".

The longer he waits, the more he snorts. And the harder it is for me not to be seen. I imagine the staff are all upstairs huddled around a CCTV screen laughing like hyenas passing around a joint.

Curiosity as to how this will end magnetises me to the spot. I'm unable to move in case I miss the ending. And the ending transpires to be well worth the wait; mainly because it's a perfectly appropriate culmination of events.

Nothing happens. Nothing at all. No one returns to the obnoxious angry man who's not so much a person as a huge honking annoyance. Why should they return? If he behaves as badly as that then surely he has no right to expect further interaction with the staff or humanity in general. Eventually he wanders off neglected towards Sugar/Eggs/ Home Baking. Then he turns right into an adjacent aisle and self-scans a bottle of what looks, at my range, to be clear spirits.

Perhaps a more perfect ending would have been a store announcement over the tannoy by the diminutive Asian girl: "Hello shoppers. Saffron is now 90% off in the 'Reduced for Quick Sale' section in Aisle 24." There are only 23 aisles in this branch of Sainsbury's, but watching him trying to locate Aisle 24, and at what point he'd literally explode in the process necessitating a "Clean Up in Aisle 23", would make for great staff-watching CCTV entertainment.

I return home. "Oxford City lost again," I say. "I know," says my wife, "and so did Oxford United." Neither of us mentions that it's a Saturday. "Got anything for tea?" asks my wife, looking at my battered bag-for-life. I produce a packet of double-gunned reduction-labelled crumpets.

"Yeah, but what I really fancy is a slice of that cake we brought back from Cornwall. The saffron cake." "Oh I gave that to Sandra and her kids," says my wife far more matter-of-factly than I consider appropriate.

"No saffron cake?" I lament. "Oh well," I say lugubriously. My wife blinks her dissent at my selfishness. Then pushes two crumpets down into the toaster. Internally I'm behaving like the man in the supermarket. But crucially I don't let my behaviour escape into the outside world because I don't wish to ruin anyone else's day. Including mine. Nor am I a total, utter…"

"Knob," says my wife, "of butter?" and plonks it on my crumpet, demonstrating that we're lucky to live in a time and place where if one food isn't available (such as the utterly unessential saffron) then countless others likely are.

Rude people of the world: F**k off.

HOW MANY COLUMNISTS DOES IT TAKE TO CHANGE A LIGHTBULB?

I've just reached the summit of a step ladder when the house phone rings. "Oh, swear word!" I remark to an empty kitchen. My wife is upstairs listening to Radio 4's *Saturday Live* and is therefore oblivious to the needy ringing of the living room phone.

I descend the step ladder, light bulb in hand, as quickly as I can without compromising safety. Like many people I have often wondered how and when my inevitable death will occur - but I particularly don't want it to be caused by tripping when rushing to answer a speculative call about PPI. Picking up the phone after its tenth - and potentially - final ring, I shout a breathless "Hello?" which is meant to communicate: "This is an inconvenient time."

"Is that Richard O. Smith?" asks a palpably Northern Irish accent. Once I actually received a landline phone call that wasn't from a salesperson or fraudster; that was around the turn of the last century. Therefore I am cautious to engage in conversation with any phone stranger.

"This is JP from *Saturday Live*." His distinctly Northern Irish tones are consistent with BBC Radio 4 broadcaster JP Devlin. Yet my fraudster filter is set so high after perennial criminals' attempts that my initial thought is: "Hmmm… that's a new one. Fraudsters are now impersonating the voices of well-known broadcasters to obtain a false familiarity and presumably my password. Perhaps John Humphrys will call next and press me aggressively: 'I have to ask you again, Minister, what was your mother's maiden name and first pet called?'"

"Who was that?" asks my wife when popping down to the kitchen in search of snacks.

"Was that your other woman?" she asks. More in hope than concern. I've never understood why some (or, in France, all) married men have a mistress. Why would you want to have two women who hate you instead of just one?

"Oh, JP from *Saturday Live*," I say with false insouciance. "Yeah, right," she replies. "Really it was." My wife's expression doesn't require accompanying words. But she says some anyway. "Why did he want to speak to YOU?!" Her tonal implication registering off-the-scale incredulity. She's fairly dubious that I'm worth a fraudster's time, yet alone that of a celebrity.

"The show's producers asked if I'd do an anecdote on the show." "Why?" asks my wife, insensitive to my fragile confidence. "Cos I do, er, you know, comedy and, um …you're right, I have absolutely no idea why they'd want me on national radio," I concede. My euphoria at being asked onto live Radio 4 has now audibly crashed.

At this point a distinctly unwelcome crashing sound comes from the kitchen, as if illustrating a metaphor with a sound effect. "Oh, the light bulb must have rolled off the side," I say.

My wife rolls her eyes, before asking: "What anecdote do they want?" "The Russian wedding one." "Yeah, that's a good story," she agrees.

JP calls back and I recount the anecdote about being the best man when my friend from Lincolnshire married his Russian fiancée. Consequently my best man's speech was delivered in English (to big laughs in all the right places from the English contingent), but I had to pause after every line to allow the bilingual groom to translate into Russian. My gags - that had mostly killed in English - provoked only stormy faces from the bride's Russian friends and family.

After I'd just said: "I won't elaborate too much on the number of the groom's former girlfriends, other than to say who knew that the number 89 would turn out to be his lucky number?", a Russian guest whispered in my ear, "You realise, Richard, there is no tradition in Russian culture of ridiculing the groom in a best man's speech." Oooops.

"That's really good," JP assures me. "It should be on sometime between 10.10-10.30am," he says, as long as it's to the producer's taste - implying that this is such a formality it's like asking a panda if he likes bamboo.

At 10.30am *Saturday Live* gives way to *Kitchen Cabinet*. They don't include my anecdote. Considerately, JP Devlin emails me afterwards. "Sorry we didn't have time to include you," adding: "You sound like you've done a lot of weird and wonderful things - certainly more varied than me!" Which, er, I haven't. "Are you sure JP contacted the right Richard Smith?" asks my wife, somewhat unsupportively in my opinion.

"I'm not surprised they didn't include you," she declares later. "I meant the OTHER Russian wedding anecdote you do. The one about the groom warning his horse and bride that he might shoot them on the count of 'Three!' That's funnier."

"Three!" I say, which actually makes my wife laugh. "See, much funnier," she says. I re-enter the kitchen and discover the spent - not replacement - bulb was the one that smashed. Things are looking up.

HAVE I GOT VIEWS FOR YOU

A girl with enviable long thick hair stands to inform everybody of her name and, supposedly, ask a question. Although we're in the cavernous Oxford University Exam Schools, the arrival of the roving microphone mid-way through her comments makes little difference to the volume. Which is exhilaratingly loud. "My name is Lucy and I'm an...." she thunders before pausing, suddenly predisposed as if she's had a panicked realisation that she forgot to lock her front door.

Since this is not an Alcoholics Anonymous meeting, everyone leans forward to display their interest in how her opening sentence will conclude. Particularly as there are about four hundred people in the room. And one of them is *Have I Got News For You*'s Ian Hislop, who is sitting directly opposite - about as distant from her as he usually is from Paul Merton.

"My name is Lucy and I'm an undergraduate student," she eventually finishes. Given her age, attire and attitude, and since we're in a university building, this is hardly a revelation of traffic-stopping magnitude. Presumably sensing this disclosure requires an upgrade, she continues dispensing personal information after another long pause. "And I am also a..."

This had better be better, we think. "...lesbian." Again, this may have produced a mild shock if she'd been here fifty years ago to orate it, but not today.

Perhaps some elderly retro members of the Oxford audience - doddery dons and portly port- partaking professors still consulting pocket watches as they're reluctant to embrace this modern fad for wristwatches - might have reacted with "What!? First radios without wires, then transportable cordless telephonic devices, and now lesbians with long hair!" But I seriously doubt it.

So she goes again, with a third and final attempt to captivate the audience's interest. "This week I was denied going to my college's Bop dressed as a homosexual as I was told it infringed the rights of a safe space."

Everyone in the room is now thinking the same thought: how do you go to a Bop (basically a college disco - it's *such* an Oxford thing) specifically dressed as a homosexual? Sadly she doesn't elaborate on that point. "So then I announced I was going as a Thai lady boy, but I was told this infringed the rights of the Trans community and was also deemed racist and guilty of cultural inappropriation."

"Right," muses Ian Hislop, aware like the rest of us that this doesn't actually constitute a question. Instead Hislop, ever the consummate communications professional, asks her a question in order to move the conversation forward. "What did you go to the Bop as, then?" This was hardly a risk-neutral question. Given what we've learnt of Lucy so far, she may well have replied, "I blacked-up and went as despot African mass murderer Idi Amin." Mercifully her actual answer is more prosaic, if rather odd.

"So I went as Becky the fish." Realising this doesn't mean much to the four hundred other people present, she continues with unwavering volume and confidence. "So, like, I dressed up as a fish and said I was, like, called Becky." Okay. And an audible 'phew' for not being offensive. "A lesbian fish called Becky," she qualifies, unnecessarily. Again she doesn't explain how the fish costume managed to convey gayness, or whether this was deemed pescaphobic by the college authorities.

I suddenly recall once seeing a cartoon from *The New Yorker* magazine. It depicts a moderator on stage who has just thanked the day's speaker for delivering a talk. The caption reads: "Now, Ladies and Gentleman, it's time to open up the floor to slightly shorter speeches disguised as questions." You don't half get a lot of this type of thing here - Oxford has an unwelcome proclivity for it.

Sitting next to Lucy, her friend's head nods repeatedly, bobbing up and down like a cheerleader's ponytail as she visibly agrees with absolutely everything her companion is saying. It's a nebulous speech that will soon be in danger of being longer than Ian Hislop's. Lucy is speaking about perceived micro-aggressions when the *HIGNFY* star grabs the conversational steering-wheel and reverses us out of Amorphous Avenue into Perceptive Place.

"Well," says Ian Hislop calmly, after the microphone has finally been grappled out of Lucy's unwilling hands, "people often take offence. Not for themselves, but on behalf of someone else." This earns a round of applause.

"That's a good note to end on," says the Principal of a nearby college moderating the event. "If there are no more questions then we'll curtail the event there." Lucy raises her hand to come back in. "No one has any more questions then?" he checks.

She's sitting in the middle of the second row, arm held more noticeably aloft than the Statue of Liberty. "Okay, so if there are definitely no more questions please join me in thanking Ian Hislop for a fascinating talk." The last time I saw someone with their hand raised that desperately was when I was five years old at infant school: exactly ten seconds before my classmate Gregory Harrison wet the floor.

I decide that I like the event's moderating Principal a great deal. After concluding proceedings formally, and wisely ignoring Lucy's raised arm in case it prompts another uninterruptible diatribe of Political-Correctness-baiting costume anecdotes, he concludes the formal part of proceedings. His closing sentence I find particularly endearing. "If you are an invited guest of St Edmund Hall then please make your way to the college where a drinks reception awaits you attended by our guest Ian Hislop. Otherwise, I'd advise you to just gate-crash it in the traditional Teddy Hall way." I duly gate-crash it in the traditional Teddy Hall way.

Soon I'm ensconced in a function room so crowded that it's impossible to remove a jacket no matter how much the temperature rises. "Bloody gate-crashers," I remark to a smartly suited man who I have no option but to accidentally elbow as I slalom towards a drinks table. A table that appears to be getting further away rather than nearer whenever I try and move towards it. Since we have no option to move from each other's immediate vicinity, I start a conversation with the stranger. "Did you know that when Ian Hislop started on *Have I Got News For You* Margaret Thatcher was still Prime Minister?" I say. "That's interesting," replies the man.

Then I spot a waitress. "'Excuse me, excuse me!" she exclaims, hip-swivelling past everyone like a tricky winger. She's carrying a tray of hors d'oeuvres. I immediately activate an old Homer Simpson trick that has served me well at social functions over the years as an impoverished bread roll-pocketing freelance writer. First keep an eye out for where the food is entering the room at any catered social function. Having then situated yourself immediately outside the located comestibles entry point it's possible to get a first helping off the trays. Plus you're ideally positioned to get a second grab when they return to base.

Loquacious lesbian Lucy is pinning someone to the wall. His hair is flurrying behind him like a World War One flying ace's scarf as she thunders her inescapable opinions into his face. Her silent sidekick, very much a Boo-Boo to her Yogi, is nodding enthusiastically at everything she is bellowing. [BTW: I've often wondered why Yogi Bear wears a hat, collar and tie - but no shirt or trousers?]

Speaking to Ian Hislop seems impossible. He's garlanded by a throng of well-wishers at least three rings deep. Therefore I deem him unreachable. Suddenly I recognise a familiar face inside the inner ring engaged in actual conversation with the *Private Eye* editor. It's my wife.

He appears to be laughing at something she's saying; though it's impossible to eavesdrop given the general murmur of chattering in the congested room. Yet Lucy, at least twenty metres away, is somehow still audible. After countless "excuse me's" and "pardon me's," I reach Hislop's audibility range. Everybody wants to know about *Have I Got News For You*. Hislop says he can't believe how long he's been doing it. "Do you know that when we started Margaret Thatcher was still Prime Minister?" Yes. Yes I do.

Then my wife reaches forward and deliberately pats the celebrity editor, panellist and documentary maker's head. Gentlemanly he chooses to react with humour and smiles.

Waiting at the bus stop with my wife an hour later, I say a sentence I hadn't expected to use in my life: "Why were you patting Ian Hislop on the head?"

"I told him he has such a cute bald patch," she answers as casually as if I'd just asked her what time it is. Right. Why? "Because everyone else was asking him how long he'd been doing *Have I Got News For You*, so I thought I'd change the subject and tell him that he looks like a grown up *Just William* and that he should wear a cap like William." Suddenly my envy of celebrities decreases markedly. Then a group of students walks past our bus stop dressed in Arab headdresses, presumably going to a fancy dress party. I feel sure Lucy would have something very audible to say about them.

An acquaintance spots me boarding the bus and asks me where I've been. "Ah," he says on hearing about my evening, "Do you know that when they starting doing *Have I Got News For You* Margaret Thatcher was still the Prime Minister?" Yes. YES I DO!

A SCRAGGY DOG STORY

"It'll make a lovely birthday present for Hannah," says a girl in the queue at Blackwell's here to buy a book supposedly written by, er, a dog. "That'll be the best pressie ever," agrees her companion, before adding with excessive enthusiasm, "What else could she possibly want?" The receipt?

Hence they grab another copy from a table creaking under the weight of books. The two friends of the absent Hannah are both magnificently attired. One is wearing a retro flapper dress and has clearly made an effort to look her best when meeting a celebrity. Both plan to take selfies with the famous author.

A good twenty minutes later they reach the front of the queue to encounter Tuna the dog - a four-year-old adorably scraggy Chihuahua-Dachshund cross. Well over a hundred people - and one dog (another Chihuahua) - have come to see Tuna in the flesh/fur.

Tuna is an undisputed celebrity. He has 1.7 million Instagram followers. Refreshingly he doesn't appear to have let his fame affect his behaviour. I ask a Blackwell's staff member, also called Hannah though not the one with an imminent disappointing birthday present, how Tuna behaved backstage. Digging for a journalistic exposé of a celebrity behaving badly, I ask if there were any Green Room tantrums. Did he demand that the red ones were all removed from his Winalot mix? Alas not. "He's been adorable," confirms Hannah.

My bright smile is shadowed by annoyance. I catch myself harbouring pangs of professional jealousy towards a tiny dog who is a vastly more successful units-shifting author than me. I've done book signings at many stores, including this branch of Blackwell's. The nearest I got to having a queue was when my wife had to wait behind someone who mistook me for a store employee.

To be fair to my canine nemesis, he demonstrates remarkably placid behaviour, content to be picked up and photographed repeatedly by human strangers for two hours. I've worked with many celebrities in my time and most human celebs would not be happy to put in an uninterrupted two-hour shift at the fan-face.

Every few minutes Tuna's owner stands up and introduces herself to the queue: "Hi, I'm Tuna's mum." This is biologically unlikely. She is Courtney Dasher, 34, from Los Angeles. I consider people who refer to themselves as being "from L.A." arrogant in expecting us to comprehend their lazy abbreviation. You don't hear people from Chipping Norton proclaiming, "Hi, I've just flown in from C.N."

Three years ago Courtney's life changed forever when "I fell in love with a dog," she writes on her blog. "He has funny teeth that stick out, a crumpled chin and a neck that looks like it's been soaking in a bathtub for days! I believe that he was discarded by his original owner. I don't think that they saw the beauty in him."

His mum - and I suspect actual author of the book since Tuna would have difficulty typing given his noticeable lack of fingers - stands proudly next to him, directing photographers. She's dressed exuberantly, exhibiting a Californian confidence in her mannerisms and fashion choices. Her hat has such a wide brim it's unlikely she would be able to fit into a lift.

The decibel levels of cooing is disconcerting. Readers request that their newly purchased books are, er, pawtographed by Tuna. A paw shaped rubber stamp has been manufactured for this singular purpose in order to save this member of the canine literati from the indignity of having to sign/paw books personally.

His *New York Times* bestseller Tuna Melts My Heart: The Underdog with the Overbite bundles several incidents from Tuna's average day - captured in captions beneath photos. Mainly his day involves sleeping, eating and undergoing more changes of clothes than a catwalk model. Anthropomorphism is clearly the key here as Tuna is dressed in human attire throughout. Then about fifty pages in, something actually happens in the plot. They lose Colin. Colin is Tuna's favourite toy. So, on the next page, they buy a new Colin. Drama over. Resolution. Rather than unnecessarily elongating the search - an oft-used manipulative plot device - they sort out the jeopardy immediately. Credit to them for that.

The hardly epic plot doesn't so much boil as simmer slightly before turning colder than iced gazpacho. But that doesn't matter - no-one is buying this book for its prose. A persuasive image of Tuna's cuteness captures him lying on his back grinning a toothy smile. He looks goofier than Goofy.

As I depart Tuna's "signing" our eyes momentarily lock in a quiet steely gaze. The mutt is giving me a look I decrypt as "if only you had my marketing, eh?"

While I walk to the bus stop, Tuna and his entourage are chauffeured back to a luxury hotel suite. "There's just been this cutey-wutey likkle doggie on the local BBC news," my wife greets me with highly uncharacteristic diction when I return. "There were hundreds to see him in Blackwell's. That was loads more than you got there," she points out. Helpfully. With more characteristic diction. Looks like I'm in the doghouse tonight.

Blackwell's proudly tweet that their hallowed bookshop has hosted authors such as Virginia Woolf, Alice Walker, Terry Pratchett - and now a dog. Surely they meant Virginia Woof, Alice Walkies, Terrier Pratchett. And Fido Dogtoy-evsky. (You're welcome.) It's okay, I won't attempt any more pawful puns.

A few "signed" copies of Tuna's book are placed onto Blackwell's shelves. And one copy, inscribed "Happy Birthday Hannah!!" should be available in a charity shop soon.

LEARNING TO LEGO

I try to be an unfailingly good person. Ideally this would mean becoming a crime-fighting caped superhero spending my free time rumbling baddies. Preferably abseiling into their secret lairs, rescuing gender-neutral princesses (I'm so 21st century) and shooting evil henchmen (sorry, henchpersons) in the face while making wry sideways remarks to camera such as: "It's time to take out the trash!" Or nowadays - still on message: "It's time to take out the recycling!"

And recycling is another way I display my All Round Good Guy credentials. I was delighted when separate food/glass/plastics/paper recycling was brought in. I wouldn't mind if the logical ultimate conclusion to household recycling was introduced: 118 separate bins, one for each element in the Periodic Table. Okay, maybe I haven't completely thought that through.

Staying in sync with the shifting social politics of the age is another exemplification of how I strive to be A Good Person. What men and women expect of each other are constantly shifting sands in the changing tides of fashion. Remember Milk Tray Man? Today he'd be done for breaking and entry, criminal damage, trespassing on a railway and stalking. He'd also get his own hashtag callout for his sexist attitude and commitment to unhealthy diabetes-risking snacks.

But I'm yet to become an action superhero. Instead, being an unadventurous and physically unspectacular sort, I've had to lower my ambition and implement a series of micro goodnesses. A compromise, yes, but one that still allows me to imprint a positive difference onto the world. This mainly involves being polite to people, raising my hand to zebra crossing stoppers and not starring at the arse of my friend Jane whenever I'm behind her in a cafeteria queue. Magnificent as her arse unquestionably is - it would inspire Michelangelo to reach for his chisel - this would constitute behaviour inconsistent with me being A Good Person.

One of the (hopefully many) micro good things I do occurs in supermarkets. I locate the barcode on my purchases and deliberately place them on the conveyor belt facing upwards. There is always time to do this awaiting your turn. Especially as the person in front is invariably staggered to discover there is a compulsory requirement to pay for their scanned goods. "Pay? For the goods I've just picked and packed. Really? What, here and now? Oh of course, I remember that happened once before," thereby entailing a self-frisking dance whereby they theatrically locate their wallet or purse via the medium of mime.

"Have you a loyalty card?" Yes, yes they have. But not the foresight to imagine that it will be used in this, of all places, the store for which the loyalty card belongs. They produce a fan of cards resembling a magician about to do a trick. No one seems to spot the dichotomy of possessing multiple loyalty cards for countless different stores. It's like committing loyal infidelity. "Well I only cheat on my wife with the same fifteen other women I met on Tinder, so she's lucky to have such a dedicated loyal bloke like me, really."

These people shouldn't be in the supermarket delaying me. Instead they should opt for the supermarket's home delivery service - of which Milk Tray Man's girlfriend was evidently an earlier adopter. And just like modern recipients of store home delivery service, she didn't get what she ordered either: "How can a box of chocolates be considered an appropriate substitute for my requested tray of milk?"

"How are you?" says the cashier when I eventually reach the front of the queue, sometime narrowly before the end of the current geological age. "Fine," I reply, before always asking how they are. Another micro goodness of mine. By their reaction it appears no-one else has ever done that before.

Nor have they experienced any previous customers placing their shopping barcode upwards on the conveyor belt before. "Surely some people do that?" I say. "After all it's a win/win. Saves you work, saves the shopper time." "No, only you." They confirm I'm unique. And for once, they mean it in a good way. Hopefully.

"Since you're nice to us, you can have extra Lego cards," says the cashier. She gives me a fistful of them. I'm so touched I fight back tears. I've never obtained an Oscar, BAFTA or Cycling Proficiency Certificate. But now I have been selected for bonus Lego cards. And you can't put a price on that (well, technically 99p for a packet of four, but my point still stands.)

That night I recount the experience to a friend over snacking - dinner parties are too much arsework - informally from the fridge. Sniffing each 'Reduced For Quick Sale' item that I'd purchased from previous supermarket visits confirms their fitness for consumption. I discover a festering blueberry yogurt whose 'Use by' date is so old I'm surprised it doesn't appear in Roman numerals.

In the kitchen BBC Radio 4 is chattering away to itself in the background, then claims my full attention when mentioning a book prize on *Front Row*. Because it namechecks an author whom I know personally. It transpires she's won another major national literary prize.

"Wow," says my friend, "I saw you doing a double act with her at Blackwell's bookshop." This is true. It's good to be reminded of my star status - albeit a remote star in a faraway galaxy orbiting her comparative sun. "There were like only thirty of us in the audience." This is true. The author is Katherine Rundell. She's infuriatingly talented and, as my snacking companion fervidly points out, "now incredibly successful and famous".

This implies I should be jealous. But I'm not. "Do you keep in touch?" he asks. "She texted me a couple of years ago," I say, as a euphemised 'no'. "She's genuinely really pleasant," I add, "and *Rooftoppers* is a seriously cool book for any Young Adult readers." And not so young adults too, in my case.

"No bitterness then?" he checks. "No, she deserves her success," I enjoy being able to say truthfully. "Besides," I observe, "I bet she's never been selected to receive quadruple Lego cards in Sainsbury's."

The next day my friend Matt rings me. Seconds before we conclude the call he remembers something: "…Oh…are you still there?" "Yes," I reply. "It's a long shot but you shop at Sainsbury's sometimes, don't you?" "Yes," I confirm, "concluding that if this is his idea of a long shot, then I should definitely investigate making some wagers with him. "I don't suppose you were given any Lego Cards?" "Well, as it happens this is your lucky day."

It transpires his ten-year-old daughter has been eagerly collecting them. "Yeah, apparently they stopped doing them yesterday, and lots of her school friends reported they were given tonnes for free on the last day to clear them out. But we didn't go shopping yesterday so she feels she's missed out."

A few minutes later I hear the key turning in my front door. My wife puts down a bag of shopping and announces: "I heard that *Oxford Lives* comedy podcast you did about the year in review." "Oh, thanks," I say, "did you like it?" "It's okay - but I thought you were only funny in just a few places."

"Yogurt?" I say, handing her a blueberry flavoured one from the fridge.

I'm still a good person.

IN OTHER WORDS: GETTING YOUR TEETH INTO NEOLOGY

My wife has just returned home from the dentist after enduring a deep filling in the front of her mouth. The anaesthetic has yet to wear off, noticeably impeding her speech. She sounds like a ventriloquist's dummy.

"Would you like a bottle of beer?" I ask, hoping she'll repeat it as "gottle o' geer" given her temporary inability to pronounce the bilabial letters 'b' and 'f'. "Gollocks," she replies.

"That's neology," I say, for which I receive the same word "gollocks" again in response. Pointing this out fails to elevate her mood.

"You'll have to ring my sister for me," she adds, barely comprehensibly and far too casually for my liking. "Can't you ring your sister later?" I plead. A simple "no" nullifies my whimperingobjection.

She indicates that she's in some pain and rattles a packet of paracetamols to stress this point. "Can only eat soup," she says. "There's some geetroot soup left." "Hmmm…." I say peering into the fridge, "we've only got beetroot soup."

"Gastard," she scowls. Wow, what a gitch.

Sensing she is no longer willing to see the funny side of this until starting to feel better, I apologise in an attempt to defang my wife. After microwaving the borscht - or 'gorscht' as my wife insists on calling it - she falls asleep in a chair.

Coincidentally this is my second encounter with neology and neologisms today. Earlier I had given a talk to a retirement group. Afterwards an attentive member of the audience approached me. I'd optimistically brought several copies of my books along in anticipation of sales. This turned out to be the most pointlessly optimistic gesture since the Bon Accord FC manager's pre-match pep talk before playing Arbroath in 1875 [look it up, non-football fans!].

It's not to buy a book, but ask a question. "That word you just used in the Q&A: What's that word when it's at home?" says the elderly man, sprucely. It's an archaic expression, given its dependence on the improbable likelihood that words have homes - which is almost as unlikely as millennials having homes. "Huh? Err…" I say, realising both of those aren't actual words either, "what word was that?"

"The word you used at the end. Knee-something."

"Neology," I confirm.

"And that's the study of knees, is it?" he says.

It's not a great joke, but since it is clearly identifiable as an intended joke, I laugh politely.

"It's actually the science - or art - of making up new words," I say, adopting my best Susie Dent on *Countdown* mannerism. Only without the not-too-pleased-with-myself humility that she brings to the role.

"Oh," is all he is prepared to offer our struggling conversation. Which, although not technically a word, has certainly been coined before.

"Or I could have just made up the word 'neology' of course!" I add. I offer a big smile to convey the message that this remark is intended to be a joke. Just like a live action smiley face emoji, transferred from the virtual to the real world. He doesn't reciprocate my polite laugh.

"Besides, when would you ever need to make up a word?" he asks, inferring no-one would ever need to do this. "To cheat at Scrabble?" I suggest. It is still a few hours before my wife's dentist experience that will prompt a flowering of neologisms. Again he doesn't respond. Instead he walks away. Without buying a book. Obviously.

The neologism that I'd used in my talk was 'shoffice' - which is a handy new noun for the shed that my publisher uses as an office. Technically it's a portmanteau but I don't want to risk having to explain that as well. Once safely beyond earshot I brand him a tooker - another self-invented neologism (you're welcome) for 'touchers and lookers' i.e. those who don't buy books from the author's post-talk signing table but flick through them grubbily and even snigger their approval.

Back in my kitchen my wife awakes. After being asleep for an hour her powers of speech are yet to return to normality. She informs me that the dentist has advised her "to limit jaw mobility", which must be the poshest way ever of telling someone to shut up.

"I admired your neology earlier," I say. I particularly liked the word 'gollocks'."

"Good," she says, before adding: "and I want to thank you for ringing my sister for me. That was a kind thing you did." Concern is imprinted on my face. Spotting that I'm wearing the expression of someone who's just realised they've left their phone on the bus, she says: "You DID remember to ring my sister, didn't you?"

"Gollocks," I reply. Busted, I flounder energetically, slippery but ultimately futilely like a fish in an angler's hands - and bracing itself for an imminent club to the head. "Umm, er… errr…the line was engaged," I plead. A Swiss cheese left on a rifle range would contain fewer holes than my defence.

"That's total gullshit!" replies my wife. "You need to ask how her bathroom regurbishment is going after the flood," she orders. Wisely, I don't observe that 'regurbishment' is another "new word neology". Alternatively, I decide that instead of neology and tautology, another ology is required: apology.

ANOTHER FIDO MESS

A teenager is being pulled along our street with involuntary haste.

She's struggling to restrain a powerful dog on his lead. To the casual observer she resembles a water-skier rather than a dog-walker, as she blurs past our kitchen window while leaning back at an unintended 45-degree angle.

My wife and I step off the kerb to vacate the whole pavement for the smartly unformed schoolgirl and her canine puller, allowing her to ski past at uncontrollable speed. We don't have to wait long for her to be out of earshot.

"That's so-and-so's daughter," says my wife as the girl flashes past, doing well to recognise her facial features distorted by such an intense G-Force. The girl's long ponytail is trailing behind her horizontally, as if her hair too is struggling to keep up. "You know, from no. 45."

The last time I saw the daughter from no. 45 she had pigtails and a Peppa Pig toy. That felt like 18 months ago, yet must have been nearer a decade. "But she's supposed to be little," I protest. "Surely she's at least three feet too tall to be her?" My wife exhales a pitying sigh and summarises how time works.

Unpacking the shopping I approach a difficult subject. "Seeing no. 45's daughter and how she's suddenly, er, twelve?" "Fifteen," corrects my wife, before reciting the actual month and date of her birthday."

"Really? How did that happen? Anyway, seeing her just now made me sad that we don't have one of our own to watch grow up."

"We're not getting a dog," says my wife. "No, I mean… " "I know what you mean," retorts my wife with growing anger, invisible steam whistling out of her ears, "and the world is overpopulated as it is, with numerous children tragically unloved. Besides, children are massive poo factories. Though hopefully not by her age."

Having previously seen the girl from no. 45 once every 13 years, I see her the very next day being towed by her ferocious furball. She stops outside our window and is easily audible spitting unpleasantries into her phone, featuring a sentence mainly containing "like", "(unprintable)" and "(also unprintable)". Some of her noun and verb usage was certainly not picked up from Peppa Pig's vocabulary.

Two hours later I wheel out the bins out for collection in the morning. Then I see it. Right there. Awaiting my squelching size-12 Timberlands like a landmine.

A curled dog turd has been deposited on the edge of our driveway. It's enormous and probably the second thing after the Great Wall of China visible from space.

So huge is the animal's deposit that I question whether the girl has recently bought a dog or just found an unextinct woolly mammoth.

"I was wrong," concedes my wife. "Fifteen-year-olds can still force you to clear up their crap." Rather idiosyncratically my wife photographs the mutt mess - which looks like a decidedly strange activity when making small talk to our neighbours who are also wheeling out their bins. "Well," I say matter-of-factly, "Jeremy Corbyn's hobby is photographing drain covers. My wife likes to photograph…"

Ablaze with anger, my wife emails her pooch poo pics to our local Councillor. I point out that sending an Oxford City Councillor a photo of doggie doodoo may reasonably constitute a hate crime. Nevertheless she emails her pictorial evidence. I'd like to take this opportunity of apologising to Councillor Michelle Paule.

The frantic dog walking continues over the next two evenings. Until the third day when it rains, resulting in the schoolgirl's mother passing our window. "See," says my wife, "truculent teenagers refuse to go out in the rain and make their poor mother walk the dog instead."

We debate about telling the teenager's mother. "Yeah, let's grass up a 15-year-old who knows where we live. She'll probably push it through our letterbox next," cautions my wife. "But we need to confront her. Speak to her when she walks the dog tomorrow," orders my wife.

The next afternoon is resplendent in uninterrupted sunshine and the teenager is back holding the lead. She walks in a jerky fashion, following her dog with the mannerisms and footwork of someone who is losing a tug of war contest. They stop briefly outside our drive. Needless to say I bottle the confrontation with the dyspeptic youngster. Thankfully our four-footed enemy doesn't leave a calling card this time. "I'll definitely speak to her tomorrow," I say, bluffing conviction.

On the following day we see her mother walking the dog. "Didn't realise it was raining," I say. Dismissing me as a coward, my wife marches out and interacts with the mother. Turns out the same dog has just pooped outside their house too - and their pet isn't the culprit. "So it's not the tetchy teenager's dog after all?" I state. "Now," shouts my wife, her anger reignited, "where's the camera?"

Again, I'd like to apologise to Councillor Michelle Paule.

TURNING OVER A NEW TEA LEAF

Intense drama can erupt from the most mundane of situations. Recently I experienced a scene that felt like it belonged in a gritty - all grit and no oyster - movie. Yet it originated from the most humdrum of unpromising circumstances. The whirlwind that picked me up out of ennui came from nowhere - before almost instantly depositing me back down into the banal reality I'd so fleeting departed. Afterwards I stood for several seconds, panting like an over-excited dog. And wearing a big "Did this really happen?" look.

Let's start at the beginning; a few moments before I became dislocated from reality. It's a regulation Monday afternoon in the characterless Oxford suburb where I live and work. Long may it stay characterless. That's why I live here. If I want vibrancy, noise and my over- familiarities challenged, then I'll bus to the city centre. (Take note estate agent language-misusers, for an area to be actually 'vibrant' you need to live on a fracking site.)

At about 4 o'clock I take a calm stroll to my local supermarket. It's what we homeworkers do to achieve daily human interaction and obtain some beneficial exercise in our otherwise deskbound sedentary existences.

Plus, you can improve productivity by taking a break - honest, boss. For the last seven uninterrupted hours I'd been editing text and reached a stage where I could no longer trust myself to recognise several letters of the alphabet. To edit text well you must stare at the words on a page with the intensity of a Frenchman studying a wine list the day after his Dry January ends.

Since I need milk - and after all, life is nothing but a series of connected timeslots to fill between necessary milk runs - I arrive at the store. Fifteen minutes later I'm waiting at the Customer Service desk since my supermarket's Own Brand Essential No Frills Economy Pie from the Sainsbury's Joyless Range has been scanned at the full price. Not the 'Reduced For Quick Sale' price that entirely justified my attraction to it in the first place. Similarly my tea bags have also been charged at full price, ignoring the yellow reduction sticker displaying their perilous proximity to a 'Best Before' date. Therefore I'm clutching my receipt and anticipating a partial refund.

If this was a heist movie the director would be busily establishing normality for the forthcoming juxtapositioning of serenity and jeopardy. For now all appears routine.

It's at this point that the terrifying shouting begins. Instantly I'm tingling with anxiety.

An unshaved man in his 30s runs into me with a cartoonish thwack. He doesn't quite knock me over, but only because it's more of a glancing blow than a full-on ram. I quickly conclude he probably didn't plan to run into a stranger, but if you're going to sprint around in a supermarket then such behaviour does rather increase the chances of knocking someone over.

A cashier hollers: "Code red! Code red!" [I've altered the actual security word used for, ahem, security reasons. You see - I'm a responsible adult.]

Let's just say their actual security code word is better. Incidentally, to avoid mass panic, all commercial theatres have a longstanding code word in case of fire. In one theatre where I'd supplied material for a gigging comedian the code word for a fire outbreak was - and I promise this is true - for staff to announce over the P.A. system: "There's a Mr. Fire in the building." Impenetrably cryptic and its meaning deadlocked, I know!

A uniformed cashier screams: "HELP! GET THE SHITBAG!" - the situation providing her with a welcome alternative to referring to customers as 'Sir'. Within the space of four words her need for assistance has transmogrified from vulnerability to retribution.

This, I realise, is a mighty serious situation. And will delay my £1.49 refund. Two supervisors have materialised from the back of the tills. They have the look of former mortals transformed into superhero guise. They bawl: "GO!" Four more uniformed staff appear as if summoned by a bat beacon lighting the sky.

Suddenly everything in the scene becomes cinematic. Even more uniformed staff materialise at the entrance of the building. Genuinely I had no idea so many people worked here - certainly not at previous checkout times when I've waited holding a single satsuma behind fourteen people tutting like a human beatbox.

How come when you're going through the checkouts there's usually just one tired girl on duty by herself with a look in her eyes communicating: "Please go to soft furnishings and bring a pillow to suffocate me with. Please."

Relieved of their supermarket customer-care personas, the staff are now action heroes and springy crime fighters, leaping around the place as they rush towards the store entrance. And this means they're allowed to shout in the workplace. And run. In a corridor. Probably with scissors too should the need arise. And it's likely, if they catch the thief, they'll beat the utter Own Brand Essential Pie Filling out of him.

For every obnoxious customer they've ever had to smile at tolerantly, this is Payback Time. "I know what you're thinking. Did he price six special offers or five? Well to tell you the truth, in all this excitement, I kinda lost track myself. But since this is the most powerful price gun in the world, and some of these reductions would blow your mind, you've got to ask yourself one question: do I feel lucky? Well, do ya, shitbag?!"

"THIEF!" bellows a member of the public requisitioning a role for himself in the unfurling drama. The thief and customer-barger has run to the main entrance. Seemingly everyone joins the chase behind him. More members of the public enrol in the pursuit - like bank clerks joining up for war.

Realising I only have a few seconds to make a decision, I decide to get involved too. I follow the staff platoon now swelled by vigilantes. This is the nearest I'll ever get to joining a proper Wild West posse. If we catch the thieving toerag maybe I'll be entitled to have an honorary sheriff badge pinned on my chest by the Deputy (Store Manager). But the chase has already commenced so there's no time to swear me in as special sheriff.

I rush outside. Excitement lubricates my leg joints. We move after the carrion. I sight the thief. He's well ahead. But we're gaining. He swerves around abandoned trolleys. He's sprinting. Yet his pursuers are getting closer. Much closer.

A woman spots us running towards her and panics. She loses her trolley - quite literally.

Ironically, should you want to purloin any stock from the store, now is your chance. Seemingly the entire staff are outside the shop, positioned on the opposite side of the retail park chasing a scumbag across a car park. Instead of having to retain professional politeness while some tedious complainer berates them for only having unsmoked not smoked paprika, the staff now get to chase a customer and potentially kick him to death by the bins in a CCTV blind spot.

There's certainly a lot of shouting involved. "GET HIM!" A corpulent cashier, breathing heavily, is tailed off at the back of the group, barely able to jog yet alone run. She leans forward, places both palms on a nearby trolley handle for support, and pants louder than an asthmatic porn actress. She's quit the chase. Two minutes later I eventually overtake her.

Pursuing the assailant hardly requires the tracking services of a scout. He's leaving a trail of Hansel and Gretel breadcrumbs behind him (if Hansel and Gretel were over 18 and possessed proof of ID) in the form of nicked bottles of spirits. Remarkably only one breaks.

He reaches the retail park's perimeter fence. Is he determined to be caught? Surely there's no way of escaping now? The pursuing mob are seconds away. Or minutes in the case of me and the heavy breathing corpulent cashier lagging behind. Inevitably he'll be nicked shortly. And you can't spend Nectar points in the prison shop.

Instead the pilferer climbs a wire fence with the desperation of a wild animal escaping the snapping jaws of a predator. Then he sprints without looking across a busy dual carriageway, slaloming between braking cars. Motorists hoot aggressively yet impotently. It's a genuinely terrifying scene. I'm primed to avert my gaze at any second as a fatal collision looks inevitable, splaying him against a windscreen like a summer bug.

Unlike most heist movies, this one ends unsatisfactorily with the baddie getting away. But he risked his life - and that of the motorists at school run time on the ring road. Wisely the supermarket staff opt not to follow him onto a busy road. At least one records his dissent towards this collective decision but is talked down after climbing the fence.

Back inside the store they process my refund. "Seems a bit trivial now," I say. The man smiles. "We nearly got him. Next time, we will," he says." I believe him. "The cashier should have turned over your tea and pie reductions," he says. Sensing a further explanation is required from my intellectually-absent expression, he adds, "To scan the reduction stickers that had failed to obscure the original barcode." He gives me the refund.

Returning home I plonk my shopping on the kitchen table. "Was it busy?" asks my wife. "Yes, surprisingly so." "See anyone you know?" "Well, I did bump into someone," I say. And rub my shoulder for emphasis.

"Who?" asks my wife, the wattage on her curiosity suddenly increased. "Oh," I add as matter-of-factly as possible, "There was a heist, then a mass staff and vigilante chase, the thief ran across the dual carriageway and lots of speeding cars nearly crashed and killed him." Calculating that my wife has already received enough intensely dramatic news - her coffee mug had stopped midway from table to mouth - I decide not to tell her about the £1.49 partial refund.

What have I learnt from the experience? Mundanity is highly underrated.

A SCROLLING STONE: THE MOVIE STAR ENCOUNTER

This month I was upstaged by someone famous.

I happen to be leading 22 members of the New Jersey Symphony Orchestra along Broad Street. As you do.

A percussionist is asking where he can buy Oxford fridge magnets. One of the violinists wants to know which college is associated with Harry Potter.

I have been asked to give the orchestra a brief tour of Oxford while they break their journey travelling between the previous night's concert at the Barbican and their St David's Hall, Cardiff, engagement.

Marching them briskly towards the Sheldonian I encounter further regular tourist questions: How many colleges are there? What's the oldest one? How old is the University? Is Boris Johnson real?

Leading them to the Bodleian's Old Schools Quad the group become architecturally starstruck and gasp loudly their positive impressions. To such an extent that I'm forced to remind them this is a functioning library, so politely request they reduce the volume of their gasps.

Standing next to the 'Silence Please' signs I whisper information about the Tower of Five Orders - or Tower of Four Orders in my case because my brain will only provide me with four of the five classical architectural styles demonstrated. Thanks brain.

Then I explain how joining the Bod involves having to affirm out loud that you'll hereby swear not to introduce to the library fire or flame nor kindle therein. Which is not very modern at all, is it? Not being able to read with a Kindle in the library. Also, it's surely significant that in every other library in the UK it's an assumed given that arson is not permitted.

We turn a corner and see a side door open to the Divinity School. Four orange-bibbed security men march out, sharpening my attention. My first instinct is that they're going to move us. Instead they divide and stand a respectful twenty metres away. Next, a woman strolls casually out of the same door and speaks into her phone. This lady is quite difficult to ignore given she's wearing a huge white wig and regency frock. Does her bustle look big in this outfit? Yes, rendered extra big as it contains a protruding radio mic. Oh, and she's one of the most famous film stars on the planet.

"This is the Sheldonian," I announce, "named after Gilbert Sheldon, a grocer's son who rose to become Archbishop of Canterbury in an age when moving between the classes was rarely achievable." Sensing I'm losing the audience as they all get their phones and cameras out, I continue nobly. That's nice, I think, they all want a photo of me as a souvenir of my excellent guiding.

Instead they all film the lady from the regency period as she scrolls, somewhat anachronistically given her costume, on her smart phone. The global superstar is on the cusp of audibility. She ends her call and we make brief eye contact.

"Do you know who that woman was?" asks a bassoonist with a breathlessness that I hope she doesn't demonstrate professionally. "No," I report.

Almost everyone in the group tells me in perfectly timed unison - hey, just like an orchestra - who the lady is. She is Emma Stone, star of controversial Oscar loser *La La Land*.

I tell them about Rachel Portman, formerly of Oxford's Worcester College, who was the first female composer to win an Oscar - assuming they had the right envelope.

"You sure have a beautiful city here," says a cellist. I nod proudly, as if Oxford's splendid architecture is an accomplishment down to me. Though I noticeably take the credit. "Weren't we lucky to see her? Timing is everything," she says. Later I discover Emma Stone is here filming the movie *The Favourite* with Olivia Colman.

Oddly this is not the most upstaged I've been while conducting a tour. That happened a couple of years ago outside Balliol. Just as I was reaching the culmination of a routine I noticed my entire audience avert their attention from me. I tried waving. They didn't turn back. I tried saying, "Hey, look at me. Me! Give ME attention!" like Donald Trump as a toddler. And Donald Trump now.

Then a man led a camel past my tour group. You get blasé about seeing odd things in Oxford, but this was a whole new level of distraction. Determined not to get the hump (you're welcome), I carried on as professionally as I could. Later I discovered the camel was promoting a Middle Eastern food fair.

They've been a friendly and engaging group so I'm happy to walk the NJSO back to their coach. Just as I'm about to stop waving as the bus diminishes into the horizon, my brain suddenly provides me with the word 'ionic', the fifth classical architectural style. Timing is everything.

THE BOOM OF THE UNKNOWN SOLDIER

Predictably my lone occupation of the bus's peaceful top deck doesn't last for long. At the next stop a family of four board and noisily herd upstairs with the subtlety of startled mammoths.

An obvious brother and sister combo occupy the front seat immediately opposite me. I always find it hard to age children, but I decide he may be around his final year at primary school, and his sister at the very beginning of secondary school. But it could easily be a year either way.

"So you're saying that it's morally unacceptable to wear fake fur?" he asks, pressing his sister like he's interrogating her on a radio programme rather than siblings chatting aimlessly on a bus. "I believe it's morally wrong to wear fake fur, as it normalises the alternative," she responds. Impressively. But, it transpires, not well enough to win the point. "So what you're saying is, if I've got this right for the listeners…"

At this stage the parents intervene. We're all used to eavesdropping classic parenting soundbites in public ("put that back", "mind that lady", "hand your weapon to the nice officer") but as far as I'm aware the sentence that their father utters next is a first in overheard public parenting: "Stop interviewing your sister!" Their father has the air of a man whose tether's end was located a considerable time ago.

At the next stop a part platoon of army squaddies gets on. They have obviously been drinking, adduced by the volume setting on their conversation. Mercifully they don't come upstairs; but remain audible, voices booming out like indiscriminate shellfire. They may as well be sitting on the top deck directly behind me.

Regrettably they have a vulgarian amongst their party. I'd like to be the person who goes downstairs and calls out his misogynistic humour, although since they're five boozed-up professional fighters, I decide to generously allow someone else to have the feel-good factor of intervening - self-sacrificial as that gesture is. You're welcome.

One of them suddenly shouts to a fellow intoxicated squaddie: "You've never seen *Die Hard*!" and then stumbles over an intended topping to his remark: "That's like, er, like…." Suddenly the bus falls quiet. His search for a simile is clearly going to take a while and requires absolute silence.

"Would you wear a leopard skin print top?" asks mini John Humphrys. "Yes, as it's a pattern rather than an animal skin. That would be causal effect." Since when did ten-year-olds know expressions like "causal effect"? When I was their age I was still leaving crayon marks on the landing wallpaper. The parents now seem content with the interviewing, as it at least renders the unpleasant waft of alcohol fumes and scatological language fluttering up the stairwell if not inaudible, then at least incomprehensible.

"Never seen *Die Hard*! That's like…umm… "The squaddie's search for a simile is still ongoing. At least the distance between Witney and Oxford.

Finally, the simile is ready. Expressing exasperation at his colleague's *Die Hard* unfamiliarity, he bellows: "That's like saying 'I've never breathed'." No. It. Isn't. For starters, had you never breathed then that's a fairly compact description of death. Dead people don't tend to go to the movies (zombie screenings notwithstanding). Admittedly I wasn't expecting genius to erupt. But this is an appalling simile. Also, it's not even technically a simile. Again, I generously allow someone else to have the satisfaction of pointing that out to him. You're still welcome.

If that amount of outrage is deemed necessary for not seeing a Bruce Willis action film, I'm intrigued to hear his reaction when discovering his fellow squaddie hasn't seen Ingmar Bergman's 1957 Swedish-subtitled monochrome masterpiece *Wild Strawberries*. "What? You've never seen the existential Scandi portrayal of an accessible metaphor for the peripatetic axiom? That's like… er… like… give me ten minutes. Or better still, your email address."

"We should have got a taxi," says the loudest squaddie somewhere near Botley. Yes, that's a statement the whole bus agrees with. Finally the bus docks in Gloucester Green. I allow the junior interviewers to descend the stairs ahead of me, pass through a cloud of lingering alcohol fumes and walk to my destination: a lecture room at the Ashmolean Museum.

After settling into my seat I hear an unmistakable voice behind me. "But surely holding that position is merely endorsing a heteronormative narrative." No, it's not one of the squaddies. That would be like… er, like… give me a minute.

It's junior Emily Maitlis. Their father is wearing an expression that says, "Whose stupid decision was it to educate my children?" You can guess which two hands shoot up first when they request questions at the end.

A WHITE ELEPHANT IN THE ROOM

I am a graduate (3rd class) of the University of Life - or, as it was called in my day, the Polytechnic of Life. This can sometimes cause an audible leaking of my self-esteem whenever I interact with today's better educated youngsters. Therefore I was surprised to be in possession of some common knowledge recently that a current Oxford University undergraduate palpably did not have.

Five of us are conversing around a lunch table. Four are enforced members of the 50 or over club amongst a lone 19-year-old. The teenager stops the conversation mid-flow to clarify a phrase I have just used: 'a white elephant'.

"Surely you've heard of 'a white elephant'?" gasps one of the (we've already established, much, much) older adults, with emphasised disingenuousness. "Nope," confirms the obdurate teenager.

We express collective shock at this blind spot in his knowledge - especially as my perceived image of hubristic teenagers these days is to overhear them yelling lines like: "I removed Google from my phone - don't need it anymore, since I already know absolutely everything!"

"Okay," he concedes, after hearing all four non-teenagers present provide heartfelt evidence that the phrase 'a white elephant' definitely does exist in the English lexicon. "Where did the expression originate?" he asks. This is definitely a good question, whereas my impending answer is definitely bad.

"Allow me to explain," I begin with a blustered authority that I do not possess before braking hard four words into my reply with the realisation that I am ignorant of the expression's origin. Hence I dither with audible awkwardness - still making noises although saying nothing: "Err… um… hmm." "Yes?" he presses. None of my fellow 50-somethings throw a conversational rope into the hole I'm digging for myself.

"Well, it probably originated when a bloke was helping a friend with, er, a job…" "What sort of job?" asks the teenager, like a prosecuting lawyer enjoying toying with a defendant who has repeatedly changed his story under cross-examination as to how he happened to be outside a bank holding a bulging bag of money while denying any connection with the alarm ringing inside.

"Maybe a DIY job," I continue. Unwisely. "A-ha," nods the teenager as the other four at the table flinch at my self-induced humiliation, but significantly still don't help me. "So he says, 'I've brought an elephant. Furthermore, I've painted it white. Thought it might come in handy.' But his friend says, 'I fear that white elephant may be superfluous to requirements,' and his mate replies, 'Really? That's a lot of Dulux I'll never get the money back on.'"

"Sounds plausible," says the teenager, his tone soused with sarcasm. "Okay, so that might be a huge guess." "Or a huge lie," clarifies the teenager. "Of elephantine proportions," adds an adult. Still unhelpfully.

"So you don't know where the expression originates?" he says, his tone conveying a dead heat between contempt and disappointment. "No," I admit far too late.

This prompts smartphones to be unholstered like the draw in a Wild West shootout. I am the only person at the table who doesn't own one - as a freelance writer my phone is so old that it would probably be mocked by Alexander Graham Bell. Everyone taps away in a race to be the first to discover the origin.

After googling it transpires that albino elephants were traditionally revered in Burma, Cambodia and Thailand by monarchs - yet exploited for a sinister purpose by the Kings of Siam (now modern day Thailand).

Acknowledged enemies of the Siam royal court were given a present of an elephant. However, the upkeep of the enormous free elephant was expected to be ruinous to the gift's recipient. I assume the king didn't insist on gift-wrapping, or the wrapping-paper expenditure would be ruinous to him too - plus the impossibility of retaining suspense with the shape of a gift-wrapped elephant ("Go on, guess!" "Er... is it a tennis racket?").

You can see how being forced to live with an elephant could provide practical problems. Certainly installing a cat-flap for an elephant would compromise household security. And indeed bankruptcy often befell those gifted an insidious white elephant by the King. Hence the term 'a white elephant' grew to mean an object was damagingly unnecessary. Although some sources caution that the King of Siam's rather peregrinated approach to administered justice is likely to be apocryphal.

"You don't hear the expression 'white elephant' much nowadays," one of our party speculates. "We used to run a white elephant stall at our school's fundraising events," says the only teacher in our party, "but not anymore."

This is a good point. It confirms that 'a white elephant' has two meanings: bric-a-brac as well as a superfluous object. With the rise of charity shops, plus multiple stores where everything is £1 (and not forgetting their aggressive capitalist under-cutters: the 99p store, whose customers must enviously observe whenever they pass the Pound Shop, "pah, it's alright for some!"), I suppose people have less inclination to buy from white elephant stalls. "I wonder when'll be the next time we hear someone use the expression 'white elephant'?" says one of our party.

I don't have to wait long. The next night I am invited to a "Drinks among the bones" event. I am concerned this might be an event organised by the fashion industry with numerous professional models present - all refusing the tiny hors d'oeuvres because "I ate a blueberry two days ago and consequently I'm full." Instead it transpires to be a networking event where wine is quaffed under dinosaur skeletons in Oxford's Natural History Museum. A woolly mammoth skeleton is on display and his bones are almost white - albeit marginally discoloured.

Someone at the previous day's lunch discussion approaches me with his stepson, and points: "There's a white elephant in the room."

"We're not mentioning it," I reply.

His stepson is the 19-year-old who 24 hours earlier was unaware of the phrase. "Sorry my explanation yesterday turned out to be a bit of a red herring," I say. Then I pause, before adding, "A red h…" "I know what a red herring is!" he says.

SUPERMARKET CHALLENGE

It still counts as very early when I wake - given today is a Sunday. Tottering downstairs in my semi-awake and unshaven state, I resemble a grunting Neanderthal stalking the savage savannah in search of a, ahem, milky macchiato with sprinkles.

Immediately I discover we're out of sprinkles. It's hardly a doomsday scenario, I grant you, but I was hoping to deliver to my wife's bedside a Starbucks café-quality foamy drink with extra over-the-top-ness. Although it's never truly possibly to replicate the exact Starbucks experience in your own home - for starters, I pay my taxes.

Opening the fridge door illuminates the kitchen. Nothing can prepare me for the shock about to erupt. There Is No Milk.

In the kitchen sink is an upturned milk carton. Prior to bed last night this was residing in the fridge, containing sufficient milk for two vital morning coffees. Either burglars have expertly gained entrance with no visible signs of a break-in overnight and swiped nothing but a nearly finished milk carton, or my wife has snaffled the last of the precious milk as a bedtime drink. Either way she's not getting that bedside macchiato. With or without sprinkles.

Strange, isn't it, how food and drink cravings only fit certain times of the day? You always want a coffee first thing, and a kebab exclusively at 11pm. No one ever leaves the pub at closing time declaring: "I could murder an apricot."

The kitchen has now become a crime scene. My wife must take her position in a police line-up next to famous milk stealers from history alongside a blue tit and Mrs Thatcher. There's nothing I can now do except contemplate a long walk to Sainsbury's - after I've unrolled yellow 'Crime Scene - Do Not Cross' tape in the kitchen.

My wife believes that I am entirely responsible for maintaining milk in the fridge and hence must ensure a constant supply. This surprises me as I've been looking to shed my milk responsibilities ever since I was reluctantly appointed a milk monitor in 1973 - still the highest position of public office I've held. Thankfully Margaret Thatcher the Milk Snatcher came to my rescue and put an end to milk monitoring - like so many other industries.

Nevertheless I have a plan to rectify my milk negligence. My nearest Sainsbury's supermarket has always opened on Sundays between 10am-4pm since time immemorial. And probably time memorial too - whatever that is. Hence an operation of military precision is devised. I need to leave home at zero nine fifty hours precisely. Leaving at 9.49am precisely would ensure I arrive at the store with the minimum of footfall. Supermarkets only have a six-hour Sunday opening window, and it can get pretty busy. Leave it any later and an intended visit to 'Milk/Butter/Yogurts' can see you swept off your feet by an enormous wave of people that beaches you in the crisps aisle.

"Anything else we need from the supermarket?" I ask my wife. She delivers a firm "no", before contemplatively adding: "Maybe just one other thing." That "one other thing" soon constitutes five new items. "By the time I've put on my jacket the list has grown to seven items - precariously close to disqualifying me from accessing the express checkout.

I'm about to leave, to catch my 9.49am departure window. "You'll forget without a list," declares my wife. Hence I dutifully jot down the items, even though I'll now be late. Every minute arriving after 10am, I calculate, will add a further two minutes in the checkout queue. Of course I could use the self-scanning facility, but if I want a woman with an automated soulless voice barking repetitive directives at me and refusing to compromise, then I can stay at home.

"Unexpected item on shopping list," I say, as my wife scribbles down 'dark chocolate!' "How dark?" I ask. "Chocolate so dark that its surface is incapable of reflecting light," she replies.

Arriving at the supermarket at 10.03am due to my list compiling delay - "No-one looks cool with a shopping list," I had protested ineffectively - I see the shop still in darkness. A large disgruntled crowd is milling around purposelessly outside. I soon learn why.

Apparently the store has recently changed its Sunday opening hours from 10-4 to 11-5. And the resultant horde emitting steam like a frustrated express locomotive stuck at a red signal rather proves the store was ineffective at communicating its change to the trading times.

"I've been sitting in my car for fifteen minutes already! Un-be-lieve-able," fulminates a fifty-something female, forcing out her words through airwaves constricted by anger. It's not actually too difficult to believe someone once sat in their car for fifteen minutes, but I decide not to comment on her deployment of the description "unbelievable", given her beetroot complexion and rising vexation.

A nearby man responds to her with equivalent volume: "I've come from Abingdon," he says, "ABINGDON!" as if Abingdon represents three days' trek by pack mule through bandit country, rather than a five-minute drive along the A34.

Another man peers crestfallen at the locked door and then shouts inarticulately like someone angrily hollering at a rejected god. It's the sort of response appropriate to returning from a night in an air raid shelter in 1941 to discover that your house has been destroyed by the Luftwaffe.

I decide to leave the brewing drama before the mob starts lighting flaming torches and demanding a lynching of some unfortunate weekend checkout-worker.

"That was quick," says my wife. An expression she dispenses with such regularity it risks becoming a catchphrase throughout our marriage. "They've changed the opening hours," I explain meekly. She responds by adding another two things to the shopping list.

An hour later I dutifully return to the store. Fortunately there's no sign of the rabble, or a swinging silhouette in the strengthening breeze of a lynched supermarket employee who bravely unlocked the doors at 11am rather than 10am.

Grabbing a basket, I collect ten items and sweat like Keith Richards going through customs as I approach the '8 items or less' checkout - resisting my inner grammar pedant's desire to announce it should be '8 items or fewer'. As the chirping bleeps of surrounding checkouts sound like hungry fledgling birds in a nest, I prepare myself for humiliation.

At least I think I've remembered everything. The cashier tolerantly allows my ten items, ignoring my 25% breach. Momentarily I allow myself to bask in the well-earned smugness of a mission successfully accomplished. Yet also internally acknowledging that I'm going straight from now on; my life of rule-bending is just too stressful to justify the rewards.

"Forget anything says my wife?" when I return home. "No," I reply proudly after a fractional delay to check that I most certainly haven't.

"How about this?" she says, holding up my handwritten shopping list that I obviously forgot.

"Coffee?" asks my wife. She peers inside my shopping bag like an intrigued bear pushing an investigating snout into a picnic basket. "Why did you get a duplicate milk?" "A what?" I check. "I got milk last night at the Co-Op on the way home. Didn't you notice we were getting low?"

THE SPERM DONOR

I am at a lunch party in Cowley. I know there's no such thing as a lunch party, but we are having one anyway. It's for people who are insufficiently refined to have a dinner party, but also wish to be less tired for work the next morning. Our hostess, usually known for a wine consumption unhampered by medical guidelines, is demurely sipping tap water from a pint glass.

Unbeknown to me, our hostess is attempting to have a baby. Being a bravely modern, unflinchingly independent woman, she has decided to forego the orthodox requirement of having a male partner for her baby. Well, other than right at the very beginning of the process.

She announces her intention over the lunch table. All the men present immediately volunteer free use of their sperm. This she interprets suspiciously as an unsubtle attempt to sleep with her. "I'm going through a professional organisation who provide the service - after I have attended prerequisite counselling sessions to discuss the full implications and ramifications of my decision," she says. "That's great," say all the males present, aware this may not be the first time she has issued this carefully crafted statement to prospective donors.

She immediately replenishes our glasses with wine and hers with water. "That's why I'm not drinking," she explains.

"Well," adds a man with a complicated name that I am too frightened to repeat in case I mispronounce it, "if it doesn't work out there's plenty of sperm available from me." "Thank you," she says, identifiable sarcasm trickling into her tone, "if the long-standing professionally run company with access to thousands of legally vetted donors proves unsuccessful, then I'll be in touch." Failing to spot this as the knock-back it was blatantly meant to be, the man nods contently and wears an aura of smugness. "Think I've got an imminent mission for you boys," he appears to be implying to his groin.

"Now, who would like mint sauce?" says our hostess, her demeanour communicating a strong wish to change the subject. "Do you mind if I ask a question?" says the man with the complicated first name. "Is it about the mint sauce?" asks the hostess, more out of longing than expectation.

"How do... you know... er...?"

"They use an insemination device. I don't meet the donor. Have you got that?" Her patience is now hanging by a single frayed thread. Only an irredeemable imbecile would fail to pick up on the signs and continue travelling along this narrow gauge rail of conversation.

"How does the donor... er... donate?" I ask.

"How do you [swear words deleted] think he donates?! That's the sort of question I'd expect from my niece. She's eight."

"They give you a little cup thingy," says Weirdly Named Guy, before adding, "So I've been told."

"Wow, cool," says the other male present.

"I'll certainly have some of that!" I say, pointing to the mint sauce. It's contained within a little cup thingy which now makes it appear slightly off-putting.

"Believe me," says our hostess, "if there was any way of doing this without involving a man I really, really would."

Our hostess is a competent if unconventional cook. I spoon mint sauce onto my vegetarian sausages resting on a bed of cabbage speckled with a pepper-like spice that definitely doesn't taste like pepper.

"Hope the cabbage is okay," she says. "I meant to season it with pepper, but think I may have used nutmeg instead."

"It tastes fine," I lie. "Did you see *Masterchef* this week?" I ask, keen to help with changing the subject.

"No," says Weirdly Named Guy. "So, how do you choose a good-looking man?"

"I'm not allowed to see what they look like. That's part of the confidentiality arrangement."

"Wow, that's brave," he responds.

Our hostess now has a dilemma. Anxious as she is to stamp on this conversational topic and move on, she also doesn't want to leave the originator of this last comment unpunished.

"Why is that brave? I'm looking for some healthy sperm, not to cast someone in a fashion shoot."

"Does the donor get to see you?" checks Other Guy Present. "No. No they don't. That's a no. NO!"

Other Guy Present fills the empty silence by revealing: "I used to be an airline pilot." The reason for this intriguing past-tense usage remains teasingly unexplained. "I had a penchant for air hostesses," he says, revealing possible clues for his 'used to be' status. Yet in spite of his anecdote receiving bumpy turbulence, he's in for the long haul. "They don't call it the cockpit for nothing."

I ask: "If you sleep with an air hostess, does she stand by the front door when you leave, pointing out the exits and saying 'thank you for choosing to shag Diane today'?"

Our hostess is distracted from her eye-rolling when the doorbell rings. "I'll go!" she says.

My wife enters, blowing a storm of apologies for her lateness. "At last, another woman to balance up the numbers a bit," proclaims our hostess, hoping out loud that the emotional intelligence levels amongst our party will be now raised.

"She's planning to have a baby with a sperm donor," announces Weirdly Named Guy to my wife. Realising I have to introduce him to my wife, I attempt to say his name and stumble over the strange syllable combination midway. I endure the embarrassment of being corrected.

"I know," says my wife casually. Our hostess nods, as if saying "See, it's no big deal." "I have so many questions," says my wife. "Do you get to see what he looks like? How does the donor, er, you know, donate. Where do you…?"

Our hostess positions a wine bottle over her recently emptied water glass and holds the bottom aloft until nearly a full pint of white wine has entered.

ICH BIN EIN BELIEVER

It started with an advert. "Three Germans are coming to Oxford next month," it read, "and require a local resident to speak English with them." Hmmm, I thought, I can do that. Job adverts usually insist on pesky qualifying criteria that invariably I don't possess (skills, qualifications, trustworthiness).

Yet the twin required job skills here are living in Oxford and being able to speak English. This means I need to undertake considerably less CV embellishment than usual. Especially as they are offering to pay £25 for a three-hour day.

I text the Daily Info (yeah, it's that one) advert placer excitedly. "I can help you practice English," I text. This, my wife points out, is an appalling solecism, since 'practise' is the verb I should have selected. Whereas the utterly separate, and majestically different word 'practice' is a noun. Clearly I need to practise my practice.

Bad enough, I concede, but rendered worse if such an error is contained within your opening six words when specifically teaching English grammar. "It contains a howitzer... I mean... a howler," I admit. "And no World War Two references either," cautions my wife.

They reply instantly and say I've got the job. It's a Ja. That's German efficiency for you. It then dawns on me that teaching someone a foreign language may require some actual preparation on my part. Just because some of the teachers at my school didn't always formulate any lesson plans - if they had I might now be able to differentiate between my practice and practise usage (with practice) - this doesn't mean I shouldn't. Mind you, our school was so rough the teachers frequently played truant.

The 'i' before 'e' rule in English - so useful for whenever you want to mis-spell 'deceive', 'receive', 'conceive' (this is also a three-word tactic sometimes deployed by broody women to get pregnant without their partner's consent) - actually comes into its own here. Advice, advise. Licence, license. Practice, practise - they are all separate noun and verb clauses. "It's not a clause," says my wife.

"For you ze clause is over," I say. "As I said, no Second World War jokes," she reaffirms.

When the day of the Germans' visit arrives I bus into Oxford to meet them. I get there early as, needless to say, I'm expecting the

Germans to be punctual. Crumbling the stereotype, they arrive ten minutes late. Solveig is here with her aunt Heike and her cousin. Wolfgang is 13 and only prepared to look up from his phone three times a day in order to locate food placed on a table in front of him.

Solveig and her aunt communicate with smiles, warmth, and positive body language and not a hint of stereotypical German over-confidence. She swears too. Which surprises me since surely nothing ever goes sufficiently wrong in Germany to justify swearing. Particularly when attending football matches involving their national team. However, this turns out not to be the case at all. Solveig has a list of (ungrammatically expressed) hang-ups with being German at the moment. Angela Merkel in particular is given a blitzkrieg… (sorry, last one).

Solveig repeatedly informs me that she is 44 years old. Which is odd, because she doesn't look ein Tag over 24. "Vier und zwanzig Jahre?" I ask. She laughs rather than answers my question - possibly due to my pronunciation being mystifyingly incomprehensible. We never quite understand if she has made a deal with the devil for eternal youth, or simply transposed the numbers in her English vocab. Until she offers to pay for coffee and cakes. "Here is a forty pound note," she says, handing me a £20.

Having pointed out that twenty = zwanzig, and forty = vierzig, I feel I've accomplished a successful first day as an English language teacher. I've taught her two English words. Admittedly she technically knew the words already, albeit the wrong way around. Now, according to the OED, there's only another 171,998 words of English vocabulary to impart to her before Tuesday.

That night she sends me a text. If the policeman in 'Allo 'Allo was German, most of her message would be good enough, unedited, to make the show's script. She genuinely signs off with "Many grieves, Solveig."

For the next day's tutorial I decide to walk them around Oxford, imparting conversational English vocab on our stroll. "This is a famous Oxford college." "Ja." "This is spectacular architecture." "Was ist architecture?" I look it up on my phone. Turns out the German word for 'architecture' is 'Architecktur'. "Architecktur," I repeat. Their minds look blanker than Wayne Rooney on Only Connect. I show them the word on my phone. "Ah, Architecktur!" they chorus in sudden comprehension. "Das war was ich frigging well gesagt habe," I mutter.

Germans are actually difficult to insult. Turn to a German and declare "Zwei Weltkreige und ein Weltmeisterschaft" ("Two world wars and one World Cup") and rather than become offended and agitated, they'll meet your intended rudeness with an outpouring of glowing gratitude. At last, they'll think, we've encountered an English person who has shown the courtesy of learning a foreigner's language.

After four more minutes of sightseeing, Solveig asks a question: "Können wir jetzt ein Kaffee trinken?" "Mit einem Schnaps," adds Auntie Heike sensibly. After my noble attempt to show her a particularly fine example of an Ipswich window on Oriel College's façade, it appears their enthusiasm for Tudor fenestration is unmatched by that for strong alcohol at 11am. I didn't expect concentration problems from a class with an average age of 44 (or 24). Decidedly it's not going well if they require hard spirits after only ten minutes. "We believe in you as a teacher," they kindly inform me, adding some more billow to my sail; significantly after we've downed whisky chasers with our mid-morning cappuccinos.

That afternoon I sheepdog them on a reluctant walk in Worcester College's indulgently large grounds. A squirrel porters some nuts in front of us, causing the reactive cry: "Ein Eichhörnchen!" They invite me for breakfast the next morning at Keble College where they are staying on B&B terms. When I overhear what I recognise as the word "Eichhörnchen" I say "Ah," anxious to show my astute language learning skills, "you're talking about squirrels." They convulse into laughter, spasming to such an extent that I start to scan the room for a defibrillator.

After fully fünf Minuten Solveig and family manage to speak again. Turns out "ein Hörnchen" means "a croissant". Ha ha and bloody well ha. For the next ten minutes they amuse themselves by picking up the bread basket and offering each other "a squirrel". It's the funniest thing in German history since Kaiser Wilhelm inadvertently got a bratwurst stuck on his helmet spike.

To me, those two words are so similar it can only be a word trap. If I ran a patisserie in Germany, I'd certainly keep some prop squirrels out the back for comedic interplay.

After three days of my teaching them English, Solveig and her aunt's language skills have started to bloom. On the other hand the teenager appears to have learnt exactly one English phrase: "Where can I plug in my phone charger?" In exchange he's taught me that although the German and English words Wi-Fi may be identical in spelling and hyphenated appearance, in Germany it's pronounced as "wee-fee" - which is what I call the 20p entrance requirement for some public toilets.

On their last day in Oxford we go for a goodbye coffee near Radcliffe Square. After we hug they are about to depart from the Heathrow airport bus stop in Queen's Lane, when Solveig spots some wildlife moving in a tree outside the Vaults café. "Ein Horchen!" she shouts, and both of her fellow countrymen collapse into shoulder-wobbling laughter. Even the teenager fleetingly retargets his gaze from the phone and giggles profusely.

Who says Germans need to practice/practise (I'm still genuinely unsure) at having a sense of humour?

THE MEDIA WHORE

Recently I have noticed myself becoming a bit of a media whore - although some people are perhaps beginning to object to this longstanding phrase. Therefore it might be more compliant with modern political correctness and snowflakery if this expression receives a 21st-century makeover. My friend Helen the psychologist has a suggestion.

I once told Helen, significantly when we were both leaving a BBC studio, that she was also becoming a bit of a media whore. While she was deciding which side of my face to slap - before likely opting for both - I pointed out that this long-established phrase is devoid of any sexual undercurrent or occupational aspersions. "I prefer," she said with hands thankfully now on her hips rather than my cheekbones, "the phrase 'media sex worker'."

As an author with books to promote, I'm forever standing kerbside under the streetlight of media glare, soliciting for punditry work. Subsequently I appear to have become the go-to-guy for a quote covering any media story occurring in my neighbourhood.

This happens regardless of my relevant expertise. When a Roman pottery fragment was discovered in a local garden, a newspaper rang me up for my thoughts. I dutifully pointed out that my inability to establish whether a vase is from the 1st century AD or TK Maxx ought to disqualify me from commenting. Nevertheless they insisted on printing my "insights".

Later a proposed temporary shortening of my local bus route results in another call for a soundbite. I respond: "I hope temporary won't calcify into permanence." Buzzing with pride at my (not remotely pretentious, obviously) wordsmithery, I repeat the phrase. Fanning through a paper two days later I find the piece with my quote. It's been changed to: "I hope this is only a temporary thing." Bah.

Now this expert witness work has spread to covering national media issues. Because a few years ago I wrote a book about Britain's most eccentric sports, this ensures time-starved producers contact me for appearances on local radio stations whenever a location in their area is staging some mildly eccentric sport. Hence if a small Suffolk coastal town tries to solicit national media attention by hosting, say, a pantomime horse Grand National, then their local radio station will approach me: "Can you appear on our breakfast show tomorrow for five minutes?"

Often this means going to Summertown where there's a special studio reserved for appearing on other BBC stations. Once I had to wait for this same studio to be vacated by the Bishop of Oxford - fellow media courtesan - after he'd done *Thought for the Day*.

This explains how I've become a regular on BBC Gloucester. That's right, people - living the showbiz dream. Ahead of my latest appearance they call me. "Will I get paid my travel expenses?" After a short pause while they recover use of their upper bodies after profuse giggle-stifling, they reply with an adamant: "No!"

Arriving in Summertown the person (wo)manning reception informs me: "You'll be collected by Will shortly." Sure enough a disconcertingly young male appears and leads me to the lift. We go to the 3rd floor, get out, walk around. "Not here," he remarks indifferently. Re-entering the lift, we descend and step out onto the 1st floor. "Not here." We go up again. Life is certainly full of ups and downs - but not usually this literally. At Level 2 we exit and turn right. "Wrong way," he says. Eventually, we find the studio just as I'm considering finding somewhere to make camp for the night.

"Thanks Will," I say, quite generously given the circumstances. "My name's not Will," he corrects me. "Oh, sorry." Then I realise that the woman in reception called him Will, which I'm sure was not in any way channelling the inept and mercifully fictional BBC assistant in the comedy *W1A*.

Departing the building I hand my visitor badge to a receptionist distracted by a ringing phone. "Okay," she says to the caller, "I'll get Will to collect him." Might be a while before he finds his way back to reception, I think.

Returning home after my five minutes on BBC Radio Gloucester I optimistically ask my wife if she heard me. "How?" she reasonably enquires. "Well, you could listen online by..." "Too much faff," she interrupts, disloyally in my opinion. "Besides," she continues, "I was listening to Radio 4. There was this fascinating item on *Woman's Hour* - they had Helen on it."

A THISTLE STOP TOUR

I'm already late when I turn a corner on my bike and encounter a road block. About twenty primary schoolchildren are riding bikes in an organised group. All are stationary and clothed in bright yellow high-vis.

Leading the group, a teacher proclaims her profession by wearing a luminous yellow jacket emblazoned with the solitary word 'Tutor'. Maybe everyone should wear a jacket announcing their job on the back: 'accountant', 'baker', 'does something unspecific in IT', 'estate agent/assistant to Beelzebub'.

Nearby, a group of schoolchildren, uninvolved with cycling proficiency training, frolic noisily in a playground behind railings. They too are all dressed in high-vis. Such is the national proliferation of high-vis jackets that it seems everybody will - I estimate sometime by the year 2025 - be adorned in high-vis. The only person left in Britain not wearing it will, paradoxically, be Britain's most noticeable man. And probably get run over by fledging cyclists gawping at him.

A necessary roadblock detour makes me slightly late reporting at the reception desk of a large Oxfordshire publishing house. My tardiness results in me being the last arrival on their list. Hence by process of elimination I'm greeted with: "You must be Richard O. Smith?" by a friendly lady with a big white clipboard and smile.

The reception area is adorned with enlarged covers of books by authors deemed more successful than me. Including a book by someone who (in order to prevent any rapacious libel lawyers - I can think of several words to appear on the back of their high-vis jackets - getting even richer) I'll refer to as Ms Overrated. Professional jealousy can be a bitter toxin.

Strolling further along the reception area reveals more poster-sized covers of her bestsellers. Bitterness risks burning a hole in my stomach like leaking acid in a ship's hull.

Another friendly woman introduces herself and announces she'll be leading the tour. Twelve members of the public have signed up for the rare opportunity to go backstage at a famous publishers. My arrival completes the dozen. Like a lot of my chosen activities, I am predominately attending on the off-chance that the experience may be potentially column-worthy. However, as a columnist I need to act undercover. A writer should be an invisible observer, clandestine and refraining from anything that risks blowing journalistic cover.

"Are you going to be writing one of your columns about us?" I'm asked by a woman on the tour. "Er, possibly," I reply with sudden agitation. "Do you remember me?" she asks. "Yes, of course I remember you," I say. I do not remember her. A convivial lady in her early 60s, she informs me that she once saw me speak at Oxford's Town Hall and we chatted afterwards at my book-signing table.

"I like your columns," she says. I like her too. Especially her excellent taste in columnists. But this has rather outed me as a journo. A bit like meeting one's contact from MI6 on a park bench and saying: "The weather is unfeasibly hot in Sofia, Grey Squirrel," only to receive the reply: "Are you the spy from MI6 I'm supposed to meet here to exchange classified documents?"

I might as well be wearing a high-vis jacket declaring the word 'Columnist - Here to Take the Piss' on the back. If our tour leader has taken in this information that there's a journalist amongst her group, she emits no visible signs of acknowledging it.

The tour starts immediately, moving at a challengingly quick pace. Having sheep-dogged us along a lengthy communal area, our guide then ignores numerous wide and spacious potential pausing places to address the group. Instead she leads us down a busy and impractically narrow corridor. And then selects this, of all places, to stop. Drawing a deep breath, she begins guiding: "This is the area where… sorry, come through… designers have workstations… it's okay please proceed… on a hot-desking principle… do continue past us… where… what was I saying?"

We continue along an even longer corridor - covering 100 metres fractionally outside of an Olympic qualification time. Workers have signs ready to place on their desks stating: 'In use', 'On leave', 'At lunch', 'On conference call'. There's not one for 'Surfing the Web' 'Updating Facebook' or 'Trolling celebs on Twitter'.

One workstation is proudly adorned with a Tartan Army throw, bagpiper figurine and poster depicting a thistle emblem. "The bloody Welsh get everywhere," I remark.

Our guide stops beside the thistle poster to enable those at the back of our group to catch-up. "Right," she announces in a tone seeping with impatience, "we're now going to see our international division." Off we march again, the pace so intense that when I see a water cooler I flirt with the idea of tipping a cup of cold water over my head like a marathon runner.

At the international department I'm professionally aggrieved to see Ms Overrated's books being proudly displayed. Our guide points out her impressive global sales figures and generally basks in Ms Overrated's grating greatness. I deflect my desire to verbalise dissent by imagining myself clubbing the displays with a nearby fire-extinguisher.

Only three of us make it to the next stopping place. Natural exhaustion has presumably accounted for the rest. This doesn't seem to bother our tour guide as she commences her prepared spiel. Presumably if the others have perished from lassitude en route, then she considers this is the cleaner's problem for tonight.

Eventually the other tour members arrive. "We [pant] couldn't [puff] keep [pant] up." It's a fair point. It is like the primary school cycling proficiency group I saw earlier were being led in a peloton behind Laura Trott on Lance Armstrong's drugs.

Next we walk through an external courtyard where building work is taking place. For this we are instructed to don hard hats and, with the inevitability of darkness following daylight, high-vis jackets. I'm handed a yellow bib that is so small it would have been tight on one of the primary school learner cyclists.

"Any questions?" asks our guide. "Yes," I think to myself, "why are we going so fast?" Fortunately the rest of the group has lots of actual questions about the building and publishing operation. I'm not sure if they're genuinely interested in discovering the answers, or just determined to ask unending questions as a stalling mechanism to gain vital restorative rest.

"Which author are you most proud to be associated with?" asks an exhausted elderly man.

"Oh that's easy," she answers with the sort of enthusiasm you'd normally reserve for experiencing a lottery win, "we are so lucky to have Ms Overrated."

I make an involuntary noise and attempt to remove my high-vis straightjacket - which Houdini would have struggled to shed in under thirty minutes given its XXXS size.

As we're handing back our visitor's badges to reception, the woman who recognised me earlier asks a question. "Are you going to be writing one of your funny columns about our tour?" "No, I don't think so," I reply with some certainty, "There's a danger it might make me sound bitter and resentful with bilious professional envy." She sweetly reassures me this could never be the case.

BOHEMIAN BOOKSHOP BLUES

My friend Rebecca and I are trying to support a famously eccentric Oxfordshire bookshop. How much the bookshop desires our support is proving tricky to ascertain.

"Please can I buy a book by the deceased poet John Berger, please," says Rebecca, electing to top and tail her sentence with a double 'please'. Presumably in a sensed requirement to placate the bookseller. Nevertheless the bookseller is visibly unimpressed. A thought reader would confidently translate: "Not again. Someone tried to buy a book yesterday too. How can I stop this happening?"

For a bookseller his response is on the unlikely side of staggering. "I'd rather not sell books as part of some celebrity death cash-in."

Luckily there is another person working in the bookshop who takes over the transaction. She reassures Rebecca with demulcent tones that her intention to buy a book in a bookshop does not constitute an act of outlandish aggression, and finds her the desired volume.

This lady looks magnificent, attired in a dress of kaleidoscopic patterns accessorised with flowing titian hair braided with flowers, like she's stepped out of a Rossetti painting. Her dress coruscates chaotic colour that would reasonably prompt a parading peacock to advise her, "Tone it down a bit, luv." She, it soon transpires, is the well-adjusted, normal one.

"Are you his girlfriend?" the bookseller asks Rebecca. "Er… no," she says, justifiably taken aback. "Would you like to be his girlfriend?" pursues the bookseller. "Probably not. I'd have to ask his wife and my husband first." Most people would recognise this as a knockback and a subject closer - given that it's a knockback and a subject closer. But not the bookseller.

"I bet you do," he says - as if he's an author puppeteering his characters in a plot rather than interacting with real people from real life in a real bookshop. Assuming this bookshop is real. A view which I'm decreasingly confident in holding. I look around the small shop and spot the mystifying presence of not one but two pianos competing for space in the tiny retail area.

Then a customer, dressed like a man visiting from the 18th century, ceases sipping his tea and flails his arms in panicked agitation like someone suddenly regaining consciousness on a raft when approaching an unexpected waterfall. His conduct doesn't appear unnecessarily odd given the eccentricity of the shop. "Wasp!" he shouts, like a tail gunner spotting a Messerschmitt.

The owner rushes into action, opens the door and chases the wasp out - shouting aggressively at the insect as it literally buzzes off. It is easy to imagine him conducting a similar approach to customers.

After a few seconds a contextual calm is restored. The elderly man sips his tea again and I decide to speak to the bookseller as I'm supposed to be participating in an instore event. Although I really want to speak to the loudly dressed woman, as she appears to be verifiably sane. The shop offers a pleasing panoply of gorgeous books, rare and wonderful, and is a delightful place to have coffee. Though it may be trying a tad too hard not to be mistaken for a chain, given how unmistakably it wears its bohemian principles on its tie-dyed sleeve.

I have agreed to do a free gig to help support the shop and get some needed paying customers inside. "Will you invite anyone to the event?" I ask. "No, they won't buy anything." "Er… what about…" "No," he says, before my mouth has a chance to formulate exactly what my what about was about.

"Have you considered being dead? It might help sales," he suggests. Obviously he's joking. I think.

Suddenly Wasp Averse Man announces, "More tea!" and the lady from a Rossetti painting picks up a flamboyantly hand-painted tea pot that somehow now looks suddenly drab compared to her cacophony of colours. All the scene is missing is one of the tea drinkers wearing a top hat displaying a "In this style 10/6" price tag. Although Alice would have made an early decision to vacate this bookshop on the grounds that everyone here was just too weird.

We use the distraction to escape from the shop. Once outside, Rebecca and I walk briskly without looking behind us until we are around the corner. There we stop, with our backs against a wall, panting with relief like cartoon characters who have just survived a chase sequence.

"Apparently that bookshop has a reputation for being eccentric," I say. "Really?" asks Rebecca, with the sarcasm key very much depressed, "How?"

THE BAD GIG

"Before I introduce our speaker I have to report some sad news. Margaret passed away at the weekend and her funeral will be at the crematorium a week on Thursday. Now, would you please welcome to the stage our speaker for this afternoon, a comedian no less… Mister… Richard … O…Smith… yeerrhhh!"

Cue the sort of lacklustre applause that accompanies a doubt fault at Wimbledon. My introducer's prelude, having started as a sombre eulogy, performed a handbrake turn midsentence and somehow morphed into an introduction from *The Muppets*.

Somewhat understandably, the audience look on the sad side of crestfallen. Momentarily I consider saying: "What? Did someone die?"

but reject the line on grounds of (a) taste and (b) a substantive risk I'll be sconed to death. Yeah, I did type 'sconed.'

This later detail may appear quirky. But I'm addressing an over 60s teatime club in rural Oxfordshire. Everyone gets a scone and a cup of tea included in their admission. Not bad for a £3 entrance fee. Though they have to endure a failing comic. That would be me.

They're likely quite a conservative group - that's both with a small 'c', a large 'C' - and likely an emboldened 'C' too. On the wall facing me hangs a formal picture of the Queen. Her expression is about as conducive to comedy as the audience's.

Their organisation is as English as an England batting collapse on a rain-affected Bank Holiday. When I gently ridicule a ruddy faced man resembling an over-roasted brisket, he appears agitated. His complexion is so red the most likely explanation is he was grabbed by both ankles and dunked in a vat of beetroot juice.

He picks up a knife menacingly. Just as I consider ducking, he uses it to butter his scone. Phew.

Then I deliver a joke that usually does well. Though it's perhaps a marginally post-watershed gag for 3pm in the polite afternoon. Yet I'm getting desperate for a response, so if I can use shock tactics to jumpstart the audience into life, then I will. But today the gag falls; it drops emitting the metaphorical noise of a knife clattering on a scone plate. Only ruddy faced man Beetroot Boy laughs. As he tells me later, somewhat anachronistically: "I like a bit of blue, me."

After nearly half an hour of nobly battling the audience on all fronts it's announced that the tea is ready. I was supposed to do 40 minutes, but I'm happy to accept a truce. After enjoying scones beforehand, participants now witness cakes being disrobed and muffins undraped. The resultant frenzy resembles a UN food drop in a siege zone.

After chatting to a several genuinely friendly members, I start to inch towards bags and coat to begin packing up my things. But I'm spotted by the chairwoman and ushered back. "Since you went down so well, we wouldn't mind if you'd kindly do another ten minutes." "Or maybe five minutes," adds a rather formal lady who I later find out is the society's President/Commander-in-chief. "Well, er… I'm not sure if…" I flounder. "Excellent," says the chairwoman, "just another ten minutes," she confirms. "Or five," reiterates the President.

Sometimes it really is difficult to gauge, blinking in the stage lights, how well you're going down. Occasionally audiences mainly laugh internally. Sometimes they smile. Or just nod. That's fine with me. My basic requirement from a gig is to get out alive. Which is still quite entry level, admittedly, when it comes to showbiz ambition.

I go back on. The same man introduces me again and shows that he's determined not to repeat his earlier lacklustre introduction. He certainly doesn't. This time he's even worse.

"Err thank you ladies and... er... gentlemen. It gives me great pleasure... and has since I was a boy." Beetroot Boy laughs profusely. The President tuts and rolls her eyes skywards. Clearly my mistake is not to do risqué material from the 1950s. "It's time once again for Richard..." [this is awkward] "Richard... again."

Thank you. I say. Without particularly meaning it. Normally I'd add a joke, but if he has genuine memory issues then I'm not going to risk making that call. Besides, I've got enough material in the bag - just as long as, unlike my introducer, I can actually remember some of it.

On my way to "the stage" (in reality a bit of floor without chairs) a nice lady asks me if I'd like another scone. "No thanks, but they're very good." "Some to take home? Go on. Go on." "Well I... That's very kind of you." Like Mrs Doyle gone rogue, she doesn't return and I see neither her nor any promised scones again. This is a Category Ten disappointment: as a freelance writer I'd earmarked them for tomorrow's dinner.

I decide to farm the audience for material. Ordinarily I'd pick on audience members and risk the clichéd comedian's question: "What do you do for a living?" And which point every single person in the room would provide the same undeviating reply: "I'm retired." Therefore instead I ask: "So do you hate the village next door, then?" "No we certainly do not," says a woman indignantly. "We just don't have anything to do with them." This remark does at least generate a big laugh. Though significantly mainly from me - her weapons-grade irony remaining unspotted by the majority.

Afterwards I stand behind a small table while optimistically offering my books for sale. There are thirty people pinned to the furthest away wall, while I have the rest of the hall to myself, lonelier than someone in an infectious diseases isolation ward.

My dejection is mercifully tempered by the warming consolation that they did ask me to do another ten (okay, five) minutes, so they must have liked me after all. It's a surprisingly soothing thought.

Eventually Beetroot Boy wanders over to my impromptu bookstall for a browse. Reading the back cover of one of my books, he laughs out loud twice, tells me it looks "very readable", that my talk was "hilarious", but doesn't buy a copy. He introduces himself as Graham. "I was surprised and pleased that they asked me to do another five minutes," I comment. "Oh," he says, "that's because the hot water wasn't ready for the tea. Sheila had forgotten to turn the urn on. That used to be Margaret's job." I join the rest of the audience in looking crestfallen.

After it becomes even more apparent that no-one is going to buy any of my books, I still wait for several more improbably optimistic minutes before packing up. The organisers thank me, and several people kindly say they really enjoyed my talk, "as it's good to get a speaker who is funny. We get a lot of charity spokespeople and they're not funny," says the chairwoman. I imagine she's correct. "So here are some photos of a catastrophic landslide in Zambia. Anyway, this Irishman, Scotsman and Welshman go into a pub and…"

The President wanders over. "Would you please do one thing for us before you go?" "Yes," I reply prematurely, ahead of discovering what the thing is that I have to do. "Would you draw the raffle? We just have one winner each month." "Of course, I'd be honoured."

While waiting for the shoebox of ticket stubs to be brought over, the President feels obliged to make small talk. Which soon expands from small talk into big views. "The problem with so much of this so-called modern comedy is it's all so rude," she huffs disapprovingly, powered with the spirit of Mary Whitehouse.

I draw the raffle. "Number 69," I say. "Who likes 69? Come on, there must be someone? Don't be shy." The President puts her hand up. Only Graham laughs.

SHITTY SHITTY BANG BANG

I appear to be in a meaningful relationship with the actress and supermodel Lily Cole. Such is her commitment to our *coup de foudre* that she has opted to have my name tattooed on her foot. This I find slightly perturbing, so we argue about the appropriateness of her tattoo decision. After all, I worry that - should I find someone better and move on - Lily will be unnecessarily limited in her choice of future fish in the sea to ones called "Richard".

Oh, I should probably explain that this occurred exactly as I've described. Albeit in a dream. Then, just before I wake, Lily becomes agitated and yells: "I can't stand this banging anymore."

Meanwhile, back in reality, it's aggressively early on a Sunday morning. I open my eyes at 4.55am to two intense sensations. My bed is seemingly bouncing up and down like a space hopper to an accompanying banging sound. And my wife is giving me a look of contemptuous curiosity, wearing the same expression she'd reserve for analysing a newly appeared stain on her favourite outfit.

Bang. Bang. Bang.

"I said, I can't stand this banging anymore," says my wife.

I snap into consciousness. My chances of escaping back into my dream and seeing if supermodel Lily and I can make up after our tattoo-based spat is not going to happen. "It's not even 5am," says my wife. "This has been going on for several minutes already. I think it's nearby."

My part of Oxford is reverberating to what sounds like an industrial steam hammer so close that it's seemingly coming from inside my bedside cabinet. Next door's dog is doing the sort of whimpering he normally reserves for Guy Fawkes Night.

It's intrusively loud. A return to sleep is simply not an option. Everywhere is booming relentlessly with metronomic regularity. "Have they started fracking in our kitchen?" I ask.

"We need [bang] to ring [bang] the police [bang]." My wife dials the non-emergency number 101 and reports the incessant thunderous thumping. It's the sort of sound that results from workmen making a serious attempt to crack the earth into two halves.

The police agree that at 4.55am this constitutes anti-social behaviour. Especially as it's a Sunday. When my wife holds the phone outside the front door to demonstrate the noise levels, they concur it's sufficiently loud to justify immediate investigation. My wife is surprised to discover that she's reached a police call centre not in Oxford but Milton Keynes. She's also surprised they can't hear it in MK.

Apparently this innovation is "more efficient" in accessing police services. In the same way that moving our fridge from the kitchen in Oxford to Milton Keynes would be "more efficient" whenever we wanted to access some milk.

Wearing the minimum of clothes you can get away with in public - usually reserved for fetching in milk, depositing in bins or going clubbing - I head off on my bike in full investigative mode to try and source the epicentre of the invasive pounding.

Living where I do in high density housing renders the tumult hard to track, as it reverberates, rebounds and echoes like a squash court. Eventually I trace the cause of the commotion to a south-westerly direction.

I spot someone I know. She's wearing an inadequate pink dressing gown, loosely tied, and picking up a cat. As she bends down I hastily avert my gaze fractionally too late - I can confirm she has no tattoos - and conduct a conversation while staring stubbornly at her wheelie bins. "We've reported the noise to the police," I inform her. "Good. It woke me up," she says, before adding bizarrely, "Is it someone walking along the street bashing a big drum?"

My mobile rings. It's my wife to inform me that the police have rung back and traced the noise. Apparently the railway has permission to embed huge stanchions trackside on consecutive Sunday mornings when the line is closed for engineering work.

That evening we go to bed exceptionally early to try to compensate for our lost sleep. I sink deep into the beckoning softness of the mattress and anticipate a lovely 5-star
vacation in the Land of Nod. "By the way," says my wife with startled urgency: "Who's Lily?"

"Who?" I poker bluff. "You were saying her name this morning during the intense banging."

Lily's starring role in my dream can be explained. I'd seen the "flamed-haired beauty"TM in a theatre play two days earlier in London. My front row seat enabled me to spot a tattooed name on the end of one of her (about four feet long) model legs. I decide to tell my wife the truth: that Lily had appeared uninvited in my dream - finally proving that Oxford people don't just dream about spires.

"Ha, you and supermodel Lily Cole!?" chortles my wife. "In your dreams!" Er, exactly.

TEDDY, SAID HE, GO!

We've all done it. The frankly-I'm-indifferent-about-catching-this-bus shuffle. Yes you have.

I was fretting along a crowded city street when I spotted my homeward bound bus waiting at its stop. My heart pounded, as did my increased footsteps on the pavement. The bus was ninety seconds walk away, but there were still half a dozen people to board. Could I make it? I reached the back end of the bus. The door was still open.

I drew level with the boarding doors. Immediately they swooshed shut. The indicator light winked at me. Off went the bus. Without me. Leaving me standing on the pavement impersonating Edvard Munch's favourite life model: "Nooooo!"

Through the departing bus window I could see spacious empty seats mocking me. Inside, the passengers glowed with warmth and contentment. Suddenly my eyes focus on an expensively dressed attractive woman giving me a sympathetic look through the window, as if to communicate: "You poor dear. But I don't think this is your bus. Look at the front: the destination is 'Success'."

Crestfallen, I feel like my life has been leached of purpose. I turn around and a woman holding two torn carrier bags scowls: "Typical!"

Numerous people sitting on the wall waiting for other buses had observed me. Their judging eyes feel like limpets on my back. My problem is I'd gambled on the full blown run for the last ninety seconds. If you select to sprint then you have to catch the bus. Failure simply no longer becomes an option. Now I feel the searing humiliation from waiting passengers who had witnessed my belittlement.

My coolness had been recklessly gambled away on just one missed bus because I'd made the decision to dash madly. Left to contemplate the burn of my ignominy, I vow next time to walk coolly - then I could pretend I wasn't really interested in getting the bus at all. "You know what, I'd prefer to wait on the pavement for fifteen minutes. Yeah, I would. Oh it's starting to rain and I'm umbrella-less. Good."

Staying here and waiting at the bus stop is no longer an option after everyone has witnessed my indignation. Embarrassed, I scuttle away. Finding a quaint shop nearby I enter on impulse. Quickly I realise there's a risk represented here by being a rucksack wearer. Narrow aisles and shelves piled with fragile glassware alert me to the imminent danger of expensive breakages. My presence here is akin to a trombonist announcing he's off to practice in a phone box.

Making a mental note to come back when I'm rucksackless, I return to the bus stop having calculated it might now be time for another bus departure. Ahead I see another no. 3 indicating to pull out. I'm at least sixty seconds away so decide to visit another adjacent shop. One with less precariously shelved glassware.

Inside, a middle-aged American woman is asking for a teddy bear. "I was in this lovely Ox-ford college just now," says the lady, pronouncing the word Oxford as two distinct syllables worthy of a pause in the middle in that peculiarly American way. Although we're all in Oxford (sorry, Ox-ford) at the moment it is a frankly unnecessary inclusion in her sentence; she was unlikely to have been in a Cambridge college ten minutes ago. "And they had a divine teddy bear wearing a jersey that says 'TEDDY'! So awesome."

Quite reasonably the shop assistant, at one of those indistinguishable souvenir shops that all tend to sell the same sort of stock, waits for the lady to conclude her query. Not realising, just like me, that this had constituted the end of her query.

"Well," says the American - pausing for a reply that currently shows no signs of forthcoming. Mainly because she hasn't asked an actual question yet.

Finding herself somewhat zugzwanged, the store assistant is nevertheless now expected to provide a response. "In which college did you see the teddy?" prompts the shop worker. She doesn't know. "Did you want to buy a teddy?" "YES!" It appears that on this shop's premises all customer queries must be conducted by the Socratic method. There should be a sign.

"We have some teddies over here," says the shop assistant, gesturing inadequately towards half the entire store, while concealing the truth that she'd rather be looking at her phone than the American Lady.

"Do they have a cute jersey saying 'TEDDY'?" "No," admits the shop worker, almost certainly deciding only at the very last moment not to add the line: "In the same way that if you buy a scarf it doesn't have 'SCARF' written on it!"

Then I realise that I may be able to help. There could be a role for me. Although this would involve interacting with strangers and as any regular reader of my columns will know, this rarely works out well. Neither for me nor the strangers. Rather than just being guy-who-sprints-for-buses-then-pretends-he-wasn't-fussed-about-catching-them, I need to show I can contribute more to the world today.

I step up to the crease (not plate - as American Lady would say - since we play cricket in this country not baseball). And I initiate Operation Stranger Interaction.

"Maybe you saw the teddy at Teddy Hall?" I say, addressing the American woman and shop worker. "What, teddies have their own hall in Ox-ford?" she snorts. I knew this would go badly. Why do I ever leave the house?

"Sort of," I say, to give myself more thinking time ahead of a hopefully better response that my brain will be formulating imminently. Any time soon would be good, brain.

"You probably saw it in St Edmund Hall, a college known as Teddy Hall," I say, sounding almost authoritarian. "That's so cute. Isn't that cute?" she turns to say to her husband who has wisely disappeared to another part of the shop. Probably to hyperventilate.

The shop assistant interjects and advises the American Lady: "Why don't you **go** there and ask them?" (Code for: "'Get out of my shop, now!"). "Do you think they are for sale? Because it was behind a case." "I really think you should **go** and ask them," says the shop assistant. She's so visibly keen for them to leave her shop and allow her to return to doting on her phone that the next strategy may involve activating the fire alarm.

"We went into several colleges this afternoon. Where's Teddy's own hall?" As the shop assistant drops her head to avoid eye contact - and since phone messages aren't going to check themselves - I step in and give the American couple directions.

I return towards the bus stop. In the distance I spot my bus. There are still several passengers to board. I don't run. Instead I walk normally. It feels good to be acting like the cool guy for once. Strolling casually, I reach the back of the bus. It pulls away as soon as I pass the rear. If I'd run I would have caught it.

THE GOLDEN RUMPUS - MY CELEBRITY HUMILIATION

I'm never meeting celebrities again.

In future, unless I'm actively working with a celebrity, I'll be crossing the street without looking for oncoming traffic in my rush to avoid them. I suffered a mortifying humiliation - as you'll see. Although it's only partially (well, 99.9%) my fault.

Last summer at Kellogg College I found myself standing next to an internationally famous author. Momentarily neither of us had anyone to talk to as we both held empty fizz flutes awkwardly. This ought to have been an ideal opportunity to engage in repartee as sparkling as our champagne. But there was a problem. With the champagne.

This is because they were serving that most dangerous of all the different types of alcohol: free alcohol. Especially given I'd just consumed five gratis glasses of the bubbling idiot-maker potion.

"Hello, my name is Risshhhard… and… er." Four faults and a refusal just from attempting to say my name. It's going well. "Ish a writerish too." He probably didn't want to hear about my writer's peccadillos even if he could comprehend what language I was attempting to speak.

Several seconds too late, I stop talking. I withdraw myself, concentrating really, really hard on not walking into a wall that someone has inconsiderately left in the room.

Over a year after that self-induced humiliation I'm sitting in an auditorium at Brookes University awaiting an appearance by the same celebrity. The audience is instantly hushed by the house lights being lowered. He is introduced with: "Be appreciative to Oxford's favourite living son." "Hey!" I catch myself thinking, "That's a bit insensitive. I *am* in the audience too, you know, and can hear you."

Philip Pullman - disappointingly not wearing dark materials - proves to be an engaging speaker; his sentences glisten with insights.

He reveals his own daemon would be a magpie. "I'm a great fan of stealing," he declares. I pat my pocket to ensure my phone is safe. "What do other authors represent to you?" asks someone evidently trying a bit too hard to come across all Oxford-y. "Other stories are like a street of open houses with the residents away," opines Pullman. Wow. Seen a plot or paragraph in a Philip Pullman book you recognise from elsewhere? Call Crimestoppers on 01865…

We're treated to an exclusive about the next instalment of Oxford-set novel *La Belle Sauvage*, titled *The Secret Commonwealth*, which depicts its main character Lyra as a 20-year old Oxford undergraduate. And a bad tempered recalcitrant 15-year-old character called Alice will also figure in the story. "Every teacher has encountered an Alice," comments the *Golden Compass* author, who was an Oxfordshire middle school teacher for over a decade.

Asked how he maintains his optimism, he replies: "Spending time with grandchildren and reading Proust." Though I suspect he didn't mean simultaneously - reading the pop-up edition of Proust's 3000-page bookshelf-buckling epic *In Search of Lost Time* to toddlers would be a tough gig.

Inevitably there are many in the audience requiring writing tips. They won't be leaving disappointed. "Tone is fundamental in a story, structure is superficial."

"I don't like travel. Don't like going anywhere. I prefer to stay at home and make things up." Or, as his literary hero Proust put it - probably better - "The real voyage of discovery consists not in seeking new lands but seeing with new eyes."

My plan is to ask Pullman to dedicate a copy of *La Belle Sauvage* for a friend's birthday. However the title is French. And I don't speak French. Whenever I try I mispronounce words and people laugh. At me. And not in a nice way. Next door's daughter has laughed profusely at my French pronunciation before. She's eight years old.

After queuing for fifteen minutes I reach his signing table. Tripped by anxiety, I make a humiliating mistake. Vibrating with nervousness I ask: "Please can you dedicate my copy of *La Belle Sausage* 'Happy Birthday, Grahame' with an 'e' on the end." A flicker of shock appears in his eyes. His look is easily decipherable: "You realise what you called the book?" He graciously signs it nonetheless. With an 'e' on the end.

Avoiding eye contact - and hopefully any further indignation - I scurry away, wondering if I should be covering my face while expecting my trousers to fall down clown-style to complete my ignominy. There's not been any champagne to share the blame with this time. You sausage, Richard.

TALKING 'BOUT MY GENERATION X

I have a Top 10 of least favourite Oxford pavements; but no one tends to be interested in my list (particularly at parties and speed dating events).

So I'll just cut to the top spot. Are you ready for the big reveal? (*Dramatic pause... drum roll ... go to ad break.*) My least favourite Oxford pavement is the stretch in Magdalen Street linking Debenhams' corner to the Randolph Hotel. A very short patch of pavement, but invariably a very long walk.

I am currently navigating this corridor of the damned at a pace resembling a knackered snail. Nearby an odious grey-haired man is remonstrating with someone. This can't be pleasant for that someone, I think. Then I notice it's me he's remonstrating with.

"Are you getting this bus?!" he asks with unmissable malevolence. I have spent the last five minutes shuffling fractionally forward in a long bus queue. The bus driver is processing passengers' fares with the urgency of a second class stamp. Indeed a second class stamp would easily deliver its accompanying cargo to my intended North Oxford destination quicker than this bus.

"Yes," I reply confidently. "Where to?" he demands. The bus' destination is marked on the front, back and side in large-lit letters. I debate whether sarcasm is called for. I reject it. "Summertown," I say. "Ohh!" replies the stranger, as if this piece of newly relinquished information has convicted me before a jury of fellow queuers. It's also obvious from his tone that he shares no similar qualms over rejecting the sarcasm option.

Even though there are still ten people ahead yet to board the bus, he evidently thinks I have somehow caused him to risk missing it by not millimetring forward quickly enough on this maddeningly overpopulated footpath.

Not for the first time I'm grateful for Britain's restrictive gun laws. Had this been America, the temptation to nip into a nearby store to complete a semi-automatic weapon impulse purchase would have been hard to resist. There would certainly have been time for the transaction, shooting and subsequent arrest before this bus departed.

After a period of time so long it requires naming by geologists, I reach the front of the queue. There the driver takes my fare with the urgency of a sloth whose mis-set alarm has gone off way too early.

Smarting from a stranger encounter with random rudeness, I go upstairs. The front right seat is surprisingly vacant so I select it. A few seconds later the unwelcome sound of the rude OAP funnels upwards the stairwell. Unburdened by self-awareness, he's now remonstrating with the bus driver. His voice booms out intermittently like a battlefield gun.

The front seat across from me is occupied by two millennials. They are stereotypically on-message for millennials as they're bemoaning their future prospects of owning a house. That's what happens when you opt to spend all your available income on turmeric vegan lattes and avocados. Still, I'm old enough to remember a time when pork wasn't pulled and neither avocados, nor the patriarchy, were smashed. Right, sisters?!

If I had millennials still living at home, it would at least enable me to constantly shout at them: "Oi, stop treating my house like you rent the place!"

Nonetheless I contemplate the bristling unfairness of the rude OAP downstairs not having to pay for his bus fare, whilst these two representatives of Generation Rent have to fork out the full amount.

Disembarking the bus, I still have twenty minutes before my meeting. Hence I do a quick bargain scan in M&S and find a fish pie significantly reduced. At the checkout two people are ahead of me. One is a grey haired Baby Boomer slightly similar in appearance - and, it transpires, mannerisms - to the rude pensioner I'd encountered earlier at the bus stop.

"These rules are batty," he denounces belligerently. "We have to check age appropriateness for selling alcohol as the cashier is under-18," says a lady summoned by the checkout girl's buzzer. "That's ridiculous," retorts the Baby Boomer who is attempting to buy several bottles of wine. And a small packet of nuts. The latter presumably in a sensible attempt to line his stomach before consuming the six bottles of booze. "Completely batty," he grumps before harrumphing off clinking with agitation, his face wearing the expression of someone determined not to enjoy life.

The other person in front of me is a millennial. "Afraid we'll have to check the alcohol age purchase", the supervisor informs him. "Yeah, that's cool," he says graciously, before politely adding, "no problem."

So much for millennials being the generation of oversensitive snowflakes with an outrageous sense of entitlement.

HERR OF THE DOG

Exiting a supermarket on Oxford's Botley Road I spot Ralf panting loudly at two women. He then proceeds to rub their legs. It's okay. Ralf's a dog.

Ralf's owners are repeating the same two words to an increasingly bemused member of staff positioned near the baskets in the doorway. "Hunt Vaseline?" says the taller of the two women with an unmistakable Germanic accent. She is accompanied by an older woman who is no doubt either her mother or grandmother. It's a tough call to make, and the wrong call will either flatter her profusely, or flatten me profusely depending on how much offence she chooses to take. Thankfully it's not a judgement I'm required to vocalize.

"Ja, hunt Vaseline," repeats her daughter (or granddaughter) to the uncomprehending supermarket employee. Adding the word "Dummkopf!" at the end of the sentence would have been superfluous given its hitherto tonal implication. Like an English person abroad unable to obtain a local's comprehension, she opts to repeat the exact same words. On-ly sl-ow-er. AND LOUDER.

By now it's obvious to me this must be a Google translate issue, and "Hunt Vaseline" probably resulted from a "Find petroleum jelly" search. If so the Germans are reassuringly upfront about their need for buying lubricants in public. By repeating it slower "Hunt Vaseline" is revealed as containing an extra syllable. Then it strikes me. They're saying: "Hund Wasser hier?"

I am not used to stepping up to situations, taking control and sorting them out. I'm usually an inadequate background cowerer, a social parasite reliant on others to initiate solutions. But this time I can be the cool control-taking sorter-outer. Yeah, today I am going to be THAT guy. Plus I can impress a six-foot tall German woman - or at least her Grossmutti.

"Ah, ich verstehe," I say in comically mispronounced schoolboy German. "Hund Wasser hier?" I ask. "Ja," they chime harmoniously, suddenly alight with comprehension. "Hund Wasser ist hier," I declare. They look around, immediately noticing the lack of promised Hund Wasser in the vicinity specifically designated as "hier".

I want to say "outside" but am impeded by my German vocabulary being limited to "ja," "nein", "Achtung Spitfire" and about 20 more words. Even the word for "table" - which used to be one of the first nouns taught in any language class - evades me. Thankfully Hund (dog) and Wasser (water) are among the twenty I know.

I motion for them to follow me. The dog isn't so sure. The two German women look more sure that I'm worth following than the dog does, even though it's actually in a dog's job description to follow people. After whispering something in German, they decide to follow me. Outside the store I turn right into a plant display and show them, camouflaged among garden accessories, a bench painted a sea breeze blue. Next to it is a bowl of water for canine usage provided by the store.

"Ah, danke," they all say - apart from the dog who slurps thirstily, draining the bowl expeditiously. I sit down at the bench and say out loud words 18 and 19 of my German vocab. "Ich heisse Richard." "Ja," they agree, oddly. They don't tell me their names. But they do introduce Herr Ralf. He's clearly deemed more akin to my intellectual level. If he knows the German words for 'fetch', 'sit' and 'stay' then his vocabulary is already more extensive than mine.

They depart soon afterwards, enabling me to use word number 20 of my German vocab: "Auf Wiedersehen," They smile for the first time and repeat it back to me. Momentarily I consider saying goodbye to Ralf, which would surely be: "Auf Wiedersehen, pet."

Left alone at the bench to ponder, I'm surprised how shocked I am to encounter Germans who cannot speak fluent English. English people are lazily monolingual and expect every encountered local to understand everything we say. Moreover we imagine this from people who probably grew up in East Germany where interacting with Westerners was forbidden for decades.

A lady in her early sixties approaches the bench with a small white dog and sits down opposite me. When neither of us can stand the silence any longer, I speak.

"He's nice," I say. "It's a she!" she barks curtly, surprising me with fierce sudden rudeness. "Sorry," I muster, apologising for not being able to genderise a tiny dog from above. I depart the suddenly unfriendly bench and wait at the adjacent bus stop. A few minutes later I am ascending the steps to the top deck when I realise what I should have said to the bafflingly rude lady: "Oh sorry, I didn't realise you're a bitch."

Literally *l'esprit d'escalier*, I could have said - were I not so monolingual.

ONE HIT WONDER

"I think he's phoning a hitman!" I inform my wife clandestinely.

Admittedly it's not a sentence I was expecting to use today. Or on any other day in my entire existence.

Unsurprisingly my remark concerns my wife a lot. "You should say 'hitperson'," she says, elaborating, "hitman is suggestively sexist," before rolling her eyes. At me. As if failing to frame my nouns within gender neutrality is the biggest crime being witnessed here.

We're travelling on the top deck of a bus out of Oxford town centre. Fully two minutes earlier a man with an unnecessary loud voice had started conducting a prolonged phone conversation with someone who is quickly revealed to be a brother or sister. "You know the man that's been providing our mum with all those cheap flights, free hotel bookings and other stuff?" he says, before leaving the minimal amount of time for the unfortunate news receiver on the other end of the phone to presumably reply with the most abridged of affirmatives, "Well guess what? He doesn't exist." Admittedly that is quite a bombshell.

"That's right," he says - after leaving the other party in the conversation no response time whatsoever to say anything that he's now agreeing with. Hence we're unsure what he is agreeing to. But this man evidently has news and wishes to exploit the status this grants him.

"Anyway," he concludes, "he's been arrested." He doesn't elaborate on how someone who doesn't exist has been arrested. "No," he says after a micropause only long enough to allow his sibling to express a maximum of one syllable, "he's already spent the money. All of it, apparently. All gone. Our mum won't get a penny back."

Onlookers are gawping in fascinated revulsion. At least that describes the behaviour of my wife and me. It's one of the most alarming phone calls I've ever overheard. Yet its occurrence exemplifies modern shamefulness in conducting the most private of conversations in public.

On my commuter bus it's regularly possible to hear people booming out their credit card details: "AND MY SECURITY PIN ON THE BACK OF THE CARD IS 734!"

Once en route to Aylesbury to do a comedy gig, I had unwisely selected a quiet seat at the back corner of the bus. The seat lost its 'quiet' description two stops later when a shoal of undergrad girls boarded, darted to the back of the bus and surrounded me. Either I was invisible or they felt no compunction to alter the decidedly post-watershed content of their conversation. And it was only 6pm: that no-man's land between late afternoon and early evening when the lights are flicked on in houses a few minutes before the decision to formalise night's arrival is declared by drawing the curtains.

I recall it was a late spring evening as the bus strained uphill past South Park. Peeking through the window rewarded me with a glance of Oxford's architectural majesty. Subtle honeysuckle scent drifted through an open window in the approaching twilight as the bus made a complaining noise climbing higher. It groaned past emptying parks and filling pubs. Lace curtains flickered in the windows of neat Georgian houses starting to light up like sparkling dollhouses bathed in orange-peel incandescence. The skyline of Oxford appeared as timeless as the seasons themselves. "This guy I met on Tinder last week had the thinnest dick I've ever seen," broadcasted one of the students to the entire top deck.

Anyone sipping water on that warm evening would have instantly deposited it on the neck of the unfortunate occupant of the seat in front. Prudish these girls were not. Later, somewhere between Oxford and Thame, I was forced to overhear an engrossing conversation on how they planned to uninvite a member of their social group from an upcoming holiday for the sole reason they termed her "a cockblocker". They didn't mention what type of vacation they'd booked, but I assumed it wasn't a week's cycling holiday incorporating brass-rubbing around West Country cathedrals.

Back on our current bus journey things are about to develop. "Look, I'll ring you later when I get in," says the man involved in a fraternal discussion, relaying the impression that the current environment is a tad light on privacy settings. On account of it being a packed double decker bus in rush hour.

In the hope of making conditions more compliant for continuing with his conversation, I pretend to be distracted by my phone. "Hello?" he says, "are you still there?" Good, this means the call is continuing. My wife and I catch ourselves involuntarily bowing forward, hoping for more audibility and therefore clues. "I think it's time to, er… you know…" I recognise the reticence of a man stumbling to find a euphemism, and that time is now. "You know… we have to engage… the expertise of the man at the garage. Yeah, he's done this sort of thing before. What? Let's say he's been recommended. Look, I'll ring you later. Sorry the news wasn't better."

He alights at Iffley Turn and crosses the road in a hurry, with the distracting mobile phone still pressed to his ear. Stupidly he crosses the road in front of our bus just as it's pulling away. A car coming from the other direction narrowly avoids running him over. The vehicle was so close to splaying him over its bonnet that some of my fellow top deck passengers gasp. Maybe the mother-swindling conman has hired the bloke at the garage first to kill the man on our bus? The plot thickens but never congeals.

"Bah," says my wife, "why couldn't he live nearer to us, then we could have got five more minutes of the conversation." And thereby, she infers, potentially enough clues to solve it.

"Where would you find a hitman?" I say on our walk from the bus stop to home. My wife doesn't answer. "Sorry… a hitperson." "How would I know?" answers my wife, now the noun has been modified for gender neutrality. I'm relieved that after twenty years of marriage her answer doesn't reveal an expert knowledge of previous research. "Not in the Yellow Pages, I guess," she says. "Of course it's not in the Yellow Pages," I agree. "No one's looked for anything in the Yellow Pages since J R Hartley and Jeremy Thorpe."

Teasingly my wife ruminates aloud in a Columbo-wrapping-things-up tone. "Maybe the man - the man with the expertise at the garage they need to recruit - is…" she begins. Then pauses like she's buffering. After four seconds of silence it's obvious her theory, and therefore her sentence, has collapsed under the weight of its own implausibility.

"Yes," I encourage her, "go on," desperate for insight. No matter how speculative and unlikely that insight may prove to be.

"Maybe he's a man who's a mechanic and therefore good at fixing cars. That's why they need to recruit his expertise. That's all. It's as prosaic as that."

I find her response terrifically disappointing. And lose no time in telling her so. "The man? He?" I repeat in the tones of a disappointed parent addressing their child after finding cigarettes in a schoolbag. "Why make the automatic assumption the mechanic is a man?"

"Fair enough. That's true," says my wife. Hinting that would be much worse. Even though I was failing to be facetious.

For the next fortnight we both keep an eye out for the man on the bus. Although I wouldn't go as far as admitting having deliberately hung around town to enable me to catch a similarly timed bus as the one where we overheard the conversation - that doesn't mean I didn't do it.

About two weeks after we eavesdropped the dramatic phone call - my wife spots someone on the top deck. He looks like the same man. After studying the stranger's face with the intensity of a North Korean passport official who's just won Employee of the Month, my wife makes a declaration.

It's not him.

We also check the local news regularly in case a known conman has been found drilled with holes like a Swiss cheese used for target practice. Needless to say there's no such story, and we both reluctantly conclude we must be confusing modern Oxford with Raymond Chandler's 1940s Los Angeles.

Neither my wife nor I see the mysterious man on the bus again. But I do see some of the undergraduate girls again. A month later I'm chugging up Headington Hill on the same number 280 when they board the bus outside Brookes University. This, I pledge to myself as they make their way noisily towards me, is the last time I sit at the back of the bus. Going to school teaches you life's basics: counting, reading, writing and that sitting on the bus' backseat is the preserve of the naughty cool kids.

"It's empowering for women if we sign up," says the tallest one who's identifiably their pack leader. "Yeah," agrees one of her sub-lieutenants, "as feminists we should go," before adding, "and there's cheap Prosecco." I don't discover what event they're referring to, but I'm convinced that their motivation is to be positive female role models - plus the swaying presence of Prosecco - ensures they all enthusiastically agree to attend the mystery function. This leaves me feeling guilty for misjudging them last month; they're not vacuous after all, but evidently feminists motivated to promote gender equality across the sisterhood. "Women need to stick together," says Pack Leader, before adding in somewhat unsisterly manner, "although I'm not attending if that bitch Claudia is going." At this point a 'ding-ding' chime rings out. Either someone has pressed to stop the bus or an irony bell has just been loudly struck.

"I could have killed Claudia last night," confirms Pack Leader. I know about a bloke at a garage who may be able to help with that ambition.

MARGINALISED AT OXFORD

A college library is staging a display of their literary treasures. These secular relics include a signed 1st edition by a historical A-list author - apparently she was a close friend of a former college Principal.

Apologies for not naming names but there are identities to preserve here, as will become apparent. Particularly one undergraduate's identity. And for Alaina's sake, we don't want her to be identifiable. No, Alaina isn't her real name. I don't want anyone retrospectively having to stand (very silently) on a librarian's naughty step as a consequence of this shatteringly indiscreet column.

An undergraduate in a college sweatshirt is guarding the exhibition. Although should anyone try to steal a priceless book and make a run for it, even when giving chase in hot pursuit it's doubtful whether Alaina would be prepared to put down her phone. Or stop texting.

The exhibition she's supposedly guarding focuses on marginalia. One era's graffiti and vandalism is another period's museum artefact. It's somehow pleasing to acknowledge that a naughty late-medieval schoolboy's obscene doodling would have resulted in both a sore thrashing by an unimpressed teacher AND an Oxbridge college's exhibition dedicated to his work several centuries later. An outcome that any number of "But, Sirs" would have failed to convince his medieval master at the time as he went off in search of a bigger cane.

"Yeah, it's totally cool to take photos," says Alaina obligingly in response to my request. I thank her, and snap away.

Ten minutes later a lady - profoundly more senior in age, status and demeanour - saunters briskly into the room and immediately adopts the authoritative mannerisms of an old-school librarian ordered from Central Casting.

Although not owning horn-rimmed glasses and a hair bun, nevertheless she no doubt believes a librarian's right hand is for three purposes only: operating a date stamp, placing in front of lips to emphasise "shush", and slapping readers who dare to pollute the library's monastic church-mouse-in-slippers silence. Not only do I not mind such librarians, I welcome them as resistance to increasingly noisy libraries.

"Remember Alaina that no photography is allowed in the exhibition." Alaina doesn't respond. But that's how I learn her real name. "Like we said during the briefing." Still colossally nonplussed Alaina offers no reaction or response. It's as if whatever operating system runs Alaina's brain is currently buffering slowly while it receives a vital upgrade. "An hour ago?" prompts the matriarchal librarian. "Of course," says Alaina as casually as she can convincingly muster, which involves an impressive amount of mustering.

If Alaina had any concerns that I was about to turn informant and snitch, then she is safe. Besides, we now possess a shared secret - the estate's lax gamekeeper and poacher in cohorts against the Lady of the Manor.

Words don't seem to flow naturally from Alaina's mouth - probably because like most modern teenagers she prefers to communicate via texts, emojis and shrugs.

"Can I, like, get a drink?" asks Alaina. "Yes, but remember no drinks allowed in the library," reminds Her Ladyship. This news is clearly a first-time discovery shock for Alaina, but to her credit she reacts in the same insouciant and unimpassioned way as before: "Cool." Impressively she continues texting with her right hand under the desk while looking in the other direction to hold a conversation.

I continue walking around the fascinating exhibition. After ten minutes Alaina returns and performs a changing of the guard with the more senior woman.

No sooner have the proper librarian's urgent footsteps disappeared than I hear the distinct swoosh of a can being opened. In her defence it's a red energy drink - not a can of Special Brew - but it still enables me to admire Alaina immensely; this rule-breaking bad girl of librarians.

Twenty minutes later I depart. Outside the room I spot the senior librarian approaching me. Realising she'll reach the exhibition in about five seconds, I sense this is my chivalrous chance to try and save Ariana from being busted, red-drink-handed. "Er... that's a fascinating exhibition," I say - thankfully not having to lie. "Thank you. Have you signed the visitor's book?" "NO! I WILL DO THAT NOW!" I boom like an appalling am-dram performer overcompensating for lack of amplification - and acting talent - in a village hall.

Alaina clearly doesn't require my crude early warning alarm. When the librarian and I re-enter the room there isn't a sign of her drink can anywhere.

But she is taking a photo of one of the books.

LUCKY GYM

Often imagined as time spent at award ceremonies and in green rooms twinkling with stars, the night time locations of a full-time writer are, in reality, quite different. My profession invariably involves hanging around supermarkets at night - waiting for the reduced food to be even further discounted.

This action conveys two ineluctable and undeletable truths: freelance writers don't earn very much, and literally cannot afford to be fussy eaters. That sentence may shock you - and not just because it contains a rare correct usage in the modern world of the word 'literally'.

If a decayed grapefruit, a broken packet of semi-powdered crispbread and a joyless Weight Watchers lasagne due to expire in exactly two hours are all the available victuals falling within a freelance writer's dinner budget, then *bon appétit*. This predicament is recognisable to all but a fortunate few creatives in the arts industries. Although one struggles to imagine touching the delving hand of JK Rowling in the bargain bin when competitively beating her to the last "Reduced for quick sale - now 10p" mould-speckled courgette in a Tesco Extra at closing time.

Hence I was recently attracted to a university experiment where volunteers were pledged to receive a free breakfast and lunch. It transpires that not only is there such a thing as a free lunch after all, there's a free breakfast too. But surely there are more catches than a Yale lock factory?

After exchanging emails for further experiment details, I pass the intensely thorough screening process to determine eligibility: are you male or female and aged between 18 and 80? Yes I am. I allow myself to experience a swelling of pride at passing such a strenuous audition.

Arriving at a university gym for my first experiment session, I'm directed to wait in reception. A girl, fumbling through her purse, is being fined £3 for missing last week's yoga. This concerns me. I'm in my mid-50s and have never been to yoga once - that's going to add up if I'm fined accordingly.

Two passing gym bunnies fire me a withering look of unfiltered contempt. They clearly have a problem that a blubbery old dude like me is infecting their gym. Entering the sports hall I see six more Duracelled gym bunnies pounding running machines. This strikes me as odd - in the Victorian era prisoners were forced to exercise like this. Now it seems you pay £500 a year to operate a treadmill.

Placed in this environment, I've never felt more unfit. Consequently by the time I commence my experiment suitability fitness assessment I'm sweating like Joey Essex on University Challenge.

My instructor is impressively muscular and tells me he's a former rugby player. He informs me empathetically: "My lifestyle is very similar to yours as I do lots of writing." Judging by his vast biceps, if that's true then he must use a very heavy pen.

A machine accesses me with an unwelcome incorruptible honesty. It prints out the ratio of muscle to fat in my body, emitting a strange elongated bleep noise to signify its calculations are complete. "Think I just made the machine laugh," I say. He writes down the figures studiously. "Is it good?" I ask. He evades answering the question directly.

Next he ascertains whether my lifestyle can be fairly described as sedentary. I ask if I can sit down for this bit. "Your cardiovascular rate will be monitored next," he announces.

For this test I have to ride an exercise bike. "Every minute the difficulty will increase," says my instructor. "When velocitic exhaustion occurs…"

"… velocitic what?" I check.

"Velocitic exhaustion," he repeats. "You mean 'knackered'?" I enquire. "Yes, although I'm not allowed to call it that in an academic paper."

For the first few minutes the pedalling is easy. Then, as promised, it gets incrementally harder every 60 seconds as my instructor introduces more resistance to the wheels. He is visibly surprised I manage to complete five minutes. By the time I reach eight minutes he is now entering gasping incredulity.

"Go on. You can do it! This is amazing! Do you want to be AMAZING??!!" he asks.

Yes, yes I do want to be amazing. Though I consider this a generous descriptive prize for managing to rotate the wheels on a stationary bike for nine minutes.

Wheezing like every breath could be my last, I stop. I'm deselected from the experiment but given a voucher to cover the cost of breakfast and lunch. He coos impressiveness for my cycling stamina.

Outside I see the two gym bunnies who stabbed me an earlier cruel look. They're both smoking. I throw them a pitying look of disrespect. Everything about their mannerisms convey that the taller one was a former school bully and her companion was her mean assistant. The process of voluntarily tarmacking their lungs causes Assistant Bully to emit a deep guttural cough.

Then I go and spend my food voucher on a big, unreduced in price or fat, cake at Tesco.

AT THE DROP OF A HAT

I've arranged to meet a friend and his ten-year-old daughter at a football match. It's a big game - a Women's FA Cup tie between Oxford United and Cambridge United. Oxford's opponents are controversial. Not because of varsity rivalry, but due to Cambridge's unconventional progression to this stage of the competition.

In the previous round they had lost to their city rivals Cambridge City Women. Given the universally accepted rules of how knockout competitions work, their appearance in the next round seems contrariwise. So why are they here? Had they kidnapped the victorious Cambridge City team, left them tied up and gagged in the changing room and taken their place as imposters? A rather implausible plotline which occurred regularly in *Roy of the Rovers* comic strips during my youth. However the real explanation is almost as incredible - as I'm about to discover.

I greet the arriving ten-year-old by offering my outstretched hand to shake. This, I discovered in a book my wife is reading for babysitting tips, is how you're supposed to interact with children. Treat kids as much as you can like adults.

She shakes my hand wearily. Her face sags with sadness, revealing an absurdly large frown. Instantaneously I realise that she, a normally rambunctious child possessing the resilience of a cartoon character, has yet to speak. "I'm afraid something bad has happened that's upset us," says her father solemnly. "We're having to cope with a loss." The ten-year-old, uncharacteristically glum and lachrymose, sniffs loudly for emphasis.

Immediately I fear the worst. Are we about to explain to a small child about the inevitable death of all living things including, but not limited to, hamsters, rabbits and grandparents? After all, everyone and everything shares a flower's destiny to bloom and fade.

"She's lost her favourite unicorn hat somewhere on the way here," explains her father dolefully. This prompts her to speak for the first time: "You lost my hat." "Er... well, I don't think apportioning blame will help," adds dad, struggling for audibility above rapid gunfire bursts of "You lost it! You lost it!"

Recklessly I decide to start a sentence without any realisation how it might end. My mission is threefold: firstly to stop her saying "You lost it!" on a repeat setting, then to aid the formulation of a hat retrieval plan. Boldly my mission is then to counsel a child about coming to terms with lost stuff.

"We don't really own things permanently," I say, attempting a consoling voice, hoping to persuade her to adopt a more sanguine interpretation, "we just curate…" I stumble, realising that this may not be a word contained within a ten-year-old's vocabulary. "Er… look after stuff for a while," I continue, trying to select words that can act as padding against the painful impact of loss. "Things get passed on, change hands, bought and sold, lost and found, eBay-ed and charity-shopped. People lose things all the time. It's only stuff."

"Do you own that coat?" she asks me. "Yes, but…" "Can I have it?" "No, not really, it wouldn't fit you. And you've already got a coat." "So you own it then?" I appear to have been philosophically checkmated in two moves by a kid still at primary school. Outthought, outmanoeuvred and outplayed. Just like Cambridge United Women are experiencing concurrently, as they quickly go one-nil down. "Anyway," I say, "at least I didn't lose your hat like Daddy." The look I receive from Daddy is thoroughly deserved.

So how did Cambridge United Women stay in the Cup after being knocked out in the previous round? The rules state a footy pitch must be a minimum of 100m x 64m. Reportedly the pitch where they were eliminated measures 94m x 58.7m. Thus necessitating a re-match from which they emerged victorious. This strikes me as odd. Because for decades women have been reassuring me that size really doesn't matter!

"Daddy is going back to look for your hat," he announces. "Would you be able to do some important looking-after for me?" he asks, before labouring the seriousness of the situation at supererogatory length: "Looking after someone is a really important thing to do. You'll have to take the responsibility seriously." Yes, I think, it is and you're a tad patronising. "So," continues her dad, "if I go off for about an hour, do you think you'll be up to the job of looking after someone? You'll have to be very grown up about it."

At this point I realise he's speaking to his daughter. "So if you look after Richard, I'll hopefully be back in time to see some of the second half." I pledge supinely that I'll be on my best behaviour while he's away, and not eat too many sweets.

Using the distraction of his daughter screaming her approval of the home team's goal, her dad explains the situation to me: "Her hat must have fallen overboard on the bike ride here. And annoyingly I've lost an expensive bungee strap off my panniers too, so I'll go and look for them." Her father departs upon his search. A sort of *Lord of the Rings* epic quest, were the eponymous ring replaced by a Poundshop hat devoid of supernatural properties.

As soon as her father has exited the ground, Oxford score again. Evie Gane, playing on the left wing for the home side, is so pacey, tricky and elusive that her marker couldn't locate her with a sniffer dog and access to CCTV. Her wing wizardry leads to a second goal, leaving Cambridge's befuddled right-back in a state of spinning dizziness wondering where both the ball and Oxford's winger are currently located. The ball, it eventually dawns upon her, is located in Cambridge's net.

Soon Oxford are three-nil up. "I think Oxford are going to win," says the ten-year-old with seasoned punditry. A few moments later, Evie cuts in from the right and finds herself in an area of space so devoid of fellow humans that the Cambridge defence must believe the region has been declared a nuclear exclusion zone.

Unchallenged, she continues her run towards goal, pursued by a puffing and demoralised right-back looking determined to quit the fags, before unleashing a ferocious drive. Thhwaaack! The ball hits the near post, but still enters the goal. It's fair to say the Cambridge 'keeper was beaten for pace, given she commenced her dive two seconds after the goal net had stopped shivering.

"Yah! Four-nil to Oxford," shrieks my ten-year old companion approvingly, and waves her yellow homemade Oxford United Women flag. I shout out: "Time to start measuring the pitch, Cambridge!" The referee's assistant rewards me with a coy I-know-I-shouldn't-really smile.

"She's my favourite player," she tells me, pointing at Evie Gane. It's fair to conclude from her expression that the Cambridge right-back's favourite player is not Evie Gane. I point out that there are many other talented players on the pitch, including Georgia Timms, Flo Fyfe, Lauren Hayes, Ellie Noble, Cheryl Williams and Emily Allen.

Illustrating my point, Emily taps the ball into space, spins her marker and leaves the unfortunate wheezing defender stationary with hands on hips in resignation. Only the intervention of the crossbar stops Oxford reaching five goals.

Cambridge's full-back is so fair skinned that there must be a serious danger of sunburn whenever she opens the fridge door. This probably explains why when the sun pokes through the Tupperware dimness for the first time all afternoon, she is immediately substituted. Dejectedly, she walks off the pitch so sluggishly that a sloth would slow handclap her. Finally she reaches the bench before moss starts to grow on her.

Suddenly my ten-year-old companion jumps involuntarily. There's been a tap on her shoulder. "Have I missed much?" asks her returning father. She proceeds, breathlessly, to fill him in. "Do you want to know if I found your hat?" he asks, somewhat reasonably since he's missed most of the match for his long, and presumably arduous, quest.

There's a definite buffering delay while she locates the reason why he's been absent for the last hour. Enraptured by the footy match, it's obvious the hat drama has been relegated in her priorities. "Oh, yes," she eventually recollects, though not with the sufficiently concerned tone her father justifiably expects.

"Here's your unicorn hat," he reveals, and places it before her like Sir Walter Raleigh bringing back unfathomable things from his explorations for Queen Elizabeth. "Er… thanks," she says casually, and immediately puts it in her pocket.

"Didn't Daddy do well?" I say. I rightfully receive an I'm-not-six look. "I retraced our route and found it on the roadside about a mile away." She doesn't respond. "Actually, it was more like two miles." There's still no proportional increase in his daughter's gratitude. "Didn't find my bungee cord though," he imparts disgruntledly. "Somebody will have nicked it," he grumps. She puts on her unicorn hat, telling me: "I'll curate it better."

When the final whistle blows, Cambridge sprint off the pitch towards the tunnel, like eleven people anxious to avoid TV cameras on their way to a court appearance. Covering their faces might have been considered.

At my suggestion we make our way to the players' entrance. Unlike in the men's game, the female players willingly wait to sign autographs for their young fans - a practice that should be equally prevalent in male football.

Unexpectedly my youthful companion alters her personality from boisterous to acutely shy. This transformation amazes me, akin to Michael Palin throwing a punch, or a Dalek inviting you for tea.

I hold her hand for bravery as we march towards a yellow-shirted player. "Excuse me," I say, "could you kindly sign our programme?" "Of course," says Emily Allen, compliantly. The star striker considerately gives us her autograph and writes her squad number next to her signature.

Then we approach Evie Gane. She has untied her long blonde hair, ensuring her face is barely visible through curtains of magnificent mane. My companion, her uncharacteristic shyness now extinguished, boldly informs her, "You're my favourite player!" and asks how she got to be so talented. "I didn't use to be very good, but I kept playing and practising." I thank her for dispensing this encouraging advice. "Any time," she says, and thanks us for coming. We overhear another player telling a press interviewer, "I'm just pleased we're in the hat," thereby echoing the sentiments of my companion.

Exiting the ground, I glance back at the pitch in case Cambridge's players are using a surveyor's wheel to measure it.

An hour later I receive a heartening text. "Found my bungee cord. Someone had put it on a wall next to where I dropped it."

POSTSCRIPT: In November 2019 we attended an Oxford United Women match against Launton Ladies FC in the Oxfordshire County Cup. Oxford won 32-0. An English record? Although the goalscoring was sublime, my favourite bit of the afternoon occurred when a spectator handed Launton's good-spirited goalkeeper a black puppy to stroke at half-time to help de-traumatise her!

OXFORD IS THE PITTS

I'm strolling along George Street on a Friday evening when my subconscious brain triggers a threat alarm. It signals to my conscious mind that I'm in imminent danger.

Although I'm theoretically safe on the pavement, there appears to be a speeding black cab heading straight towards me. A taxi steers across the road and brakes aggressively, stopping disconcertingly close.

The cab spills out a giggle of girls onto the pavement. They are already blatantly inebriated and, between the four of them, wearing sufficient clothes to adequately dress one person in public.

The last one out is carrying a bottle of lager in one hand and an inflatable phallus in the other. Completing this Hogarthian 2018 reboot is a pile of vomit land-mining the pavement in front of me. At this point I think to myself: "That sweet city with her Dreaming Spires, she needs not June for beauty's heightening." Or perhaps this wasn't the exact view of Oxford Matthew Arnold had in mind?

This encounter causes me to walk faster, even though I'm early, anxious to reach the civilising presence of my chosen venue for a wild Friday night out in Oxford: an, ahem, academic lecture on anthropology. Having concluded that I've done quite enough anthropological field-studies for the evening already - thank you very much. However the lecture will soon prove to be far from the indictment of civilisation I was expecting - but an affray to the senses highlighting humanity's repellent violence.

As I wait for the lecture theatre to fill up, I dread the row behind me becoming occupied by the hen party I'd seen earlier. Though had that occurred it would have constituted the most unlikely thing to have happened. Anywhere. Ever. With the possible exception of *Mrs Brown's Boys* getting commissioned for a second series.

Inside the Victorian gothic splendour of the Pitt Rivers Museum a curator eventually dims the lights and commences a captivating talk to a meagre audience. The crowd may be small, but the subject is big. As is the museum's collection.

He enthusiastically shows us a slide of an artefact. "This is one of 55,000 objects we have at the museum." Clearly this talk may stray beyond the advertised 30 minutes if he has a PowerPoint slide of all the other 54,999.

There are some marvellously strange exhibits housed here. For instance he shows us an object that is specifically a whistle to lure anteaters. Try finding that in the Argos catalogue.

Encoring, he shows us spears, crossbows, blunderbusses, harpoons, daggers, pikes, man traps, swords and basically a lot of other stuff you'd need to dispose of quickly should there ever be a police raid on your house. "We have 3,000 spears," he adds casually. "People don't realise it's quite a hazardous place to work."

Certainly you wouldn't want to experience employee grudges in this workplace environment given the easy access to such a waiting arsenal. Those ubiquitous handwritten workplace kitchen signs

"ONLY take ONE biscuit at a time, and ONLY [triply underlined] if your contributions to the biscuit pool are FULLY up-to-date" would be rendered more unignorably ominous given the access to lethal weaponry here.

Apparently 60 Banbury Road in Oxford, we're informed, is a vast storeroom for the museum, stuffed to the rafters with clubs (the sort of clubs that Stone Age man would be interested in, not barely dressed bachelorette parties in George Street) and sticks. It appears they have a lot of sticks. More sticks than, er, you could shake an exhibit at.

At the conclusion of the lecture the curator asks: "Any questions?" No hands are raised. "Any questions at all?" I think about asking: "Two trains depart Plymouth at the same time, one travelling at 75mph over the first 50 miles…"

"I've got a few more minutes if there are any questions." Silence descends and envelopes us like a collapsed tent.

"Would anyone like to think of a question?" I twirl that thought. Since it's been a fascinating talk, I desperately want to ask a question to avoid him thinking we're unappreciative.

Thankfully someone does eventually ask a question. It's about the shrunken heads displayed here in the Pitt Rivers Museum and immortalised in the *Harry Potter* films. Afterwards I clap the speaker with hand-hurting alacrity to make the applause sound larger.

The next morning I'm about to put out the recycling when I experience an electrical charge of anxiety. Again my subconscious brain has spotted a threat and notifies me: "Stop thinking about the usual rubbish - as well as the actual rubbish in this case - and focus."

There is movement inside my house. Lots of brown dots are scurrying around on the floor tiles. On closer inspection I realise there's a huge trail of ants inside my hallway.

If only I had some way to summon an anteater.

THE CAT THAT CAME TO TEA

Previously I wrote about attending a lunch party - even though social orthodoxy insists there is no such thing as 'a lunch party' but only a dinner party. Ever the spineless conformist, I attempt to arrange an actual dinner party as experienced by other grown-ups. But no-one wants to come.

Rather than choosing to interpret this accurately as the personal rebuttal I should, instead I cling to my invitees' reassurances that evenings are difficult because of childcare, next day work requirements and, er, a repeat of *The Great British Sewing Bee* being aired at 9pm all week on the Yesterday channel.

Hence I am hosting a tea party. At least a tea party is a thing. All the best people have tea parties: chimps, Alice in Wonderland and her mad hallucinogenic friends, and even madder uber right-wing Americans with their gun ownership and Trump-endorsing habits. (Obviously the only way to guarantee all US citizens remain safe is by ensuring that everyone owns at least one gun.)

My wife greets our arriving guests. Even though it's a very small guestlist given the size restraints of our home - and my popularity - it contains two people I haven't met before.

Quickly I assume my co-hosting duties by wandering into the living room to ensure my guests have drinks. One asks for a rum and coke with ice. No, it transpires, we don't have rum. Or coke. But we do have ice. Otherwise it's perfect.

This is not a compromise she's prepared to accept so requests a G&T instead. We have that. Well, apart from the gin. There's a reason why the next person is asked to choose from a highly specific list of red wine, white wine, tea, coffee, beer, orange juice or water. Seven choices. Pick one.

However I've been over generous with the ice too early, meaning there's none left for the final order - my wife's request for an iced water. "We haven't got any ice?!" says my wife, ahem, icily. I run the now empty ice tray under the tap.

One of our guests appears to be gripping the attention of the others. Which is pleasing as it's distracting them from not receiving the drinks they wanted. He's recounting an anecdote earnestly in short stabbing sentences. "Shipwrecked on a desert island. He had no stones or rocks. Just sand. So he couldn't open any of the coconuts. Even though they were growing abundantly. He starved to death. Later rescuers discovered him dead. On his desert island. Next to a pile of coconuts."

"And a list of his eight favourite records," I add. My guests laugh - with the noticeable exception of the anecdote teller.

My wife summons me with the subtlety of calling a dog that's in Very Big Trouble. I return to our tiny kitchen. My mission is to carry through sandwiches, cakes and more disappointing iceless drinks options.

Back in the living room Coconut Man is recounting another story. His partner, who is responsible for his presence here because my wife knows her but not him, is looking decidedly uncomfortable the longer her boyfriend dominates the conversation.

He regales his 75% female audience with a misjudged anecdote about how, before meeting his current partner, he slept with a veritable United Nations of women – as if somehow keen to prove he may be a chauvinist but no way is he a racist. Turns out he's not the only one to have misjudged his audience. My wife looks furious. But his girlfriend looks positively bellicose.

"You're a comedy writer?" says Inappropriate Anecdote Man. "Yeah, I think so," I say as my confidence hastily abandons me. "You think so? Tell us a joke you've written and prove it." This meets with much more approval from the guests than from me.

It also encapsulates an occupational awkwardness encountered by most in the comedy industry. "Er, well it's my day off," I flounder. My response fails to satisfy their interest in what I deem to be very much my business.

The late Bob Monkhouse used to have a stock reply at social engagements to anyone who, upon discovering he was a comedian, pressed him to tell a joke. "If you discovered I was a gynaecologist you wouldn't ask me to take a look at the wife." Glancing at Inappropriate Anecdote Boy's partner, who is now so obviously contemplating which specific murder weapon she'll be using after they've left our house (hopefully she'll wait until then as we have light beige carpets), I contemplate a suitable response. Instead I fail.

Kindly filling the menacing silence, the other guest my wife invited and whom I haven't met before, asks me: "Have you worked with anyone famous?" My wife rolls her eyes as she knows I enjoy reeling off an immodest list and expects to hear the same well versed names. Quickly she re-routes the conversation by asking the questioner: "What line of work are you involved with?"

"I'm a model maker in children's TV and adverts," she says. This is a much better response than "I do something in IT." Everyone turns their heads away from me and towards the model maker, as if they're following a tennis match and witnessing a crosscourt winner. "Wow, she works with models," says my wife. Fittingly the model worker resembles a model herself. Looking effortlessly fabulous, she's intimidatingly attractive. She is wearing a short charcoal skirt and thick fashion tights that become more patterned the closer they get to her hemline. Her legs are lengthened by unnecessary heels, given she's tall enough to maintain eye contact throughout a conversation with a giraffe.

"I love Oliver Postgate's work," blurts my wife. Given Model Lady is aged about 24 there is no way on this earth that she will get that reference; hence I give my wife a chastising look. "I absolutely love Oliver Postgate - he's like my all-time hero," concurs Model Lady. I give my spouse a confirming, supportive look. It is not reciprocated.

"Surely everyone loves Bagpuss?" says Model Lady. "I once met someone who worked on Bagpuss and a couple of his other shows," I say. Then pause to receive any forthcoming acclaim. "Wow," she says impressed. I throw Inappropriate Anecdote Boy a look meant to convey, "Stick to listing your sexual conquests!"

My wife has changed her expression to one of acute suspicion. If I possessed an insider's knowledge of Postgate's shows, why had I failed to mention it in the previous twenty years of marriage? "You know that Oliver Postgate eventually got sacked for breaking a puppet on set?" I say. "Oh dear, what happened?" asks Model Lady. "He dropped a clanger." My wife and Model Lady turn their heads and feet towards each other and continue their conversation without me. I depart in search of dips.

"You must forgive my husband. He's a part-time comedian," I hear as I depart. 'Part-time' was harshly unnecessary, I think.

Later when I bring a rattling tray of hot drinks into the room like a nervous butler, I remark to Model Lady: "You'll have had your tea, Hamish?" Model Lady laughs. Not at my ten-per-center Bagpuss reference which she probably didn't get, but more likely because of the unrepeatably awful Scottish accent that I brazenly attempt for added - but unaccomplished - authenticity.

"When I moved to Oxfordshire I was fascinated to discover there's an actual place here I thought was pronounced Kingston Bagpuss," says my wife. "Isn't it?" questions Model Lady. "I always call it Kingston Bagpuss too." "I fear it's pronounced Kingston Bag-poo-eze," I say spoilingly. Inappropriate Anecdote Boy, clearly not having shagged anybody from there, feels unable to contribute to the conversation.

My wife and Model Lady insist I'm wrong. My knowledge that Kingston Bagpuize (as it's correctly spelt) is pronounced 'Bag-poo-eze' rather than the infinitely more pleasing 'Bagpuss' is simply because a fellow comedy writer, Guy Browning, lives there. There aren't that many of us comedy writers around. As a profession we're not known as being socially capable or attractive, hence we don't breed that successfully in captivity. Thereby ensuring our numbers are permanently low.

"They once made a feature film in Kingston Bagpuize where the residents gave their time for free," I say. No one's interested. "Called *Tortoise In Love*. It's good but like a Richard Curtis film without a budget." Still no interest. "It's about a socially awkward man who falls instantly in love with an attractive girl in her mid-20s whom he meets at an afternoon tea party. He's so flummoxed by her that he starts wittering on, bloviating endlessly, embarrassing himself... er, I'll go and see if the ice is ready yet."

Later, returning to the living room, I interrupt Model Lady as she speaks: "Too many cooks spoil..." "... prime time TV," I interject, finishing her sentence. By this stage it's obvious even to me that I'm trying too hard to be the party jester. And impress a woman thirty years my junior, voluntary prey to her beauty. Meanwhile my wife observes me with steely eyes, contemplating the best place to bury my body.

Model Lady gets out her mobile and holds it in front of her chin. Uplit by her phone screen, her face glows like Bacall's having a cigarette lit by Bogart. Of all the living rooms, in all the world, she has to walk into mine.

A few days later my wife is looking after the two boys that she regularly babysits. Both are contentedly engaged in building a model of a 16th-century Spanish galleon. They are unusually quiet and calm, although this could just be due to the glue fumes.

The galleon was a risky present from their grandmother. Risky as it assumed kids have the same interests in a post-iPad, smartphone and Netflix world as they did sixty years ago. Yet in direct contradiction to the cynicism apparently expressed by the boys' parents, grandma's present appears to be an engaging distraction. Although anything can be an engaging distraction when the offered alternatives are all homework-based.

After half an hour the younger one declares: "This is really hard." However the older boy doesn't agree. "This is great fun. I want to do this ALL the time."

"Well," says my wife, "there was a lady in my house this week who does this all day. She makes models for her job. And puppets." This has the desired effect in maintaining both boys' interest in the project. As if continuing for another twenty minutes will enable them to qualify with apprenticeships to commence model making jobs immediately upon leaving primary school.

"The model making lady I know likes Bagpuss. Do you know Bagpuss?"

"Bag-who?" asks the older boy. "Never mind," says my wife, concluding it's clearly a generational thing after all. "Who's Bagpuss?" presses the younger child. "A cat puppet that I really liked on TV when I was your age," she replies. "Oh and it's also the name of a village not far from here in Oxfordshire: Kingston Bagpuss."

"That's not Bagpuss. It's called Kingston Bagpuize," corrects the younger one, stressing the 'bag-poo-eze' pronunciation. He's eight. Told you!

NEVER ODD OR EVEN

My friend Hannah is late. This is not an unusual occurrence, yet she is now entering the alarming zone on the Lateness Scale between 'pushing it' and 'probably forgotten'. "I'm on my way," says Hannah, by way of "hello" when I call her. "Oh, good," I say, relieved that she hadn't forgotten. "I'd forgotten," she says.

Hannah has degrees from two of the world's most prestigious universities (and also one from Cambridge). But she can be occasionally absent-minded and... er, where was I?... oh yeah, easily distracted. "Order me a strawberry milkshake, I'll be at the café in five minutes." I place her order, and request a banana one for me.

Now, dear reader, it's time to set you a task. Although everyone who appears in this column's cast list is wonderfully different, can you spot which quality they all share in common? See if you can work it out. AND DON'T SKIP TO THE END FOR THE BIG REVEAL - THAT WOULD BE CHEATING. That's you told. And I'm sorry about the shouting. Okay, let's get back to the story. Meanwhile I'll get this Fourth Wall fixed as I won't be breaking through it again. For a while, anyway.

A week after catching up with Hannah in Oxford I am attending a scriptwriters' meeting in London. Afterwards an assistant producer called Anna takes me to lunch. This is not at the Groucho but a well-known sandwich café chain. The budget is parsimoniously capped at £6.50 per person. Even though I'm writing lines for a multi-million dollar film company, somehow I appear to be earning below the minimum wage. Again. "Petty cash won't let us have any more," explains Anna. It's the pettiest of petty cash.

A woman catches Anna's eye and wanders over to our table. Given that this woman's TWO sandwiches are extravagantly augmented with crisps, yogurt, fruit and a frothy coffee, it's obvious her successful life isn't capped at a £6.50 lunch limit. "This is Eve," says Anna.

At this exact point Eve, her long hair falling free of her shoulders, bites into a juicy red apple. I feel like shouting, "Eve....NO!!" but feel this Garden of Eden reference may be a tad obscure. "What, too soon?!" And hardly the topical comedy I'm here to write. "You know, from the Bible," I say, losing faith in my words before they are even out of my mouth, "Eve ate the tempting apple growing in the Eden Project." Still nothing.

"Eve has a lovely new fiancée," announces Anna. "Is he called Adam?" I say with instantaneous regret. "No," she says, before adding an unsettling: "Why do you assume that?" This is either a brilliant deadpan, or kids don't get a theology grounding in school any more.

I should point out that Anna and Eve have very successful careers in spite of both appearing to still be in the Sixth Form. Any bitterness on my part is intended. Working in the creative industries at my age serves to remind me that everyone else appears at least twice as young as me - and three times as successful.

"She," says Eve, her sentence's opening pronoun stressed with a tonal pressure in excess of a thousand pounds per square inch, "is called Elle." This now not only makes me look jarringly unfunny, but also borderline homophobic with my heteronormative assumptions.

Eve flicks her long hair back behind her shoulders. Now lesbians have long hair - no wonder the world doesn't make sense any more to people who can remember black and white TV and struggling with decimalisation. It's almost as if you can't rely on ludicrously crass reductive stereotyping anymore.

Fortunately Eve soon forgives my initial indiscretion and we proceed towards a friendly chat. Though I finish my disappointing £6.50 lunch well ahead of hers, as she has another four courses to munch through. "Would you like some of my crisps?" offers Eve kindly. "YESSS!!!" My inner nine-year-old squeals. "That's very kind of you, but no thank you," replies my 54-year-old self out of polite social reservation.

"Oh, okay," says Eve, then immediately casts aside her half-finished crisps onto a dirty plate. Social protocol now means it's too late for me to change my mind and rescue her discarded snacks. If only she'd announced earlier her intention not to finish them, I could have eaten more. Saved more crisps. Like a Golden Wonder Schindler's List.

The conversation turns to sport. Anna casually announces that she popped over to watch the beach volleyball at the Olympics a few years ago. "At Horse Guards at London 2012?" I check. "No, Rio 2016," she says matter-of-factly. Then Elle arrives and everyone frankly goes over the top in their arm-waving, hugging, kissing and general squealing. Someone trapped in a cave for several days would greet their rescuer with less enthusiasm than I've just witnessed being expended on Elle's arrival.

So, dear reader, what links this month's cast in order of appearance: Hannah, Anna, Eve and Elle? It's just a pity my friend Bob wasn't there too.

"Selfie palindrome people!" I announce, and then lose the moment by failing to press the right button on my phone for taking a selfie of our table. "What?" says Eve, inelegantly.

"You know… your names are all spelt the same backwards as well as forwards," I explain.

"Are they? I didn't notice that before," says Eve - colossally unimpressed. "Is your name a palin…" "…drome?" finishes Anna for her. "Yeah, my name's Richard Drahcir." Nobody laughs. They go back to talking about beach volleyball. With my humiliation pretty much confirmed, I start helping myself to some of Eve's abandoned crisps.

Hey, didn't I just say NOT to skip to the last line for the ending reveal?! Dammit, I'm mad. (Yeah, that's another one!)

I relay the above story to a late arriving Hannah as she gets her breath back. She's very clever. So clever she can afford to willingly admit possessing blind spots in her knowledge. "I thought a 'Palindromic name' was from Monty Python," she tells me. "Really?" I check, expecting her eyes to flash with rascality. "Yeah, I used to think it described a character played by Michael Palin." This strikes me as unlikely, but her body language conveys her sincerity.

A waitress brings over our milkshakes. Hannah slides the yellow drink across the table towards me and says: "Yo, banana boy!" Told you she was clever!

THE RADIO 4 TODAY PROGRAMME APPEARANCE

It's still unreasonably early when the phone rings. This is confirmed by the red light on the cooker displaying 6.08am as I stumble downstairs dangerously pre-caffeine for decision making. This cannot be good news. People never ring you up this early on a landline.

Answering with a cautious "Hello?" the voice on the other end speaks quickly as if to indicate (a) he's a very busy person (b) it's not early as he's evidently been up for ages. "It's BBC Radio 4's *Today* programme here," he begins.

This perturbs me. I'd read that their audience figures were in decline - apparently listeners had been migrating to other channels because of the programme's increasingly combative style. And, you know, what with all the bad news in the world. Though even John Humphrys' biggest critic would probably be reluctant to pin responsibility for all the world's travails personally on him. And if you did, you could expect to be interrupted.

But I'm surprised they're now taking the labour intensive approach of cold calling their listeners to check if they're currently tuned-in. I consider offering an excuse: "I was going to switch on the radio later. I promise." This, however, is not the subject they're calling about.

"Can you come on the *Today* programme? We'll send a car." "Er… yes," the 20% of my brain that isn't still asleep replies. "When do you want me to appear?" I ask, hoping the date will be a sufficient number of months away to allow me to be wholly prepped on whatever subject I am to pontificate about to a hastily breakfasting nation while John Humphrys sledges me. "Today," they reply. I suppose there is slight clue in the programme's title.

A friend of mine once appeared on *Newsnight* while Jeremy Paxman reclined in his chair snarling contempt and metaphorically flicking his bogies at him. So traumatised was he by the event that he's refused to ever appear on TV or radio since - the fact that he's never been asked in no way undermines the relevance of his boycott.

"In about an hour," they reply. "If we send a car can you be in the BBC Oxford studio by 8am?" "Err… yeah, why not?" I reply. The 80% of my brain that's still slumbering would be able to answer that "why not?" question in some considerable detail. But when you're asleep or drunk, you'll agree to basically anything. "Fancy swimming the English Channel tomorrow, Richard?" "Yeah, why not? Pick me up at 3am." Remembering that you can't actually swim comes later. Specifically at 5am the next morning when someone unscrews the lid on a jar of goose fat.

I should come clean here and reveal this happened to me exactly as I'm reporting, only five years ago. There's been a bit of a press curfew on this story ever since and here it's being lifted. You see I had inadvertently caused a media storm. Or media cyclone. It involved a national newspaper critic and one of my movie scripts. Let's leave it at that.

Radio 4 rings back. "We've got a car coming to you." "I'm very sorry, but I can't go on now." "Why not?" Because I'm terrified of John Humphrys (he hadn't retired then). I'll get humiliated by professional presenters relishing gladiatorial debates whilst I'm a shy writer.

Ten minutes later they ring again. Initially I stare at the phone ringing as persistently as Humphrys' questioning. "We can mention your new book," says the researcher, like a drug dealer outside a school offering your first hit for free. "I'll call back my producer for advice," I say. The producer counsels against it. He recounts a story where a colleague was invited onto the *Today* programme under a similar promise to discuss his new book, then ambushed like a mouse following the "Free cheese this way" signs erected by a group of hungry cats.

Ten minutes later they call yet again. This time it's one of the well-known presenters, not a researcher or production assistant. My wife answers the phone. "Oh, hello, it's you!" she says, before adding, "I like you." "Err… oh… thank you," he says, genuinely taken aback. That's how you flummox a *Today* programme presenter. Take note politicians.

"It's that bloke off the radio," she says, and hands me the phone. "Look, we'll put you on just before 9am and you can participate in a general discussion." I decline.

Later that day BBC Radio 5 live call. Their approach to broadcasting appears more convivial and we agree to an interview.

They ask me: "What book by another author do you wish you'd written?" This is a difficult question at any time, and I can report it is especially hard when you receive it on live national radio. "Hmmm…" I ponder. "Yes?" the presenter encourages, eyes darting at the studio clock. "*The Highway Code*," I answer. "That's an unusual choice," he says somewhat startled. "Why that one?" "Have you seen the author royalties on that book?"

POLAROID PARANOID - A NEGATIVE IMAGE OF MUSEUMS

Visiting a museum is about the closest you can get to time travel - at least in a town centre during a lunch hour.

Since my friend Rebecca and I are ardent time-travellers, we're taking in a museum's special exhibition. 'Special' in a museum context means 'you have to pay' whereas all the other (in my view, just as special) exhibitions are free.

Of late I've noticed a tendency for a 'special' exhibition to be prefixed with another intensifying addition: 'blockbuster'. A few weeks earlier I had attended a 'blockbuster special' exhibition in London. The website was very specific about advance purchasing timed tickets or risk 'substantial disappointment' at not gaining admittance. Once inside there were exactly five other people. Two of whom worked there.

Entering through the impractical tall 30-feet high front door - sensibly installed to cater for anyone bringing their pet giraffe - we arrive in the museum foyer. A friendly greeter welcomes us and instructs us where to find the 'blockbuster special' exhibition. On the right we spot a brolly safe. This impresses Rebecca. "Wow, they've got a brolly safe. That's amazing." Told you she was impressed. She locks her brolly and takes a numbered tag, with the effulgent look of someone who's realised their life has just peaked.

Prudently she has booked ahead online. Even more prudently she has printed our two tickets double-sided, thereby utilising only one piece of paper.

"Saving the rainforest?" says our ticket-tearer cheerfully. We nod smugly. "Can we take a photograph of the exhibition's poster title for social media publicity?" asks Rebecca.

"Yes, of course. It's immediately inside."

Outside the exhibition the staff are charming, well informed and smartly attired. Inside the exhibition the staff are smartly attired.

"You can't take photographs!" barks an attendant once we are three millimetres inside the exhibition room.

Sensing a particularly deep breath is required for the forthcoming negotiations, Rebecca draws one. Careful to present a smile - whereas my instinct would be to scan the room for improvised weaponry should it all inevitably kick off - Rebecca asks a question. "So have I been misinformed by the previous member of staff?" Thereby deliberately providing an opportunity for a score draw.

Simply admit 'yes', say an apology you don't mean, and everyone can get on with their unruined day. Then Rebecca can re-sheath her camera allowing both parties to depart with a point each. But no. Escalation is to be the option chosen.

"There is to be no photography!" she pronounces like Moses with a PA system, only more portentously. Fair enough. But is it necessary to orate it with the maddened bluster of someone addressing an agitated rally in pre-war Nuremberg? Presumably a large determining appeal of applying for this job was the fact it came with a uniform. Though disappointment must have quickly followed for some successful candidates upon discovering there was no accompanying armband or jackboots.

"All we're doing is attempting to photograph the exhibition title so we can publicise it on social media. For the museum," Rebecca explains. Yes, we understand if they prefer punters not to take pictures of the exhibits. The distraction is off-putting to others. Some artworks may be damaged by flashes. We comprehend that. That's why, I reiterate, we have no intention of photographing anything but the exhibition sign. On behalf of promoting the museum.

They ignore me. I wonder if I'm still set on mute - as they evidently can't hear me - but remember that's only an option for my phone and, alas, not human beings. Nevertheless I ponder checking my settings since I seem to experience this same problem at home too where my wife regularly ignores everything I say.

"But we just wanted to take a picture of the exhibition sign only," reasons Rebecca. The staff dig in their heels - which at least makes a change from clicking them. One uniformed worker's tone makes it very clear: if an issued firearm came with this uniform, then I'd shoot you - and that would definitely be allowed.

Punching air holes of humility into their stuffiness, Rebecca curtails negotiations. She puts away her phone camera and gives an emollient smile, generously given the staff have been so thumpingly rude.

Frankly we're both big fans of museums - particularly this one. So neither Rebecca nor I are about to make enemies. It perpetually amazes me how much time and effort people are prepared to invest in creating foes - such industry rarely provides benefits.

However, just as we believe the altercation is over, one of the guards' radios crackles into life. Another uniformed official has been summoned. I'm not used to being in trouble with uniformed officials at my age. For an uncomfortable moment I suspect we're going to get ejected or arrested. Or frogmarched to a cold store room where the only amusement will be throwing a ball against a wall before we start digging a tunnel with a spoon.

On the plus side, being banned from a museum would represent a significant cultural boost for me. The only other place I'm currently banned from in my unadventurous life is the Princeton University Library. Yeah, should I ever be incarcerated I really am the reputational bad boy of fellow lags and surely qualify in the prison pecking order for first dibs on the smuggled snout.

The reason for my Princeton Library ban? It relates to an incident with a particularly amorous anglophile Canadian girl called Rachel in 1996 behind bookshelf 612.6 (that's one for any Dewey Classification code fans). That's the 'Biology - Human Physiology - Reproduction' section for any non-librarians.

No, I'm not prepared to offer further details. Besides, all we did was just get a bit handsy with each other, a quick kiss-and-not-tell (she had a boyfriend in Quebec - who was French, so his likely definition of fidelity was attempting not to sleep with any women outside the northern hemisphere.) Anyway, it was entirely Princeton's fault for selling beer so cheaply in the college bar.

Although I often start sentences with "When I was at Princeton…", in reality I was only ever a visitor. A friend who left University College, Oxford with a 1st gained a postgraduate place there and invited me to stay with him. Once installed in New Jersey's famous pedagogical institution I met friendly academics (and even friendly Canadian Masters students) who'd invite me to functions, lectures and tutorials, allowing me to kind of drift into becoming an unofficial student for a fortnight in a way that was both welcoming but insensibly lax. I sense it wouldn't happen nowadays.

And I fear that I'm now about to have a museum added to my list of prestigious institutions where I'm banned. Because in Oxford they're fond of administering bans.

There's an Oxford story which the person who recounted it to me swears is true. Around the turn of the millennium an undergraduate was doing what undergraduates sometimes have a proclivity for doing: acting like a prat. Subsequently he was informed that he was banned from the Botanic Garden "for ten years".

Since he was celebrating the end of his Finals and therefore finished with exams and, crucially, Oxford, for good, this was hardly deemed much of a practical punishment. Fully seven years later he returned to Oxford with his parents to attend his younger sister's graduation.

Afterwards his family suggested a leisurely stroll through Britain's oldest purpose-built physic garden. "NO YOU DON'T," snapped an official on the gate, "it's still too soon!" Please, please may that story be true.

"Do you receive negotiation training?" Rebecca asks as unsarcastically as possible - which turns out to still be quite sarcastic - when the uniformed official summoned by the radio marches towards us with the look of someone used to breaking the Geneva Convention.

"Will you stop taking photos?" he says to me by way of a greeting. "No," I say mutinously, before pointing out I haven't got a camera. Thus rendering the question more surreal than unnecessary - like a traffic warden yelling at a bemused pedestrian that he "can't park there!"

"It's the female who was attempting to take photographs of the exhibits, Sir," says the original uniformed official. Rebecca corrects him politely, pointing out again it was the exhibition sign only that she was attempting to publicise. For them.

"There's no photography allowed," repeats the new official in an emotionless tone. At this stage I consider walking behind him and checking his back for tell-tell wires.

We escape without a ban. On the way out I take a paparazzi-type grab shot of the large sign curtly proclaiming "No Photography" and post it on Twitter. Yeah, I did have a camera on me - albeit concealed in my bag. Afterwards, in the chinking calm of the museum's inevitable tea shop, I show my illicit photo to Rebecca.

She agrees with my offered hypothesis that posting a picture on social media depicting the museum's "No Photography" sign with the accompanying hashtag #FuckYouMuseum may be deemed ungracious. "Excuse me," I say, "I just need to delete a tweet."

Yet the No Photo Nazis are everywhere. A couple of years ago I met up with the comedian Mark Steel for lunch and we embarked on a very long walk around Oxford with the principal aim of researching material for his show about the city. At his request I took a photo of him outside the Oxford Union, which in turn he asked the venue he was gigging at that evening to project onto the safety curtain pre-show.

Fully twenty minutes BEFORE the show started, I took a photo of the curtain projecting my photo. "No photographs!" shouted a woman running towards me with less urgency than if I had been attempting to abduct her child.

Calmly and politely, I pointed out that I took the photo myself, hence I'm photographing my photograph. This cuts no ice, carries no weight nor butters any parsnips. Realising this isn't a battle the world needs to win, I re-sheathed my camera and conceded yet another unjust and humiliating defeat in a series of unjust and humiliating defeats that will only ever end with my death.

Encountering people like this reinforces my belief that the human race was greenlit for development prematurely before the prototype was properly perfected. Hence God really ought to announce a product recall.

Just over a week later I'm scrolling through a local news website. There's a report on the preview night for guests and VIPs attending the very same exhibition that Rebecca and I had been so nearly ejected from. I know this because of the 18... EIGHTEEN!... featured photographs of attendees snapped in the room!

HALF-TERM MEMORY LOSS

Just as the Eurostar slides out of the station, my friend leans back and luxuriates in contemplation of her holiday ahead. With the drab grey North London skyline beginning to blur out of focus as the train smoothly accelerates towards the promise of unbroken blue skies, her teenage daughter unpops a white headphone from each ear.

This action would shock many who know her by proving that her earphones are removable. An act of surprise she immediately encores by doing something even more uncharacteristic. Something she has rarely done in three years since metamorphosing from the chrysalis of childhood to emerge flapping her wings enthusiastically towards teenage recalcitrance: converse with her parents.

"Who's going to feed Moby all week if we're in France?" asks the teenager.

Her mother, anxious not to bridle at this unwelcome information and emit discouraging signs when her daughter is actually speaking with her, contemplates her response carefully. She wants to appear calm, thereby selecting a response consistent with fanning and not snuffling conversation. But after a lengthy search she can only find one reply:

"Who the hell is Moby?"

"My new pet," she replies incredulously. After a few minutes of careful interrogation, and at least two attempts to pop her headphones back in averted, her parents elicit the following information from their enquiries: Moby is a goldfish. He was bought, with bowl and aerator, from a school friend, five days ago. "You didn't think about this feeding dilemma before we left England?"

She contemplates this question before calmly answering, "No," with a suffixed "your point being?" tonally implied. "Besides, I fed him this morning. He won't need feeding again until tomorrow." Her mother considers whether it really is necessary to give a surly 16-year-old a lesson in how time works and point out that a week is longer than a day.

Plumes of silent anger rise above her mother's head like smoke billowing from a steam locomotive.

As the train remerges from subterranea, both dry land and a phone signal returns. Her mother taps an urgent text to me in Oxford. Expediently I had been left a door key. This has become procedure whenever they go away because of the multitude of requirements discovered during previous absences. Hair curlers, dishwasher, TV and immersion heater have all previously been left on during half-term breaks. This left door key has hit Southern Electric shareholders' dividends hard.

With the English countryside exchanged for a French one, two hundred miles further south I read the newly arrived email aloud to my wife. "You won't believe this, but are you able to feed a fish every day that we didn't know we had?"

24 hours later my wife and I creep up our near neighbour's creaking stairs feeling like burglars. We are standing outside the teenager's room - identified from a forbidding sign declaring: "Keep Out!!"

We notice that we're both whispering even though the house is empty. "I'm not comfortable entering a teenager's bedroom," I say to my wife. "Nor am I," she replies, "but we have to. It's literally a matter of life or death. Besides, do you want to face her retribution if Moby dies on your watch?"

"Relax," I say, unleashing a plan, "I can just replace Moby with a slice of carrot. Or go to a pet shop and buy a replacement." Though apparently sitcom solutions don't work that well when transplanted into the real world. Oh.

I realise that I am quite scared of her - the teenager as well as my wife.

Pushing open the door meets with resistance. Her room has been booby-trapped with piles of discarded clothes and neglected make-up bags.

"Oh, she's got a great wardrobe," says my wife. "Yeah, so why has she opted to store most of her outfits all over the floor?" Fewer clothes are flung on Black Friday at Primark than in this bedroom.

I unscrew the orange fish food container to reveal there is only sufficient to last Moby two feeds! Hence I am forced to bike to a pet store on Botley Road. Googling "How to feed a goldfish" ensures I avoid over-feeding Moby - apparently one of the most common causes of death for a pet fish.

Six days later there is a timid knock at the door. "Thanks for keeping Moby alive," says the returning teenager, presenting us with a bottle of French white wine. "That's really nice of her," says my wife after the teenager has departed, "but I'd better check with her mother in case she was meant to give us a bottle of red AND white. Like last time - when she only brought us one bottle."

DEATH IN THE AFTERNOON

"Stop! It'll take your head off!" screams a man in a high-vis jacket and a hard hat. Possibly at me.

My panicky brain searches for context. Why is this man shouting such an agitated warning? Is he discouraging me from eating wasabi or am I in imminent danger of decapitation? Should I duck?

"It'll cut your head off!" he shouts. Yeah, seems ducking may be a good option.

Perhaps there's a cannon ball on the way? Has a second English Civil War finally started as the only way to resolve Brexit?

At this stage I identify the intended recipient of his macabre warnings: a cyclist determined not to respect the authority of a 'Stop' and 'Go' man. As I'm walking along the pavement, a cyclist on the road has dropped his shoulders and surged through the roadblock. Outraged, the roadworker has involuntarily swivelled his 'Stop' sign to green while arrowing insults at the cyclist's back while the latter furiously pedals away.

My wife, with whom I'm conducting a phone conversation, asks me what the shouting is about. And instantly thinks I'm both the justification and the recipient.

"There's a bit of a commotion going on," I say, instantly realising how antiquated my vocabulary makes me sound. I might as well have popped my monocle back in and added, "There's a hullabaloo and a brouhaha," seizing my chance to give two of the English language's most unpleasingly abandoned words an airing. "A what?" my wife responds. "There's been an altercation," I say. "Oh, I understand now," she says, artificially determined to prove she doesn't speak 'old'.

"Well it's a good job you've got your helmet and high-vis." She's forgotten that I decided to get the bus today and not cycle. Yet my wife maintains an almost superstitious belief that wearing high-vis and a helmet will ensure I'm permanently protected. Not just from bike accidents but seemingly all forms of danger. Including iron girders. Because the latter has been the reason for Stop/Go Man's shouting.

The road (Walton Street) had been briefly closed while a crane unloaded a swinging girder. It could have killed the cyclist instantaneously. He was probably a student, maybe only 18 or 19 years old. Perhaps in his first year at Oxford. Like most students he was doubtless full of life, hope, ambition, promise and potential, and Pot Noodle. Someone unafraid to use an Oxford comma. Yet he could have gone, his life snuffed out like a candle in a draught on Elton John's piano. His library books destined never to be returned. And all because he wanted to save ten seconds by not waiting at a 'Stop' sign.

Conceivably he didn't know why he did it either. Everyone likes to stitch together arbitrary incidents into sense-making narratives, even when there's really nothing but flummoxing randomness. Stories buttressed by our human need to impose meaning onto the world.

Witnessing the altercation between Stop/Go Man and the student affects my mood throughout the afternoon, prompting me to ruminate on the fragility of life.

It reminded me of the time I stood at a zebra crossing with a group of strangers. The light turned green. We started to cross, putting our trust in colour coded technology. Then the deep roar of an approaching car engine signified it had no intention of slowing down. Someone screamed. We all returned to our starting place. But I required someone else to do it first before I followed. I was prepared to die but not prepared to look uncool.

My takeaway message from the experience? That my brain conforms to normality. It does what most others are engaged in doing around it and replicates their behavioural patterns. And it certainly pattern matches to 'green = safe to cross' and that's it. Lazily it's not prepared to consider other possibilities. The bit of my brain responsible for alerting me to danger knocks off round the back of my cortex for a fag break whenever it sees green. Yeah, it's enough to make you see red.

We were a random group of cosmic strangers floating through time and space who just happened to all meet together fleetingly for one isolated moment - kerbside on a pelican crossing. And yet we now shared this incredible bonding experience - we nearly all died together in this unremarkable place. I'm not ready to die yet. Who is? But being English, we didn't acknowledge the moment other than by exchanging clichés awkwardly. "Phew that was a close shave. Thought our number was up there," remarked a man with a calmness unfitting to the situation.

My near death experience taught me that the urge to tell someone you love them is stronger than hate. That's why none of the doomed passengers on those hijacked 9/11 flights used their last message on earth to phone Dave from Accounts and inform him: "I always thought you were a bit of a twat." Instead they imparted messages of love.

The experience served as a reminder that we all take a turn riding on the relentless moving travelator of time. And to never underestimate the capacity of death to shock you. To those left behind its occurrence is a jolting reminder of our impermanence.

One of the reasons I bike everywhere instead of driving (other than the enforced lifestyle of abject monkish poverty one accepts when employed as a freelance writer) is that I always have a story. Cycling in Oxford is so dangerous that it's impossible to arrive anywhere on two wheels without a captivating anecdote about how I nearly died en route.

My latest swerve with death (or black Mazda) happened on Abingdon Road the very day after I had witnessed the student narrowly avoid decapitation. Having overtaken me, the car's driver immediately decided to turn left across me. I was wearing a high-vis jacket. It was sunny. If his guide dog had been driving he would have stuck a paw out the window to signal right as he pulled out to avoid me. But not this human driver. How could he not see me? How could you turn left directly across a cyclist you've just overtaken two seconds ago?

My breaks squeal like a gazelle in a lion's mouth. I thump into the Mazda's offside. The wing mirror hits my stomach. Thankfully the extra protective padding I've cautiously added over the last few years helps act as an impromptu air bag. There's an off-putting thud; it's the sound of my carcass hitting the tarmac. My bike carries on down the road a few metres without me, like it's anxious to escape the scene. As this point I try to speak. But discover I can't. It feels like all the air has left my body.

The driver is quickly out of the car and immediately apologetic. He constantly repeats "I'm very sorry" in a Polish accent. He asks me if I need an ambulance. A woman who is hugely pregnant sits on the passenger side observing me. She looks alarmed and flustered. If an ambulance arrives, it'll be a debate for the crew as to who needs it first.

She speaks to me in Polish through the driver: "Are you okay?" she ventriloquises through him. The truth is: I have no idea. My inability to speak is likely an indication that I'm not alright. After a while we both realise I'm winded. Eventually I stand up. My brain floods with survivor's euphoria. He picks up my bike. I apologise about his broken wing mirror - which he must have considered very English behaviour. He reassures me not to worry. He checks again if I'm okay. I decide to carry on. He drives off.

Then I discover we've caused a huge tailback. Someone starts hooting aggressively. That's always enormously helpful and constructive in an accident situation.

After inspecting the bike for roadworthiness I manage to cycle home, albeit with a few worrying creaks. Emitting from me and the bike. My wife applies a bag of frozen petits pois to my stomach area.

"Haven't we got a less middle-class option?" I ask. We haven't. "It's a good job you were wearing your helmet and high-vis," she says. Unlike my wife, I am not superstitious.

I decide against undermining her comforting superstition and point out that a helmet doesn't contribute much protection to your stomach. And that there are samba dancers in the Rio Carnival whose flamboyant costumes would render them just as invisible to the driver I encountered today. Had he overtaken a flashing lighthouse on a moonless night, he probably wouldn't have noticed that either.

By the next morning a colourful bruise has appeared. A proliferation of greens and blues ensures that my stomach resembles a page from an atlas. Otherwise I'm generally alright. Phew, I've survived. Though the pain continues for several days.

I'm not superstitious. Touch wood.

LIKE A FRIDGE OVER TROUBLED DAUGHTERS

There are several jobs deemed sufficiently important by their practitioners to advertise a 24-hour service. Fire brigade, doctors and police are all fairly contained within this category. There are also 24-hour emergency plumbers and glaziers, as you never know when someone may throw a toilet through a window. There is even an advert for a 24-hour deli to placate anyone discovering they're out of bay leaves at 3am.

Admittedly I have never seen my own profession - freelance writer - belonging to this category of twenty-four hour necessity. Until now.

I am contacted by a man phoning me at 6.48am. He sounds like a Russian meerkat. Plus he has a quaintly endearing verbal ploy of omitting the indefinite article from all his sentences, as if the Russian meerkats were actually Yorkshiremen. "What is rate of pay for writer?"

He is self-employed and hoping to make a cheap local radio advert. Put off by the prices of agencies already approached, he has been persuaded by the internet to have a go at making an advert himself.

For this he needs a writer who can "how you say, make story the funny." It's probably just spectacularly bad luck that his first permitted use of the definite article in a sentence transpires to be grammatically incorrect.

"I have friend. She recommend you." Teasingly, he doesn't reveal the identity of this mutual friend, so I scan my memory for any female meerkats that I know. We arrange for me to visit his house. He asks if I can come at 8am. We settle on 10am.

Just as we have both purposefully hinged open our laptops, the doorbell rings. "Man on phone said visit was arranged between 1pm-5pm," says my host. "Sorry, sir," says a man in a blue semi-uniform and a name badge, "we try our best to stick within the provided time parameters but sometimes extraneous circumstances can cause inevitable alteration." A prepared parroted response that is only slightly undermined by the fact it's barely 10am.

"This is man from water company to check why bills so high," my host informs me. "This man is writer," he says to the uniformed man. We're both unsure whether this constitutes an introduction and we should now acknowledge each other. Waterman chooses not to say "Hello writer," so I don't reciprocate.

Waterman asks my host a series of questions which are so enervating his sentences risk collapsing before he finishes them. "Do you ever fill the kettle?" "I fill kettle six times a day." He's not going to repeat the 'the'. "Do you sometimes boil more water than is used?" he asks, anxious to establish a forensic level of kettle usage.

His questions, so obviously learnt from a prepared yet crushingly unimaginative script, are delivered with the jaded reluctance of a soap actor aware he's shortly being written out of the show - so why bother continuing with this acting malarkey? Other questions are so blindingly obvious that he might as well as have asked: "Do you ever turn taps on?", "What's the predominant colour of grass?" He's the world's easiest quizmaster.

Noticeably the most significant piece of information is volunteered rather than resulting from questioning. "My two daughters use all shower water." Waterman's curiosity is poked, like a fisherman's reaction to a float suddenly dipping in the water. Instantly he's now in full Colombo mode, pacing the kitchen, occasionally turning to address an imaginary jury. My role as a typist on the corner table presumably replicates the part of court stenographer in his courtroom fantasy.

"How long are your daughters in the shower?" "Well, older one takes 30 minutes every day." "I think, sir, that your daughter's shower usage may well be the main contributory reason for your high water bills." Ya think? Sherlock without excrement.

Waterman pops to his van and returns with a water reducing shower head. "This should do the trick."

"You're sure it is not caused by leak?" "No, sir."

"Would you like cup of tea?" "Just a small one, please," he replies with admiral dedication to his water-saving ethos." Our host fills the kettle to the brim for one cup. "We do not have milk as fridge broke yesterday. New fridge comes today. Black tea?" "It'll have to be black, then," concedes waterman begrudgingly.

Our host has one last parting act of eccentricity. "Please stand against wall. I wish to take photograph." "Really… err, why?" says a visibly flummoxed waterman. "Then I tell daughters this man from water company wish you to stop using so much shower water." After replicating the conditions of a police station mugshot, waterman flees the scene, his black tea untouched. I hear him drive off at speed, after reversing out of the driveway with such indecent haste he cannot possibly have checked for on-coming traffic.

"You've been busy typing." "Yes," I say. "Can I have a look?" "Er… not yet," I say panicking, and close my laptop. Because, dear reader, I have just typed the basis of what you have read. And not yet any ideas for a ridiculously cheap radio advert devoid of definite articles.

THE GIRL WITH THE GRAMMAR TABOO

"The weather forecaster just iterated it'll rain later," says my wife over a rushed breakfast. This remark impresses and confuses me equally. I can't recall ever hearing someone express their intention 'to iterate' before. Everybody always 're-iterates', but she's going to give iterating a try first, before presumably an inevitable re-iteration later. Well done her. "Good vocab usage," I say. "Shut up," says my wife, "I'm just saying it's going to rain." Thereby re-iterating her initial iteration.

This launches a discussion about superfluous word usage. A doubling of redundant words meaning the same thing is known as a tautology. Risking being late for the bus to work, we set about listing as many redundant prefixes as we can: tuna fish, safe haven, free gift, wept tears, venal politician (okay, not always the last one).

And then there's the most used unnecessary word of them all. Albeit one that stands alone: 'literally'. Which is the most superfluously - and incorrectly - used adverb of them all. Literally.

It doesn't take long to prove this point. A few minutes later I'm on an early morning bus into town. Two schoolgirls behind me keep using the word 'literally' like an aural comma. Literally twenty times in as many minutes. One of them deploys it to emphasise virtually every remark. "That's literally so unfair," she bellows to her nodding friend, speaking at a volume normally reserved for addressing a public meeting after a fault with the PA system, "'cos by lunchtime I'll be literally starving."

Unburdened by grammatical self-awareness they continue their chirruping. The cause of her literal outrage? Chantenay carrots have been packed in her lunchbox. "I've told my mum these are, like, literally disgusting." Her seat sharing companion has a 'literally' pronouncement of her own: "This bus is literally boiling." Yes it's hot and humid, yet unlikely to be 100 degrees Centigrade in the shade.

A few seconds later The Other Boiling Girl (you're welcome, Philippa Gregory) observes through a sigh: "This bus is, like, literally taking ages." Admittedly our bus is running slightly behind schedule but unless it departed the depot at some stage between the Precambrian period and thawing of the last Ice Age, then it literally is NOT taking ages. It literally, like, isn't.

Nonetheless it's early and the pair evidently plan a full day ahead of adverb abuse.

At the next stop four more uniformed schoolgirls bound upstairs and surround me at the front of the bus. Their voices replicate the high pitch trill of an aviary. Producing their phones, they begin twin-thumb texting, typing at the speed of courtroom stenographers.

What strikes me about them, above their volume and impressive typing speeds, is how they seem so effortlessly nonchalant. They possess the collective demeanour of someone utterly unthreatened by the world. Secure and confident in their right to speak and bloviate at ludicrous volume at an age when their hearing ability is likely to be the best it'll probably ever be.

Meanwhile I, someone with four decades more experience of life, feel less secure. My floating confidence unanchored by a functioning comprehension of the future. Maybe Dr Johnson was right and a life unexamined isn't worth living; but perhaps a life overexamined isn't worth the Council Tax either. After all, aren't kids nowadays supposed to have too many tests and exams? Burdened with intolerable anxiety? Yet they appear so at ease with today. Giggling, laughing, shrieking. So demonstrably alive. Like someone determined to try all the ice cream flavours of life in one parlour visit. Or maybe that's just the inevitable post-sugar-rush talking.

Rain begins hitting the bus windows. My wife was right to both iterate and reiterate earlier. Another schoolgirl ascends the stairs then shakes her wet hair violently - just like dogs do on reaching the river bank after a dip. One of them produces a travel coffee mug. I guess this would establish her age as at least sixteen. Is there a legal age limit to sell coffee? If you stroll into Starbucks does someone say: "Oi, I ain't serving you without ID!"

The girls' chat flits from topic to topic busily, like bees hoovering the gossip and laughs out of every conversational flower they visit. Then it's quickly onto another cross-pollenated subject. Then another. It's fickle and unsubstantial - but that's 16-year-olds for you.

When I was their age I recall being worried rigor mortis-stiff. Worried about if anyone liked me, if a nice girl would ever go out with me, how I was supposed to get a job when the point of school appeared to be providing a daily reminder than I was useless at everything and therefore unaccomplished to do anything upon leaving the institution. You hear of some people writing letters 30 years later to their teenage selves, reassuring them everything will turn out alright; at least 30 years offers a delivery window Royal Mail could feasibly hit.

At the next stop more schoolkids embark. As I make a mental note never to catch a bus at this time ever again, I'm aware that the decibel level has suddenly dropped. A comparative silence descends over the top deck, like a ceasefire at the frontline.

I look around for the cause of this unexpected stillness. The reason for the abrupt hush is easy to deduce. Every girl has got her phone out and is staring at it like a hypnotist's watch.

I don't comprehend bamboozling emojis; given we have 26 characters in the English language that have seemed perfectly adequate for expressing every human thought in history up until this point. William Shakespeare didn't think: "Yeah my sonnets are okay, but if only I could have scribed: "Should I compare thee to a summer's day? Sun emoji. Aubergine emoji. #SoUpForIt #CU46 #BigWillieShake #Want SomeGreatnessThrustUponThou?"

In our day if you wanted to do a smiley face to accompany your message you had to get in your car, drive round the recipient's house, find a parking space, ring their doorbell and, when they bemusedly answered, grin insanely at them.

Nowadays there is a mystifying selection of emojis including - and millennials will know this - an aubergine emoji as the international symbol for sex. In the past you had to carry an actual aubergine around with you - and then present it to someone you fancied. And then ask them to use it to cook a nice moussaka. Alas they were more sexist times.

Should I want to express a sexual interest in someone these days I have to rummage in my bag and show them a cumbersome aubergine. No, I have no idea either why an aubergine has become the international symbol in the emoji language for sex. It certainly makes purchasing the ingredients for a moussaka mined with social trickiness.

Suddenly the typing pool ceases and the girls get back to their other preferred pastime: shouting the words 'literally' and 'like' at each other. One girl opens her mouth dentist-wide to exclaim: "That's, like, literally the oldest thing ever."

My stop is approaching so I reach for the bell. Pressing it doesn't produce the 'tring, tring' I was expecting. Then I realise why: audibility is impossible. The girls' decibel level can be recreated by sticking your head into the speaker stack at a Motorhead gig at the exact moment a squadron of Vulcan bombers perform a flypast.

But I see the red light reassuringly illuminating 'Bus stopping'. I make my way to the stairs. At this point something truly disturbing happens, nearly making me fall down the staircase.

I feel human contact on my left shoulder. Shocked, I turn around. One of the 16-year-olds has infringed my personal space and touched me. Awks. Am I going to be attacked by a pack of feral teenagers who respect no laws of syntax?

"Is this yours?" she asks, tugging my arm. She's wearing a smart blazered uniform somehow accessorized with a tie-knot the size of Anglesey.

Instantly she thrusts a folded-up black object in front of my face. It takes a couple of seconds, but I eventually recognise it. I can relax as it's a gesture made in peace. She's holding my umbrella. The very same brolly that I had just absentmindedly left on my seat.

I thank her profusely. She says "cool." Then instantly she is back with her friends giggling obliviously. Thankfully I conclude they're not laughing at my expense. I'm no longer in the scene. That's fair enough. I had the briefest of cameos in their world. But for a mere three seconds we'd found a tear between the separated parallel worlds of juvenescence and adulthood. It felt like having a meaningful interaction with a ghost or chatting with an animal - an experience resigned to impossibility and, besides, no-one would believe you afterwards when recounting it anyway.

I experience a glow of gratitude mixed with a reassurance that today's kids are going to turn out to be fine. We can trust them with the future after all. Not that we really have any choice.

That evening I enthusiastically inform my wife: "I had an interaction with a schoolgirl on the bus today," I begin. Unwisely, as it transpires.

"I hope you didn't, as I can't afford to pay the mortgage if you're in prison." "Not funny!" I say.

Realising the situation calls for some solemnity, she eventually asks: "What did you talk about, then?"

"A teenager on the bus gave me my umbrella back."

"Did you have to pay a ransom?" asks my wife.

"No, I forgot it. I mean the brolly, not the r…" "Yes, I gathered that," interrupts my wife.

"I left it on my seat. She kindly dashed along the top deck to give it back to me before I disembarked."

"That was good of her," she says. "It was," I agree, "as I really needed that umbrella today with those heavy downpours." "You've just used a tautology," points out my wife with the officious mannerism of an athletics official holding up a red flag. I adopt my customary blank expression. "Heavy downpours - the first word is redundant," she, er, iterates. "Yes it is," I re-iterate, "literally."

THE STUDENT BODY ART HEIST

I'm sitting in a tiny café balancing a tiny espresso cup on a tiny table. Unless my thimble-sized coffee is one of Alice's 'Drink Me' potions responsible for suddenly transforming me into a giant, my unusual perspective is hardly unforeseeable. After all I've been to this miniscule coffee shop before. It's akin to being in a hotel room with a microscopic kettle and sink serving as an optical illusion to make the room appear larger.

Which is all a bit weird. But not as weird as what's about to happen. Before I depart this café I'm implicated in a major art heist.

"It's time they moved to some bigger premises," foghorns a student at such volume that she's audible to me sitting five tables away - which, to be fair, constitutes a distance of only about nine feet. However, I agree with her choice of sentiment if not volume. Every time I come here I vow never to return as it's just too exasperatingly small and packed with students using it as a JCR overflow.

She has an unflattering dart-shaped chunky piercing in her right ear that looks like she was the victim of some horrendous crossbow accident. And rather than having to endure a tiresome wait at A&E simply concluded, "You know what - I'll keep it in my ear."

Piercing Girl is also festooned with tattoos. On a cold day she has rolled up her sleeves to show off a gallery of body art. Like so many Premiership footballers, this gives the appearance of someone having inexpertly doodled on their arms with a biro.

Unburdened by self-awareness, Piercing Girl and her equally loud student companion continue chirruping while I google: "Where to buy ear defenders?"

"I can't believe we have to do collections," she grumps. For those unfamiliar with Oxford parlance, 'collections' are exams. "Yeah it's, like, absolutely stupid," confirms her friend. "How can they expect me to remember stuff from, like, a year ago?" Piercing Girl wails in extravagant self-pity. "That's, like, er, like…" it's obvious to the rest of us in the café that an erudite simile is not about to be forthcoming… ."like, stupid," adds her friend after an interminable delay.

Fleetingly I catch the face of the only other person in the room who is approaching my age and thus outwardly not a student. Although a stranger, he is sitting uncomfortably close to me - as there's nowhere to sit that doesn't constitute that description. We share a "We Pay Taxes" look - though with his neatly parted jet black hair and suspiciously white teeth he looks a little like Jimmy Carr, so he probably doesn't.

Catering for pedants, the café displays a chalk sign proclaiming that coffee beans are not beans but cherries. This is correct. Pre-roasted coffee beans... er, cherries... are dark red, sweet and a close relative of the edible red fruit that we put on top of cakes to illustrate visual metaphors. There's also an errant possessive apostrophe on the sign. I contemplate approaching the counter to grammar-shame them.

At one point Piercing Girl broadcasts to the café: "Beggars can't be choosers." Although, I think to myself, if you offer a beggar a can of Special Brew or a can of Strongbow and state they can only take one, then via this experimental method it is possible to prove beggars *can* be choosers. QED.

"Yeah it's, like, absolutely stupid," says her loyal sidekick - very much a Bunny to her Raffles, or a Penfold to her Dangermouse. I'm beginning to wonder if her friend is broken, and consider looking for a string in her back that, if I pull to a different length, may finally result in her saying a new phrase.

Piercing Girl's look is completed with ankle boots, a lumberjack shirt with rolled-up sleeves, black leggings containing multiple 'designed' slashes and a purple hat. Admittedly I don't know anything about fashion, but I'm beginning to suspect she doesn't either. Perhaps students now have a random clothing generator app on their phones. Wardrobe choices on shuffle. Maybe tomorrow she will select tutu and diving boots augmented with one of those fruit hats you see at carnival time? It's a combination that Vivienne Westwood would think: "Actually, that's too weird even for me. I'll pop back home and change."

Despite Piercing Girl's best efforts to sabotage her natural attractiveness - if the fashion police ever catch up with her then she's probably looking at a long stretch in solitary - she doesn't need all these style-chasing adornments. Even though she is noticeably suffering from rosacea. This reminds me of my own acne bouts as a late teenager and how cruel nature's timing can be. The age when the young first leave home, possess independence and can seriously get into the opposite sex (other genders are available) coincides with the same moment that acne unfairly erupts across their faces like lunar craters. Perhaps it's nature's way of ensuring chastity - or at least not keeping the lights on.

Eventually the two students get up. This takes longer than you might think, since the café is so small that the table and chair moving required to reach the exit resembles one of those sliding puzzles - you know, the ones where you have to slide squares into place with only one empty space to move prior to arranging an overall picture. After fully two minutes they create a route to the café's door. Piercing Girl's sidekick emits a sigh and wanders off despondently. No doubt she has a hard afternoon ahead of her, constantly repeating her catchphrase: "That's, like, absolutely stupid."

Then one of the aproned café workers gestures towards me. Priding myself on not being solipsistic, I decide she must be acknowledging someone else. But she keeps looking directly at me. Yet given how compressed everyone is in occupying this ludicrously small café I decide her line of eye contact comfortably takes in about twenty people. She then ducks underneath the counter and starts approaching me. Obviously this manoeuvre takes several minutes to travel the necessary twelve feet, with a cacophony of "excuse mes," "coming throughs," "sorrys," "if you could just…" accompanied by countless "thank yous".

Then she speaks to me. And only me. "Sorry to trouble you. But we've just realised that something has gone missing." 'Missing' is unavoidably a euphemism for 'stolen'.

This, I admit, flummoxes me.

"I just wondered if you saw anyone taking a picture off the wall?" She points to a portion of empty wall I'm sitting beneath.

Even though the wall is painted completely white, I still scan all of it in case the picture was maybe three feet to the left and they'd missed it. Yes, I admit now that seems unlikely.

"Er… no. What picture?" is all I can think to say.

"We just noticed that the picture hanging there has gone."

Suddenly I wonder if I'm under suspicion. Do I open my bag? Enquire how big was the picture? Ask what it depicts? Or check if it's an abstract? Is it valuable? Would they like to buy a picture I've just acquired for cash only?

Hopefully it'll be one of those huge canvases so they know I couldn't currently have it in my rucksack. "It's only a small picture," she says. Oh.

Only a tiny one? That makes sense, I think. Given that everything else in this place is in miniature.

"It's a landscape of a windmill above a cornfield. It's kind of cool."

You should ask everyone else, I think. Not just me. This makes me look like a suspect: a person of interest in their enquiries. Students cease their conversations and stare at me. "We didn't see anything and we've been here about ten minutes," says a man to my right. My very close right. Then I realise that by asking me, the waitress is in fact asking the entire tiny café.

Everyone concurs it's an appalling act to steal their painting. "Yeah, we really wouldn't expect it," she says. "It may have been taken yesterday. We've only just noticed," she admits. "That's terrible," I add, attempting to sound as sincerely outraged as possible. "Sorry to trouble you," she says. Ten minutes later she has successfully slalomed her way back behind the counter.

Yet I leave thinking that the cloud of suspicion hovering above my head hasn't been completely removed by the gathering breeze of my expressed outrage.

"That's, like, absolutely stupid," I say to myself, realising I must have just caught a speech virus from Piercing Girl's sidekick. Then I have a Columbo one-more-thing moment. Maybe the best way to camouflage yourself amongst a group of students dressed as loudly as they're conversing… is to make yourself as loud and noticeable as possible. Counterintuitive, yes, but also potentially genius. Could Piercing Girl and her Bunny really be international art thieves? Nah, I think, that's, like, absolutely stupid. Or are they? They both departed seconds before the painting's loss was discovered.

That evening I tell my wife about the crime in the café. She makes a perceptive point: "If someone had stolen it, they would have taken ages to get it out of the place. It's always so crowded in there and too small for the tables they've crammed in." This is a valid observation. It's impractically small for removing anything. The thief's getaway must have taken many minutes. It would be like a nautical thief trying to lose a pursuing police boat in a chase sequence involving that famous bit of the Kennet & Avon canal at Caen Hill where there are 29 back-to-back locks.

I decide not to frequent the café again. Not because they falsely accused me of being an art thief. To be fair, I don't think they did that at all. They reasonably wanted to know if I'd seen anything. That's quite understandable. My decision is taken because it's frustratingly small. And always crowded - which is an indicator that my business is hardly crucial to them.

About a week later I walk past the café again. Countless undergrads are squashed inside, looking like one of those World Record attempts to cram as many people as possible inside a phone box. One student's face is pressed against the window, his features distorted as though he's struggling for air.

On the wall I can see a small painting. It's hard to tell from the outside but it does look decidedly like a landscape depicting a windmill on a golden hillside.

Motivated by curiosity, I go inside and enquire. Part of me still retains a desire to eliminate myself from inquiries. "Sorry, I'm new. I'll ask," says a pleasant girl with stunning hazel eyes. No one seems to know. Then, between whirls of noisy coffee-grinding, an aproned man with a hipster beard informs me: "The artist took it back for some exhibition but didn't tell us beforehand so we actually thought it'd been nicked. Do you want a cappuccino or latte?"

I scan the Lilliputian tables crammed with students. The alluring espresso bouquet beckons me like a siren's song. "Yes please, I'll have an Americano," I say, before adding at a forceful volume to compete with the student din behind me: "TO GO!"

NEVER A CROSSWORD

I'm sitting outside a café very much minding my own business. Even if it's barely warm enough for *al fresco* dining.

Incidentally *al fresco* in the original Italian means 'in prison'. That's why Italian waiters tend to snigger whenever you announce a preference for your order to be served outside. However both the quality of coffee and service in this particular café does resemble a canteen in choky.

But I'm stubbornly determined to utilise a brief, half-hearted appearance by the sun and make the most of its rationed rays. Obscured by milky cloud, it's the sort of day when, by mid-morning, you suspect the sun is contemplating knocking off early and taking the rest of the day off.

First I hear loud sighs approaching me, then the unmistakable realisation that the advancing stranger is going to sit at my table. My small private table outside a café. I decide not to reward them with a look up.

"Oh dear, oh dear," says the stranger. Fortunately to themselves. The interloper keeps emitting unnecessary noises committed to signifying a general state of fluster and disgruntlement. Then they ask a question unmistakably directed at me. "Do you know who this is?"

Forced to look up for the first time I observe the stranger is a well-dressed woman in her mid-60s wearing pink designer glasses and studying a newspaper. This in itself constitutes a result - it could have been three skinheads with swastika tattoos and a mugger's blade. Or worse, Jacob Rees-Mogg. "No, sorry," I say, hoping to divert attention back to my newspaper as quickly as possible without having to activate the rudeness button.

Then the stranger speaks again: "I think her first name is Julianne. But I need her five letter surname." Why? Is she composing a kidnapper's ransom note? Maybe she'll start cutting out letters from her newspaper's headlines. Surely in a digital age everyone has moved on with technology, apart from kidnappers who are still queuing up at Rymans to buy scissors and a Pritt stick.

"Yes! It's Julianne. I've got her!" squeals the stranger, expressing excitement disproportionate to her accomplishment, before adding in a distinctly less excited voice, "but I still need to spell her surname. She's an actress, you know." This stranger interaction started out weird and is now getting weirder.

Our seemingly random word exchange, masquerading as a conversation, attracts quizzical looks from other café patrons. One seated nearby stares mystifyingly at us, like a lion inspecting a bowl of salad left by a distracted zoo keeper.

I decide to embrace the situation rather than run away from it. Especially as the person may have 'issues', and therefore conclude I should probably be supportive. Plus I've also got half my overpriced, overrated and over-foamed coffee to finish. Before the screws… sorry, waiting staff… announce visiting time is over.

Then I see some semblance of logical justification in asking a stranger to identify someone. She is attempting a crossword in a supermarket's free newspaper advertorial. A tiny photo of a redheaded lady appears in the middle of the crossword grid. Presumably she represents a key clue.

Stranger Lady lays down her paper, right on the cusp of my side of the table. My eyes patrol the border for incursions with the alacrity of a North Korean border guard.

"To make fun of?" she says. "Pardon?" I reply. "NO!" she says with unwarranted shocking force. Suddenly the penny drops - to use an expression blissfully untouched by inflation. She's reading out crossword clues. She does it again. "To make fun of? Blank, blank, 'd', blank, blank 'u' blank 'e'." "Ridicule?" I propose after a significant ponder. My suggestion receives no response. "Ridicule?" I repeat, suggesting a credible answer to what she's saying out loud, rather than an allegation.

"No," she snaps, with unnecessary firmness, "that's not it!" "How many letters?" I check. "Eight." Hmm. Three full minutes of enjoyable silence and unenjoyable coffee sipping are ruined by her eventually declaring: "How about 'ridicule'? That fits."

Sometimes it's best to be the mature one. Even though Immature Me wants to yell "THAT'S WHAT I JUST SAID YOU DOZY BAT!" Instead I succeed in calmly saying "well done" in a voice sufficiently controlled to be almost recognisable as my own.

"Moore," I say suddenly. "More what?" she asks, visibly confused. "Julianne Moore. The actress," I explain, which rather than clarify appears to confuse her more. Given her response, I might as well have been speaking phrases suggested by a random word generator: "Amphibious landing craft. Gerbil golf. Punch that hippopotamus." But I'm determined to persevere. "Is it a photo of the actress Julianne Moore in the centre of the crossword?"

After spending several more seconds puzzling over how to communicate with as much clarity as possible, she says: "Oh yes. Moore fits. Five letters."

I gulp down my coffee in one final swallow. We say our goodbyes. Then I walk to the bus stop. Arriving home I spot my wife studying a newspaper with a biro clicked to attention. "We can win a £100 Waitrose voucher," serves as a greeting.

She reads out two clues. Then another. By the time of the third clue my brain is detecting déjà vu. "By the way, the answer to the clue 'to make fun of' is 'ridicule'," I say. Then I leave a pause to bask in my wife's realisation that she is only feet away from a genius. Rather than display how impressed she is, she merely waves away my contribution by deducing: "You've already seen it then?"

"Yes," I say, anxious to reclaim some semblance of contribution, "and the celebrity pictured in the middle is Julianne Moore."

"Really?" checks my wife.

"Of course it's Julianne Moore," I restress, "EVERYBODY KNOWS THAT!"

I inform her about my earlier impromptu *al fresco* crossword conference at a café and our collective inability to recognise Julianne Moore and write her surname into the central grid.

My wife rightly points out that in Italian 'al fresco' means 'in prison.' Then returns her attention to tackling the puzzle, having implied that she would prefer me to be *al fresco* right now rather than bothering her in the kitchen. I use the tetchy silence to ponder whether, should I ever be incarcerated in Italy, I can ask to dine outside and thereby escape.

After persevering with the crossword for another ten minutes, we push it aside. Neither my wife nor I announce that we're giving up, but it's obvious we won't be returning to it. Or have £100 to spend in Waitrose - which, with its prices and middle-class pretention, would have enabled us to buy half an artisan bread loaf and a bird-of-paradise marinated in pomegranate jus.

A week later I pick up the next issue of the free instore paper to tackle the prize crossword. "Have you heard of an actress called Amy Adams?" asks my wife. "Think so," I reply unsurely. "Of course you have - she's a gorgeous redhead. And nominated for an Oscar."

My wife passes the new crossword puzzle to me - mainly because she can't solve any of the first few 'across' clues. Last week's solution is printed underneath.

"It was her photo in last week's crossword puzzle - not Julianne Moore," says my wife.

"Oh 'b'," I say, "blank, double 'l', blank, blank, blank, 's'."

LOSING THE PLOT

"I have to be careful not to lose the plot," I announce to my wife, in a rare literal outing for that phrase. Allow me to explain.

Since September I have taken on an allotment. Like pet ownership and parenting, it transpires that selecting this life route involves accompanying responsibilities. Plus a huge amount of associated crap to deal with. The latter sentence is yet another phrase given a surprisingly literal outing - because my allotment contains a steaming mound of freshly plopped manure.

On my first visit to view the plot the Secretary charged with overseeing allotment allocations gushingly informs me how fortunate I am to be in possession of one. Spotting the pile of pongy manure inspires him to point and rhapsodise. He utters the clumsily selected phrase: "The previous owner has dumped you a present." I swot away flies and I notice an increase in our walking speed until we reach less malodorous air.

"Your timing is lucky," he says, "as vacancies don't come up very often," before contradicting himself five minutes later when remarking, "I must go, as I'm showing three more people vacant plots this afternoon." I instantly decide I like the Secretary, plot and the allotments in general, so decide to sign up and pay my annual rent. Plus a hefty deposit for what transpires to be an equally hefty key - so cumbersome it's perhaps missing from a National Trust-owned castle. "This key is designed so it can't be copied," he tells me. That's a challenge for a gang of crack international criminals, I think, should they attempt to replicate the unreplicable key to gain access to our allotment and steal some blemished turnips.

Apparently the plot's previous renter Russell has departed to Yorkshire thus rendering his patch available for me. Intriguingly I never discover why he had to quit Oxfordshire in such a hurry and move north to a county that deploys neither tact nor t'definitive article, but in my mind it's because he's a rumbled spy. And key replicator. Russell is certainly much missed by the allotment fraternity. Although it's early days, I already know I won't be.

On my first day of officially 'moving in' to my patch, an elderly and rather unkempt man - who strikes me as the type who is likely to have foregone belts in favour of string - is dumping brussels stalks on MY ground. To be fair, it is overgrown and looks like an abandoned no-man's-land separating two warring countries throughout a long forgotten conflict. I calculate it must be at least five years since work was done for it to be in such a neglected state. Swaying weeds stand aloft like small oaks. The only place where weeds aren't present is under the pongy pile of manure.

A week later I return to uproot more weeds. Although there are now weeds where the manure patch stood, there's no manure. Later I discover it had been wrongly delivered to my plot. "Are there many weeds?" asks my wife when I return from another gruelling four-hour weeding expedition. "I believe there are fewer molecules in the universe than there are weeds in my allotment," I reply. My wife is suspicious of the work involved when committing to an allotment - believing that if I want an allotment then, like a child demanding a pet, it'll be my responsibility accordingly.

In order to maintain an allotment you need time, dedication, commitment, diligence, expertise, a trusty trowel, and an encyclopaedic knowledge of what, when, where and how to plant fruit and veg. So far I have a trusty trowel.

I spend most of my free time in September, October and November pulling up weeds. This is incredibly hard work and I can confirm it's not known as The Green Gym for nothing.

A hard winter is followed by a galloping spring. Flowers bloom late this year, but when the growing season does belatedly arrive it's as if it's on steroids. Due to family illness and work commitments, I do not return to the allotment until late April. In my absence the weeds have clearly been holding an open-invite party.

I've never understood why describing someone as "being such a weed" or "acting weedily" is meant to imply timorous weakness. Having spent another six-hour shift attempting to remove weeds, believe me when I provide the following testimony: there is nothing weedy about weeds. They're some of the most stubborn, resilient, aggressive and brutal colonisers on the planet. I have scars, scratches, cuts, scabs, rashes, splinters, thorns and bruises as proof. But not a weedless allotment. That, I quickly learn, is impossible. And yet others somehow seem to manage that feat in neighbouring plots. How?

By early June I have pulled up swathes of weeds. When I return a few weeks later they're there again. All of them. Only bigger, higher and greener. My strawberries, so plump and promising in May, have now all dropped off following a violent storm. They rest on the ground, tragic and lifeless like slain soldiers lying at the side of a road. If only the weeds operated with such impractical sensitivity. My strawberries appear to possess the resilience of a June snowflake.

Life must go on. Literally. So I buy a packet of courgette seeds to replace my atrophied strawberries. I enthusiastically open a packet containing twelve chunky seeds resembling melon pips, then plant them all in a bag of Pound Shop compost, water thoroughly and follow the instructions more carefully than someone reading the leaflet for defusing their first bomb.

Fully one month later I am rewarded with a mere single sprouting courgette. I don't know whether to blame my seeds, slugs or general gardening incompetence.

Meanwhile the weeding continues. As does the ever-present background sense of despairing futility. Surrounding my allotment are pristine plots fecund with harvest festival photo opportunities. How? How come everyone else is not only relatively weed-free but producing enviable Chelsea show gardens? How?!

In fact I'm beginning to genuinely question whether it's possible to pull up weeds quicker than they can grow. Leave the allotment for 72 hours and upon return my patch is carpeted in uninterrupted greenness. Where do they come from? It may be the wind, but there are times when I'm sure I can hear the weeds mocking me.

"You know your problem?" begins the old bloke next door. Yes, fortunately I do - given I'm married, so tend to hear about my faults a lot. But he doesn't pause for an answer before continuing. "Your plot is nearest the edge, so you get all the slugs and snails that come out from their cover at night." He's probably right. Yet I repeatedly ponder one question: Why don't the slugs and snails eat the weeds? No answer is forthcoming. Especially from the slugs and snails.

And why hasn't bindweed taken over the world yet? Japanese knotweed was deliberately introduced to the UK from... well, you can probably guess the country of origin... to firm up railway embankments. Now it destroys foundations, sewage pipes, pavements, road surfaces and the sanity of the middle classes. And apparently it's not much good at binding railway embankments either.

By August only a frustrating fraction of the plants have survived snail attacks. But one success story is the humble although much venerated tomato. In February I had purchased some 'Reduced for Quick Sale' fresh plum tomatoes. I accidentally squashed them when my bag fell off my bike during a downhill descent, which caused a ghostly white stream on the tarmac when my milk carton flopped onto the road too. Rather than cry over my flattened tomatoes - and spilt milk, of course, as the old aphorism cautions - I brought my now one-dimensional tomatoes home. Proceeding to dry the seeds, I popped them into paper cups filled with compost and left them on a windowsill. There they grew.

In May I transferred them to the allotment. And now, in early August, I am rewarded with the tomatoes beginning to blush red. I pick one. It tastes delicious. Far superior to shop bought, which I'll now permanently brand as 'sweat shop tomatoes' in comparison to the taste unlocked in these wonderful home-grown orgasms in the mouth.

It seems that I'll never have green fingers - unless I paint my lawnmower without gloves. An inability to tell a strelitzia from a dandelion doesn't help either. Notwithstanding, I do manage to obtain rocket - the slightly bitter salad leaves, not the means to space exploration. I further console myself with the financial cost of the entire operation. The price of allotments is ludicrous.

Within the Oxford ring road, in a location delivering easel-grabbing views of sweeping hillsides and teasing glimpses of Oxford's spires looking as dreamy as ever, it's possible to rent 125 square metres of prime land for £16 a year. My initial urge is to sell my plot to Taylor Wimpey, but there's a risk the allotment committee may interpret this as a potential bye-law infringement. Who knew?

Determined to see a fleeting glimpse of soil beneath the weeds, I invest in some equipment to augment my trusty trowel. It's a necessary expense offset by the incomprehensible cheapness of the rent.

I experience the same gradient of learning curve at garden centres as I do at allotments. I learn quickly that garden centres have different pricing structures. Some things are cheap. Others, like cabbage plants, are stupidly expensive. I can buy a fully grown cabbage - one that's actually won the rampaging war against caterpillars, slugs, snails and blackfly - i.e. all four horseman of brassicas' Armageddon - for less than a packet of miniscule seeds so tiny they're only ever a sneeze away from oblivion.

Come September it's harvest time. I dig five roots of potatoes; pull up any anaemic carrots spared by the insects and rabbits, blight and pestilence, and head home - my failure at gardening hardly offset by my ability to use an Oxford comma correctly.

"Look what I got from Gloucester Green market today," enthuses my wife, plonking two blue carrier bags stuffed with bounteous fruit and veg onto the table. "They were selling it off for only £1 a bowl!"

Autumn arrives like a fist. It conquers all my tomatoes, turning the leaves brown and tinged with blight. But I have pulled kilos of the succulent red fruits in the last two months - my sole allotment success story.

I open my laptop and compose an email to the Secretary saying that it's time someone else got to benefit from my allotment as I won't be renewing the lease.

But I don't send it. Instead a month later I renew my subscription for another year. Those tomatoes really were that good.

NIECE WORK IF YOU CAN GET IT

For reasons that aren't immediately apparent when I return to the room having fulfilled an overly fussy coffee order ("not much milk, but more than just a smidge"), my wife and teenage niece Missy [an agreed alias] are discussing sex education.

"Missy was taught all about the birds and bees at school back in Year Seven," says my wife, by way of bringing me up to date with the conversation I had missed from the kitchen. "Yeah," Missy confirms, "I learned there's literally 250 species of bee in the UK yet over 600 different types of birds." "Thank you, Missy," I think to myself, "I'm the one who usually does the jokes around here." Deprived of my comedy role, what other purpose or skillset do I offer?

My wife laughs briefly but is visibly anxious to return to the subject's incontrovertible seriousness. "How useful was the sex education?" she asks. "Well," says Missy, her mannerisms hardly indicative of a reply containing a level of seriousness matched by the question, "they don't teach you any actual helpful techniques." I notice the cups starting to rattle on the tray I'm carrying.

"I assumed that," says my wife, reluctantly resigned to letting the subject matter disappear, disqualified on the grounds of not being taken sufficiently seriously. "It's literally a good thing I suppose," says Missy, newly aware that she should make an effort to discuss the matter with slightly more solemnity, "they just, literally, encourage you to discuss consent issues and shared gender responsibilities towards contraception."

"Did you have sex education in your day?" Missy asks me. According to Missy, In Our Day was sometime around the Bible's launch night. The Old not the New Testament. The cheeky little…

My wife gives me a clear "She's deliberately winding you up, so don't fall for it" look. "We had a doctor's wife visit us at school to provide a sex education class," I reminisce, and instantly feel I should be delivering this memory from a swaying rocking chair. "She told us: 'For boys, sex feels better than scoring a goal' while hinting strongly that most girls didn't share this view. Which didn't surprise me as back then most girls weren't into football." This is all completely true. "Plus she showed us how to put a condom on a carrot; a Chantenay carrot in my case, I recall." "Er, okay," says Missy, genuinely perplexed for once, as my wife unsuccessfully suppresses a snigger.

"Oh, and some boys presented her with a petition requesting a girl visit us from the town's girls' school to facilitate a practical sex demonstration. I remember one name had been energetically crossed off." "That's terrible," laments my wife. "Yeah, it was," I agree. "That enabled her to say it wasn't a unanimous request, so she didn't pursue it." Again this is all shamefully true. And part of the damaging gender apartheid I experienced at an all-boys school.

"Is that why," ponders Missy, "your generation is literally so misogynistic?" Missy then laughs, having succeeded in deliberately winding me up. No-one acknowledges that she's probably just made a highly perspicacious point. We concur that compulsory sex education is a responsible progression. Though her overreliance on, and consistent misuse of, the word 'literally' is annoyingly tiresome.

After watching the *Newsnight* item on sex education to its end, Missy says breezily: "I'd like to have a career in the sex industry." I check whether my wife requires me to fetch a dishcloth to wipe off the coffee that she's just spat out onto the wall. I maintain a facial expression of Mount Rushmore inscrutability. "It'll be cool to be a sex therapist," adds Missy, devilishly. My wife frowns. For some reason the reactor not the perpetrator is the one she judges to be at fault.

Missy has recently started at university - albeit later than originally intended. Regular readers of this column may assume this was due to her tertiary education being delayed by an enforced spell sewing mail bags in a young offenders' institution. But the actual reasons were much more prosaic, though apparently forbidden from publication by family reporting restrictions. Sorry.

Her previous appearance in this column led directly to her quoted words being voiced by an actress on *Woman's Hour*. Her enforced anonymity at the insistence of the BBC did not go down well with Missy, who saw it as a vital first step to celebrity status lost. Subsequently she's metamorphosed into fully-formed mature adulthood. No one saw that coming - especially her parents.

Previously whenever they deposited her at our house it was accompanied by an almost nauseous gratitude that we'll be keeping them away from her antics for 24 hours. Rather than teenage delinquency, she's now content commenting on *Newsnight* discussions.

Indeed *Newsnight* is the catalyst for their current choice of conversational subject as the flagship news programme is running a feature on sex education in schools. Apparently the UK has one of the worst underage pregnancy rates in the developed world. "Well, at least that's one thing I didn't do," says Missy, probably expecting praise.

"Will you ever write about me in your column again?" Missy suddenly asks. "Not if it means you deliberately doing something bad again to gain column-worthy notoriety, like that time when you…"

"…I don't think we need reminding of what Missy did when she was very young a long time ago," says my wife, anxious to shut me up. "You mean about 16 months ago?" I check. "Are there some things you literally wouldn't write about in your column?" asks Missy. "Yes," I reply, aware of an inevitable next question.

"Can I have another coconut snowball?" asks Missy. Needless to say that was not the anticipated question. "What wouldn't you write about?" Missy eventually asks. "I… err… dunno," I say. So much for anticipation providing me with an increased response time for formulating articulacy. "Lots of things and, er, stuff," I say, displaying the effortless eloquence synonymous with a professional writer.

"Traditionally the role of women has been to run around making men's lives more comfortable," says my wife. They both nod their mutual concurrence. I compose my facial expression carefully. "This coffee needs a smidge more milk," says Missy, with the unmissable indication that I return to the kitchen and add milk. My initial assumption that she's joking soon decays into a realisation that she does expect me to fetch milk. "Are your lives sufficiently comfortable?" I ask as I rise again from the sofa. Fine, they respond non-verbally, my transmitted facetiousness unreceived on their feminist bandwidth. They unmute *Newsnight* while simultaneously muting me in the process.

"Cos I really don't mind if he writes a column about this," proffers Missy bumptiously. "He's not writing one!" "He's written columns about me before," says Missy approvingly. "Well he's not writing anymore," announces my wife with stressed finality, before adding, "are you making notes?" "No," I say hiding my pen. "God, there are times when you really do take the biscuit," harrumphs my wife.

If anyone's behaviour has taken the biscuit over the years then it must surely be Missy's: stealing bottles of vodka out of our locked drinks cabinet, crashing a car into our wheelie bins when she wasn't even old enough to drive, smuggling a boy back to our house at 3am. And numerous other mentions in despatches from the frontline of teenage boundary-bulldozing. Yet that conduct now seems to belong to an entirely different person to the Missy of the here and now. Phew.

I go to the kitchen, fire up the laptop and start to write a column about Missy's late flowering maturity. After a few minutes Missy wanders into the kitchen in search of further confectionery. "What are you writing about?" she asks. I explain. "That's literally fantastic," she purrs her approval. "I'll leave you to it. I won't tell Auntie." A few seconds later she returns to take the biscuits. Literally.

"THEY HAVE BEEN AT A GREAT FEAST OF LANGUAGES AND STOLEN THE SCRAPS"

I never realised Shakespeare was so popular. This can't have anything to do with the generously provided free buffet laid out before me. Obviously.

Throngs of people are arriving at Oxford University's Said Business School to hear a renowned Shakespearean scholar deliver a lecture on the Stratford scribbler.

Immediately we are told to head for the surprisingly named Margaret Thatcher Building. I assume en route we'll be taking a left into the Pol Pot Lecture Room and passing the Joseph Stalin Library before convening in the Piers Morgan Room. Instead we're directed along a lengthy corridor past a dedication plaque to the controversial former Prime Minister. Say what you want about Thatcher - and you can because the dead can't sue for libel - but although I've never met anyone in my entire life prepared to admit voting for her, she did win three consecutive UK general elections. And kept us in Europe.

Needless to say my own attendance is entirely in hopeful anticipation of digesting insights into the Bard's iambic pentameter and declarative pronouncements - and not just the complimentary crayfish and rocket sandwiches. Mmmm… Smoked cheese and pastrami mini bagels… Mmmm… and fruit bowl… Mmmm. Maybe I was premature with my Mmmm for the fruit bowl.

From the lavishly provisioned buffet I pile a teetering sandwich of Scooby Doo proportions onto my plate. A man with a hairline now so receded he's probably only got one credible visit to the barbers left, parades up and down the narrow corridor where we're assembled snaffling complimentary sandwiches. And ignoring the fruit option. He builds a five-storey sandwich tower. Standing uncomfortably close to each other, we eschew conversation in preference for eating. Collectively we munch away like locusts about to start a fasting day on the 5:2 diet.

Courteously I enter Lecture Room VIII punctually. The speaker reciprocates my cheery "Hello" greeting. But even someone as unobservant as me soon notices there is a problem. Only one other person is occupying the room - a young woman in trousers so tight she probably hasn't been able to take them off since she became an adult.

Five minutes after the advertised start time, the rest of the grazing gazelles gallop into the room. Some have even brought plates of sandwiches in breach of the clear sign to the contrary Blu-tacked to the door: "No food or drink permitted in lecture rooms." Rude. One man, eating a long baguette, resembles a clarinet player and appears to be equally noisy in the process. Although the speaker is ready to start, Baguette Man proceeds to rhapsodise over his lunch. "Great Feta cheese, not too salty," he informs the startled stranger next to him.

After allowing for a generous amount of noisy chomping time, our speaker is introduced. Professor Emma Smith is a Fellow of Oxford's Hertford College and a bona fide Shakespeare expert. Those pondering why a Shakespearean scholar should be giving a lecture at the business school are given an immediate explanation: "Everything we see as literature is filtered through the economic process."

So how was Shakespeare monetised into becoming such a financial success? Smith knows. The answer is: it took a very long time.

"Until the 18th century there were no theatres outside London," announces Smith. I had no idea. She shows a map of 16th-century theatres - all located south of the Thames. There's a pub marked on the map as "bear garden". Just as I'm mentally castigating the cartographer for not employing a proof reader, it dawns on me that this isn't a typo. They really did stage sinister animal baiting in their bear (not beer) garden.

Moreover animal baiting arenas became theatre's architectural inheritance: The Globe was designed to follow the same template. It shows that theatres were unsettling, discombobulating places, unwanted by locals. "Having a theatre near you was like having a football stadium next door - these were not the refined arts centres of today," observes our insightful speaker. Indeed anyone aspiring towards respectability in the Elizabethan age would probably have been damning towards theatre. After all, theatres were places where people told indisputable lies - as fiction wasn't true, right?

Smith then conjures an impressive fact for the audience: "Shakespeare is the most valuable brand ever invented in the arts." Take that *Star Wars*, Beatles, Tolkien and JK Rowling. Some bloke writing with a feather over 400 years ago without coffee and wi-fi still beats you all. According to the IMDB he's certainly got an amazing film career for someone who died in 1616!

There's another surprising detail demonstrating how hugely theatre protocol differed from then to now. "Most theatres didn't record what play they performed." This is consistent with contemporary theatregoer testimonies. Journals and diaries from the Elizabethan age regularly chronicle going to the theatre, and record in unnecessary detail all the drinks, food and prostitutes consumed. Apparently popping out for a brothel visit was de rigueur for most Elizabethans' night out at the theatre (perhaps you could pre-order your prostitute for the interval?). As Smith states: "That's like saying I went to the theatre last night, and all people ask in response is: 'What drinks and food did you have?'" It seems no-one was particularly interested in the plays themselves.

Theatre managers recorded the nightly takings from staging their plays, showing a clear success bias for certain nights of the week. Interestingly the cost of a ticket to see Will's latest at The Globe would have set you back "equivalent to today's cost of two pints of beer". So theatre was cheaper in real terms than today. "Theatres had a pile them high, sell them cheap mentality," elaborates Prof Smith. Bizarrely the cheapest seats were at the front, and punters actually paid more money to be further away from the action.

Another principal selling point was a play's newness. "They had no interest in revivals." Not the business model we'd expect today. Particularly with Shakespeare being out of copyright and therefore free of pesky royalties - hence his plays are financially attractive for theatre companies operating with the change from a shoestring.

Then there's a 'Kaboom!' of a top fact bomb being dropped by the speaker. "Shakespeare plays that we assume as all-time literary classics and household names might well have had had only about seven performances [in Shakespeare's lifetime]." Wow. And another wow. And an extra follow-up wow.

At least Elizabethan England was an encouraging environment for new writing. And this literary nursery created a new job opportunity: the playwright. Unsurprisingly it proved not to be a very diverse profession, quickly filled almost exclusively by Oxford and Cambridge graduates. Plus ça change, plus c'est la même chose.

A rise in theatre audiences was inseparable from the rise in coach transportation. "You were very unlikely to be run over by a coach in 1608," Smith points out, "but by 1612 you really had to be careful" when out and about crossing city streets. Actuarial statistics reveal the sudden phenomenon of being killed on the nation's roads. Entering society in this same period are the first parking regulations. And the origins of traffic wardens. Furious correspondents no doubt fulminated to *Ye Olde* letters page: "Maketh me verily angry when parketh my cart for ONLY five minutes to visit a brothel..."

"Oxford and Cambridge provided a certain class of man who 'can't find jobs' who became playwrights," elaborates Smith, continuing to fire a relentless fusillade of fascinating facts.

A new spinoff industry began: the printing of playbooks. Early playbooks contained an omission we take for granted today: a list of characters at the beginning. Bootleg versions of Shakespeare's plays, primitively notated from an audience member's shorthand during a performance, also soon appeared. Unsurprisingly many were error strewn: "2B or not to 2B, that is the Kidlington bus?"

Even in the 16th century Shakespeare did well to succeed in a fledging showbiz industry without possessing an Oxbridge background. Famously he lived in Stratford. Or, more accurately, Stratford-upon-Avon. I envy people who live in places with names requiring three words. Town names that luxuriate in using an unnecessary triple amount of words - like posh people with double-barrelled surnames: Abingdon-upon-Thames, Newcastle-under-Lyme, Brightwell-cum-Sotwell, Moreton-in-Marsh, Not-in-Service (admittedly I haven't been to that last place, but they seem to have an excellent bus service).

Prof Smith estimates that only about a fifth of plays performed in the Elizabethan era were printed. Hence plays were ephemeral. Only those that were printed have survived for future generations to behold today.

At this stage our lecturer shows us a copy of Will's 1598 epic *Henry 4th Part One*. It's recorded as "perfect condition, first edition" scrawled in irremovable ink across the front, and the graffitist has even dated his/her unknowing vandalism as 1827.

There's a pause for audience gasps.

Women, of course, weren't allowed anywhere near the stage. Perhaps suspicious that all punters were going to see portraying the love interest for their hard-earned groats was a female impersonator, the eponymous Juliet in *Romeo & Juliet* was relegated to the second line in the play's title. Her name also appeared in a considerably smaller font than Romeo's.

Still, at least Juliet got a billing. No mention of the author's name appears anywhere on the surviving contemporary playbills for his work. Not once does "by William Shakespeare" adorn the covers of what we now recognise as his greatest hits. Surely the takeaway message from this is that the author was of no commercial value?

So how did he capitalise on success? By responding to a previous hit. "Like the modern film industry, you make a similar version that's not quite as good," says Smith mischievously. See *Henry 4th Part Two*. Or, rather, don't - and save yourself three hours of creeping bum numbness. Anyone intent on preserving Shakespeare's position as the high watermark of British culture might want to revisit the opening scene of *Henry 4th Part Two* - first performed in 1600 - which takes place in a brothel. Characters cavort with prostitutes while cracking low quality lewd jokes about venereal diseases and drunkenness. So surely Shakespeare isn't the sort of filth you'd allow anywhere near a schoolroom? Well more British school hours have been spent studying the Bawdy Bard's works than any other writer in history (even if most of those school hours have been spent staring out at the light from yonder window).

Yet a whole breakout industry was created around the plays during the Stratford sonneteer's lifetime. Such was the magnitude of the acting stars - but not the author - that wealthy Elizabethans would regularly hire actors from the Bard's plays to attend dinner parties. And pay the actors to be, ahem, actorly. Hashtag annoying. The diary of one wealthy Elizabethan, John Manningham, records hiring Richard Burbage, one of the most famous actors of The Globe, to recount *Richard III* at his suave kitchen supper. This would have ensured I left mid-starter.

When Shakespeare died in 1616 - famously on his birthday - there were three printed poems of mourning. When Burbage, often chosen as the leading man for many of Will's plays, died three years later, the actor received over a thousand such bereavement poems. Exit Burbage indeed. Pursued by a bare… faced cheek at taking all the plaudits ahead of Shakespeare.

Fascinatingly Smith recounts that in 1602 numerous playbills fluttered on London walls advertising "England's Joy - A New Play". But there was a big problem with the play. It was a scam. No such play existed. This was a common deception in the era - advance ticket sales for plays that didn't exist. And four hundred years before the launch of Viagogo too.

"The Shakespeare brand develops much later," says Smith. Undoubtedly the Bard's work was almost exclusively kept alive by the book trade. For centuries Shakespeare existed on the printed page rather than on the theatrical boards. "For many decades - even centuries - Shakespeare was primarily considered something to read rather than see performed," she adds.

I applaud our lecturer heartily. Outside there's still some food left. Ed Reardon-like, I secrete what I think is a smoked salmon roll into my pocket from a tray labelled "Fish". Too late I feel a mushy substance. It's pink taramasalata instead. That's going to require a high-numbered washing machine programme.

Then I notice several of my fellow freebie snatchers returning for seconds (or, more likely, fourths and fifths). One of them, an elderly gentleman with a suit that may have fitted him in an era when Frankie Goes To Hollywood were dominating the charts, says to me in a plummy academic voice: "Unquiet meals make ill digestions." I nod and smile as politely as possible.

Sensing my poorly disguised mystification, he clarifies: "Comedy of errors!" Taken aback, and with the defence reflex activated, I say firmly yet calmly: "I thought it was a really interesting talk." "Comedy of errors," he says, "that's a quote from *The Comedy of Errors*," and pauses while he seriously considers whether there's any need to add: "That's a play by William Shakespeare." "Oh, yes," I say. "Of course. Very good."

I desperately try to think of a Shakespearean quote I can contextualise and shoot back at him. But I can't. While chatting about the lecture, he knocks a knife off his buffet plate. Sensing that bending down may not be easy for a gentleman of his advanced years, I retrieve it for him. After the entire buffet table has now been stripped, including the garnish, I make my way out past Thatcher's bust in the corridor, taramasalata squelching down my left leg.

Outside I phone my wife and enthuse about the talk, recounting some of the fascinating things I'd learned about Shakespeare and his language. And how brazenly people pocketed the dried up food (or not so dried up) afterwards.

Then I realise what I should have said when picking up the elderly Bard quoter's knife. "Is this a dagger which I see before me?" Too late.

ANGEL FOCUS GROUP

For reasons that have evaded me ever since I overheard myself surprisingly saying 'yes', I am mentoring a debut sketch troupe ahead of their intended performance at a charity comedy gig.

An early sign of internal creative differences has manifested itself. By the time of our second meeting, I discover the sketch troupe are already down to a duo. The troupe - sorry, double act - are attending university at Oxford as second year science undergrads. In answer to the opening question I asked upon our first face-to-face meeting, I discover they "found me on the internet". They ask for my UNPAID (that's their emphasis) comedy writing advice. My ego, if not my bank balance, is poised to expand.

There's a touching naivety to the duo's showbiz self-belief; hope as yet unwithered by experience. While discussing their script ideas they express a desire to perform something with scientific references that a smart crowd of students will appreciate and "attack the patriarchy".

"Let's do a table reading of your sketch," I say to kick-off our latest encounter. Their first self-written sketch is nebulous, indulgently long and they appear to have forgotten the jokes in the writing process. In their rambling sketch set in a pet shop a man is buying a cat because he's lonely. Nothing happens - funny or otherwise - in the nine minutes of Beckett-type awkwardness and menace. While the audience nervously await a narrative. Or a laugh. Or a point. Or someone returning a dead parrot.

By far the funniest bits are when they mess up the reading and adlib with each other. There's also another high - and potentially unjumpable - hurdle: neither of them can write comedy.

One of the performers is called Hannah. For reasons that only my brain knows, I've temporarily mislaid the name of her friend. They are both dressed identically in black tops, black skirts and black leggings - like members of the French Resistance's drama society. Adding to their off-putting Frenchness, The One Who Isn't Hannah smokes incessantly.

"Why do all your sketches take place in a shop?" I ask. "They don't. There's one that takes place in a nail bar," contests The One Who Isn't Hannah. "That's a shop," I point out calmly. "No it isn't!" she responds - not calmly. "Well, it's on a High Street, customers enter it to buy something and are served by an assistant." "It's not a shop," she says defiantly, earning her a pleading look from Hannah to shut up.

There is a legitimate reason why so many sketches in the classic comedy canon are set in shops. It's a very efficient mechanism for getting strangers to meet and suddenly interact, with one party driven to want something while the other is determined to frustrate them in reaching their desired resolution.

"How is this funny or telling a story?" I ask at one point. "It shows men can be pathetic cat people - but women only get called cat ladies and that's so sexist," reasons Hannah. "I agree," I say, "but your chosen medium is comedy - so that implies the audience will expect some." "We're, like, radical, outside the box thinkers," pleads The One Who Isn't Hannah. "Yeah," she continues, "we're *cough... cough. Cough.*" "Good point, well made, Lisa," chides Hannah sarcastically. Oh, I think to myself, that's her name: she's called Lisa. "*Cough.*"

Like all other professions that wish to appear more important than they really are, we comedy writers possess our own extensive jargon. One example is a NTB. We highlight scripts with it. It stands for 'Not This But'. And it marks the requirement for a better joke to be inserted - at some future time when we can hopefully think of one. After a few minutes their entire script is illegible underneath a blizzard of NTBs. "As well as humour we need to include character consistency, a story arc and a resolution to the protagonists' predicament," I announce. Their faces crease with concern.

However, after seeing their self-written sketches, I decide to upgrade my job description from "mentor" to "take total control over absolutely everything". "How about if I compose a sketch for you? One that includes all the issues you want to cover: biological science, feminism, not dumbing down?" They both look unsure.

Hence I point out with intended sensitivity: "Elvis and Sinatra exclusively used outside writers." Their response is: "Who are Elvis and Sinatra?" "Kids, today, eh?" I remark. Then they fall into helpless giggles. This is a good sign. It means they have a sense of humour (always important for would-be comedy performers.) And, crucially, it also confirms they can act. Although it's doubtful that an Oxford-educated audience will be quite as gullible as me.

That night Hannah sends an email asking me to take over the writing process. Although good writing is rightly revered, I have long believed that in sketch comedy it is possible to get away with mediocre material, but never with mediocre acting.

At our next meeting I insist: "Our number one objective in comedy writing is to hold the audience's attention. And the key to good sketch comedy is good acting." No-one writes this down. Or anything else I say. But they do check their phones a lot.

"What advice would you give us now?" Lisa eventually asks. "Stop smoking," I answer. "Yeah, I'm trying to quit," she replies, evidently desperate to commence the lighting-up process. "How's it going?" asks her friend with deserved sarcasm. "Seriously," I say, "how can somebody as intelligent as you smoke?" "Er… dunno… I'll quit, I know I will." "Yeah, right," adds an enormously unconvinced Hannah, beckoning at her friend to go outside.

As luck would have it, the sketch I'm preparing requires one of them to play a male character. Since Lisa's voice is already well on its way towards being an octave lower than Hannah's due to smoke abuse tarring her larynx with a thick layer of carcinogenic asphalt resembling the M1, we unanimously decide she can portray the man.

Hannah mocks her friend affectionately by impersonating her pitch-perfectly: "Yeah, like I said… *cough* I'll give… *cough… gruff… grrrruufff… splatter… cough* up soon."

They start to bicker and I realise that the comedy troupe that apparently started out as a foursome ("I think it may have been five at one stage," muses Hannah later) could well soon be down to a solo act.

It's at this exact moment that I realise these two are funnier than most other people I've encountered of their age. And, boy (or rather, 'And, girl') can they act. "The trick of acting - remember in sketch comedy, you're basically acting," I say, attempting to select a grandiose tone, "is to deceive the audience into believing the words you are delivering is the first time anyone has said those lines."

"Why do you want to do comedy?" I ask "Cos it's challenging, brave," replies Hannah pensively. "And to take the piss out of men," adds Lisa.

Since they're now motivated to deliver this project, so am I. They can certainly act. In fact, the naturalness of their acting increasingly impresses me. When I produce some lines to fit their 'commissioned' script, they occupy the characters brilliantly. I soon become unstintingly optimistic that our sketch will work. And, as an additional justifier for all our hard work and dedication, it's for charity. "Cancer Research, by any chance?" I enquire.

Lisa has mostly dark brown hair; mostly, as large sections of her mane above each ear have been shorn off to reveal naked scalp. Fashionable as this may be, it gives the impression that her last hairdresser visit took place on a ship during a Force 9 storm. More traditionally, her friend has long chestnut hair held up with a butterfly clip. Both are required to look angelic - as the sketch requires them to portray a pair of angels. Deprived of a props budget, Hannah manages to borrow two sets of novelty angel wings from a relative. Meanwhile Lisa "requisitions" a flipchart from her college - a blatantly transparent euphemism for 'steals' and decidedly unangelic behaviour.

As if reverting back to school, the delightful duo clearly consider me their teacher-like authority figure. When Lisa makes a reference that's subtlely discriminatory against middle-aged white men, I catch Hannah wearing an amused-when-not-allowed-to-be look. Later Lisa, usually more of a classroom disrupter than Hannah, slightly raises her arm prior to asking a question. At last, I think, is she about to offer a contribution to the script? Maybe a funny gag or clever insight? Instead she asks: "Can I have a quick fag break? Only two minutes, I promise." Hannah tuts like kicking a bass drum.

Yet between fag breaks significant progress has been attained. When we started the project only a few weeks earlier, their mood oscillated between puppyish enthusiasm and cool detachment. Now they are committed, competent performers.

A week later I meet them in a coffee shop in Turl Street. The premises are so tiny we literally sit in the window sill. "Wow, is there, like, anything tinier than this place?" asks Hannah. "You're comedy talent," Lisa jokes. Hannah looks wounded. I manage to suffocate my laugh just in time. Then Hannah laughs at tricking me into thinking she was offended. See: they can perform and act comedy convincingly.

They ask me about my writing career. "I scripted a movie in the UK that Harvey Weinstein obtained the American rights for," I say, before adding: "There's an old showbiz adage: Never work with animals, children and Harvey Weinstein." They smile. Unwisely I feel an impulse to dispense some comedy writing sagacity: "Comedy sketches," I say with as much portentous pomposity stitched into my declaration as possible, "are like books or movies. Ultimately they depend on having just one Really Good Idea." They both get their phones out.

We finalise the sketch's premise. Hannah will be in front of a flipchart on stage playing the role of a female angel feedback co-ordinator. Meanwhile Lisa portrays a male angel focus group member reporting back from his breakout group.

Two days later they perform the completed sketch just to me, off-book and word-perfect. And coughless.

"You're ready," I pronounce. It's the last time I see them.

On the night itself I don't attend the performance as it's an undergraduates' event. Instead, like a WWII wing commander left behind while his crew fly a bombing raid, I await nervously for any news back at base.

By 11pm I'm concerned not to have received any updates. Surely such able comedians haven't died, shot down in heavy audience flak over Oxford? I begin to doubt the material I've written was airworthy, and conclude I've let them down - encouraged them to fly too soon when their comedy careers weren't ready to get off the ground. Therefore it's my fault if they crashed and burn.

When my phone eventually buzzes at midnight, all my nerves are jangled. It's a text from Lisa. "Sketch worked sooo well. So much love for us in room. Thanks sooo much."

The next morning Hannah texts: "Thanks... Angel sketch v v v good. Everyone thought we were v funny AND also v clever! [*followed by puzzling emojis*] Thanks so much. I want too (*sic*) continue with comedy but think Lisa cba." I google "millennial's text speak" to discover that "cba" decodes as "can't be arsed". Charming.

A few seconds later Hannah makes my phone ping again: "Lisa says thanks sooo much. And wants u to know she's decided to give up."

"The comedy or the fags?" I reply. There soon comes a one-word reply: "Fags!" Augmented with half a screen of bewildering emojis.

On the bottom line, after the final emoji, she's written: 'NTB'.

Here's the sketch that Hannah and Lisa absolutely nailed on the night:

ANGEL FOCUS GROUP
By Richard O. Smith

FEMALE ANGEL FEEDBACK CO-ORDINATOR: As you're aware, God has asked His leading angels to workshop ideas for an efficient process of reproduction for His important new species called 'Humans'. And I'll be feeding back your best ideas to the man Himself upstairs. So if you could introduce yourself.

MALE ANGEL FOCUS GROUP SPOKESMAN: Hello. I'm the male angel focus group feedback spokesman.

F: Right, so God's viewed our report on designing the fiddly bits necessary for human reproduction. And He's OK'd male humans to be fitted with a cock and balls - as per the diagram in your latest report.

M: That wasn't a proper suggestion. It was just a doodle I did on the back.

F: Hmm... that would explain the fact that NO FEMALE ANGELS WHATSOEVER voted for men to have balls. Clammy, hairy, dangly balls - wwurrrr... shudder. Focus. So today's big job for us, God's special task force, is to decide how this sex thing is going to work.

M: Okay.

F: You've just heard the female angels feeding back to the group that the female human should produce one egg a month. Seems logical, given one egg is all that's needed to produce one baby. Now, if you can feedback from the male angels' contribution to the process.

M: We thought of using a fertilising thing called a sperm that swims into the egg.

F: Excellent idea. And presumably - well obviously, given there's one just egg a month - the male will be releasing one sperm a month too?

M: Err... maybe slightly more.

F: Slightly more? Won't that be waste of resources if you release 2 or 3 sperms instead of just the one required for the job?

M: We were thinking more like 6 or 7?

F: 6 or 7? Surely that's inefficient?

M: …6 or 7 hundred…

F: What??!!

M: … million.

F: Come again?

M: That might take a while if 7 hundred million are required each time.

F: That's stupid!

M: We're guys. We prefer competitive numbers over scientific efficiency.

F: So I see.

M: So we thought that to incentivise the male to fertilise the egg, this process should provide a pleasurable experience. We've focus grouped it and we're calling it 'an orgasm'.

F: Okay. And will the female humans also receive one of these 'orgasms' while the male does the deed?

M: Yeah. Though maybe a bit later.

F: How much later?

M: Once she locates some new batteries.

F: How?

M: In a process we've provisionally calling 'having a lady wank'.

F: And where is the male human during the process of female orgasm?

M: Dunno. On a night bus home?

F: I see. I'm concerned that if the male humans constantly carry 700 million sperm in their dangly baby sacks [*shudder*], consequently they're going to be permanently obsessed with sex, thereby rendering them utterly useless as a species?

M: No, I can guarantee that will NEVER happen.

F: Hmm. What happens to the egg after the ejaculation reaches it?

M: Nine months later the woman pushes it out as a baby.

F: Right. Will that process hurt the female human?

M: No, shouldn't think so. She'll hardy notice.

F: Well I think she might notice, as your diagrams show it's equivalent to crapping a watermelon.

M: We also thought the most efficient process would be for any unused eggs to slowly break down causing blood loss and the women to be bent double experiencing painful cramps.

F: Hmm. Is that fair on the female humans?

M: Oh yes, we've programmed them to make life unbearable for the male humans while this process goes on.

F: Right. God's putting a lot of effort and budget into designing humans, so we need to get this right. Especially after what happened to his last big project for inhabiting planet earth. He's really pissed off that his previous Big Idea - the dinosaurs - went tits up.

M: That whole dinosaur extinction thing wasn't my fault. Look, how was I to know that asteroids could be dangerous?

F: You didn't consider that a gigantic ten-miles-wide asteroid - a molten rock fireball travelling at unimaginable speeds - could be dangerous?

M: Fair enough. I probably should have done a Health & Safety assessment.

F: And how did God punish you?

M: It's so unfair. Since the whole asteroid and dinosaurs incident I've had to spend my time in Heaven with a smaller harp and less fluffy cloud than everyone else.

F: Well this focus group is your chance to redeem yourself.

M: Have I redeemed myself?

F: There's no way in God's name...I mean His name... Brian... is going to adopt any of these suggestions as standard in humans. None whatsoever.

M: Why not?!

F: Because all your ideas are idiotic, inefficient, deeply sexist and chauvinistic, and recklessly stupid. Although... hang on... Which is exactly why I'm recommending them all to God for immediate implementation.

M: Really! You're recommending them to God. Why?

F: To ensure that the so-called 'intelligent design' argument is utterly and totally redundant forever!

ABOUT THE AUTHOR

Richard O. Smith (that's his real name - he wasn't christened it because the vicar dropped him into the font: "I name you Richard… Oh, S***!) was born in Boston (Lincs not Mass).

He writes across many different platforms - like a railway station graffitist. He's written for BBC TV and Radio 4 comedy shows including *The Now Show*, *News Quiz*, *Dara O Briain's Science Club* and is the principal screenwriter of *The Unbeatables* movie (starring Rupert Grint and Rob Brydon). His books include *Britain's Most Eccentric Sports*, *Oxford Student Pranks*, *Norse & Nordic Oxford* and football novel *The Unbeatables* ("Obviously I was delighted to read the book. Took it one word at a time. Great set of pages" - Mark Steel).

His book on true stupid criminal stories *As Thick As Thieves* ("Made me think I should have considered a life of crime" - Hugh Dennis) achieved a no. 1 bestseller slot. He's a Chortle comedy award winner and a former National Football Writer of the Year.

He lives happily with his wife [*stage direction: wife now puts down gun*] in Oxford. How happily, you can ascertain from this book!

THANKS / CREDITS

Immense gratitude to this book's editor Oliver Ledbury. Although you never see an editor's name on a cover or spine, there should a cultural change enabling this to become standard publishing industry practice. Because without a decent editor, there's no such thing as a decent book.

Thanks to the concerningly talented artist Andrew Manson for allowing his gorgeous painting of Magdalen Bridge *A Midnight Stroll* to form this book's cover. Have a look at Andrew's magnificent and deservedly successful work here: www.thebigorangem.com

Thanks to James Ferguson for vital manuscript input and to James Harrison for helpful advice. Special thanks to all the people who appear - maintaining a vital sense of humour - in these stories. A few names have been changed - indeed some aliases have been chosen by the people themselves.